P9-CRL-951

TRACTS

ON OUR

PRESENT MONEY SYSTEM

TRACTS

ON OUR

PRESENT MONEY SYSTEM

AND

NATIONAL BANKRUPTCY

COMPRISING STRICTURES ON

THE PRICE AND TRADE OF CORN

BY

PETER RICHARD HOARE

[1814]

REPRINTS OF ECONOMIC CLASSICS

AUGUSTUS M. KELLEY · PUBLISHERS
NEW YORK 1969

First Edition 1814

(London: *Printed for* T. Cadell & W. Davies, *Strand*,
by G. Sidney, *Northumberland Street*, 1814)

Reprinted 1969 by

AUGUSTUS M. KELLEY · PUBLISHERS

New York New York 10001

. . . .

S B N 678 00574 5

L C N 67 27467

. . . .

PRINTED IN THE UNITED STATES OF AMERICA
by SENTRY PRESS, NEW YORK, N. Y. 10019

TRACTS

ON OUR

PRESENT MONEY SYSTEM,

AND

NATIONAL BANKRUPTCY:

COMPRISING STRICTURES ON

THE PRICE AND TRADE OF CORN;

WITH

TABLES

OF THE

PRICES OF WHEAT AND BUTCHER'S MEAT.

AND OF THE

QUANTITIES OF CORN IMPORTED.

BY PETER RICHARD HOARE, ESQ.

London:

PRINTED FOR T. CADELL AND W. DAVIES, STRAND;

By G. SIDNEY, Northumberland-street.

1814.

PREFACE.

OUR progress has been orderly and natural. The suspension of cash payments has been followed by a deluge of paper money. The price of almost all commodities has been gradually and rapidly advancing; but that of corn, advancing like the rest, has latterly been checked by the countervailing plenty of our harvest, and has, at length, become so materially reduced as to alarm the landed interest into cries against the existing corn-trade laws—their insufficiency to protect our farmers from foreign competition: and yet not so reduced, but that it far exceeds the average price of common years preceding the suspension of cash payments; while, on the other hand, in order to encourage sufficiently the growth of wheat at home, it is thought expedient to prohibit, in effect, the importation from abroad, unless the average price exceed *ninety-five shillings* *

* Since these preliminary observations were committed to the printer the subject of our corn-trade laws has again come under discussion in the House of Commons. But instead of

the quarter—a price, till the wretched scarcity of 1800, (aggravated, indeed, as it probably even

ninety-five shillings the quarter, which, in the preceding sessions, were held out as a proper importation price, *eighty-four* are now prop sed to be the limit. It ought not to be forgotten, that the Committee itself had recommended *one hundred and five.* On what score of solid principles of reason and of calculation must they have argued, who could thus so soon have varied their opinions! In fixing the importation price at *eighty-four,* however, it will not, perhaps, escape the reader of the following pages, how nearly that sum accords with the author's estimate of the degree of the depreciation of our currency.[1] Uncertain what further change may take place in the minds of those who seem to have the chief management of the question, he deems it unnecessary to make any alteration in the text, written, as it was, with the apprehension that *ninety-five* shillings might shortly be the price established.—Should the present system of paper-money be perpetuated, the Legislature will probably ere long again be called upon to raise it even to a higher sum.

But what deters the Legislatuie from immediately m oderating the correction of this paper-money system; and thus at once superseding the ideal necessity of altering our corn trade laws, (unless it were to render them conformable to those established prior to the suspension of cash payments)?[2] It is idle to talk of returning to such payments six months after peace, without adopting, in the first place, means of materially lessening the quantity of paper now in circulation; by which the price of gold would be proportionably reduced, and come at last within the reach of those by whom the paper has been

[1] Refl. pp. 45. 50. App. pp. 25, 26. [2] Ib. pp. 21. 25.

then was, by excessive issues of Bank paper,) unknown to us during the whole course of the last century.*

But ere a measure such as this be pronounced expedient by the Legislature, it should be reasonably satisfied, that the end in view cannot be attained by other more justifiable means. For to say that an alteration of the corn-trade laws is absolutely *necessary* to the cultivation of a sufficient quantity of corn for our home consumption, is palpably absurd. Nor is it difficult, perhaps, to shew, that the same object may be as effectually, and much more beneficially, attained, by the due regulation of our currency. So much, however, has of late been said on this topic, and so weary of it does the public seem, that all attempts to recall their attention to it may be vain; notwithstanding its importance continues still undiminished, nay is materially augmented—ma-

issued. But it is difficult to conceal astonishment, if not rather indignation, at those who, after having all along denied the actual depreciation of our currency, have now the unaffected simplicity, if not the consummate assurance, openly to promote this scheme of raising the importation price of corn to an extent, which nothing but the gross depreciation of our currency, as well as the admission of the principle of our present corn-trade laws, could in any manner warrant.

* See Table of Prices—Reflections, p. 18, 19.

nifesting itself yet more and more in the daily operations and embarrassments of individuals and the government. With the subject of our corn-trade laws, indeed, it is most intimately connected, though, strange to say, unnoticed in the report of the Committee to whom the consideration of those laws was referred. With what motive they abstained from the investigation, nay, from the very mention of this prime fundamental cause of the late high prices, and large importations, of corn, they themselves can best explain. Be it what it may, the remedy they recommended could not, at most, perform so much as half a cure. The worst evil, that of enormously high prices, would remain.*

* Previous to 1765, the importation of wheat, whenever the price in the home market did not exceed 53s.4d. the quarter, was subjected to a duty of 16s. the quarter—to a duty of 8s. whenever the price did not exceed 4l.—and to a duty of 5s. 4d. whenever it exceeded 4l. A bounty of 5s. was also granted on every quarter exported, so long as the price was at or below 48s. Under this system, the Committee observes, "Great Britain "not only supplied herself, but exported a considerable quan-"tity of corn, and the prices were steady and moderate;"—that is, as it appears on an average of 64 years, the price of wheat was *thirty-three shillings and three-pence* the quarter. And it seems they would insinuate, that it is in consequence of her abandoning that system, and substituting another in its stead, Great Britain has not supplied herself, but has imported vast quantities of corn from other countries; and that the

It is, therefore, to be hoped, that in the further investigation of the subject of our corn-trade, that of our currency will not be neglected. And that the very occasion which seemed, in the judgment of those who formed the Committee, to require an alteration of the laws directly appertaining to

prices have been progressively, but enormously, advancing. Yet what can be plainer than that if a duty of 24s. 3d. the quarter be payable on importation, when the price of wheat is under 63s. and a bounty of 5s. the quarter be granted on exportation (as before) when the price of wheat is at or under 48s. which they now are, what can be plainer than that far greater encouragement (inasmuch as depends upon the corn-trade laws alone) is given to the growth of wheat at home under the present, than the former system? Is it morally possible, that one single quarter should be imported, to be sold at the low price of 33s. 3d.—if a duty of 24s. 3d. were payable upon it: or that if a duty of 16s. the quarter, when the price did not exceed 53s. 4d. were sufficient to restrain importation, the duty of 24s. 3d. when the price is under 63s. would be insufficient? In regard to the 8s. duty, it could hardly operate to the exclusion of foreign wheat after the price had attained 63s. if a duty of 24s. 3d. when the prices were under that sum, were ineffectual for such purpose. And the like remark is applicable, but with greater force, in respect to the operation of the lower duty of 5s. 4d. But, after all, if, in the judgment of the Committee, the old system were so truly beneficial, why did they not at once propose that it should be altogether re-established, that we again might have the blessing of abundance—*a bushel-full of wheat for less than four and two-pence.*

the former, will, when maturely considered, prompt them rather to attempt the amendment of those which immediately respect the latter.

It was from viewing the prodigious rise which had taken place in almost all articles of subsistence, and particularly in corn and butcher's meat, that the author of the following tracts conceived an argument might be drawn to prove an excess of currency. The depression of our foreign exchanges, the high price of gold and silver, together with the enormous increase of Bank paper, have all, indeed, been brought forward as evidence presumptive of the fact.—But unless it could, at the same time, be shewn, that the relative value of our money had diminished, no satisfactory conclusion could be formed; none on which we could decide as to the justice and expedience of lessening its quantity. He endeavoured chiefly, therefore, to maintain, that the price of corn and meat (making due allowance for the seasons) ought, in case there had been no excess of currency, to have continued almost stationary; but that in consequence of such excess, it had been raised exorbitantly—little, then, expecting so speedy and explicit an avowal by the Legislature as this, which it seems not very unlikely is about to be made in fixing, as it were, the minimum price of wheat at *ninety-five shillings* the quarter, or at least in effect prohibiting its importation at a price below that sum ; and thus acknowledging, by most inevitable implication, if not most directly, the gross depreciation of our currency, even far beyond the rate which he had previously ventured to surmise.*

He is well aware of, and has brought before the reader's view, the line of defence which may possibly be taken up by the advocates of our paper money system against the hard attacks which this concession favours. They will strive, perhaps, to make their stand upon the ground of taxes, population, and manufacturing preponderancy,

* Is it possible the Committee were not satisfied of the depreciation of our currency ? Suppose it not to be depreciated,—that the depression of exchange proceeds from some other temporary cause, which soon may be removed, and then that the exchange will be at par,—can it be doubted, that if such be the case, vast quantities of grain would be imported, notwithstanding these new regulations which they propose ? Can it be doubted, that if it were profitable to import wheat when exceeding 50s. but under 54s. the quarter, paying only 2s. 6d. duty, it would be profitable to import it, though not so high as 72s. and paying 24s. 3d. duty ?—How much more, when higher still, and approaching near to 95s.

The average price of 1794 was 51s. 8d. the quant. imp. 327,902 qrs.
.... 1797 ... 53s. 1d. .... 461,767 ...
.... 1798 ... 50s. 3d. .... 376,721 ...

See the returns ordered by the House of Commons to be printed, 17th of January, 1812. End of Append.

or some such points too weak for serious resistance. Pass but the law prohibiting the importation of foreign grain, except at the enormous prices, or with the heavy duties recommended by the Committee; or materially increase the present importation prices, and you leave nothing wanting to complete the chain of Parliamentary evidence (however opposite to the recorded resolutions of one branch of Parliament) sufficient to convince all reasonable thinking men, at least, of the gross depreciation of our currency, could any such have doubted it on the pre-existing evidence of like authority.

And yet it is truly lamentable to see with what facility men, honourable and just in all other respects, both public and private, have lent themselves to the furtherance of this system of iniquity; not scrupling to overlook the plainest principles of common honesty. Can they still, notwithstanding all the proofs, the fresh accumulating proofs to the contrary, imagine that our currency is not depreciated, or that, being so, it is a necessary evil, incapable of mitigation? These, surely, are opinions no longer seriously maintained, except upon the supposition of most unpardonable credulity and obstinacy, or most pitiable perversion of judgment in those who would maintain them.

Even the recent fall in the price of grain, on which they may, perhaps, just now insist, affords no evidence whatever of an undepreciated currency. For though they should affirm that the price was till lately much enhanced by scanty harvests, and difficulty of foreign intercourse; let them also bear in mind these other most important circumstances: that the produce of the United Kingdom, in 1812, was equal to the consumption for the first time since 1764,*—that last year's produce, far surpassed, by every estimate, not only that of 1812, but of almost every year within the memory of living man—that additional supplies have nevertheless been furnished from abroad; and yet the price exceeds the price it bore, in every year for a long series previous to the suspension of cash payments, hardly excepting 1795, and 1796 a period of extraordinary scarcity.† Were our currency now un-

* See Report of the Corn trade Committee.

† See the table of prices, p. 18, 19, of Reflections.—The average price of Wheat from the returns of the week, ended on the 9th of April instant, was 77s. 10d. and of the following week, 76s. 8d. Whether it will fall so low as 63s. should the present corn-trade laws remain unaltered, must in part depend upon the rate of the exchange; which has been much improved of late, in consequence of the greatly increased foreign demand for our manufactures.

depreciated, the price should rather fall below the average of many years preceding the suspension.

That the difficulty of returning to cash payments, is perpetually increasing, may, no doubt, be true. As the depreciation of our currency perpetually increases, the fresh additions to the public debt, and, consequently, the annual charges on the public, must be larger in amount than otherwise they would be; which must of course augment the difficulty of providing for the latter in an undepreciated currency. And this principle applies as well to payments under private contracts. But is not all this an argument, at least, for checking the further progress of the evil? Let those, however, and some there are, who consider it an insuperable impediment to cash payments that we could not possibly sustain the present load of taxes, first examine whether these would not be much diminished in amount, —whether the total value of the funds, from which they must be drawn, would not, *in reality*, remain the same, though charged more equally than they are at present—and, lastly, whether those funds, being more equally charged, the pressure of the taxes would not, on the whole, be less severely felt by individuals. For it is only to the extent of the real loss now borne by the creditors of Government, in consequence of their receiving payment in a depreciated currency, that the public need, in case the value of our money were restored, be subjected to any additional burthen;* which in the shape of taxes might then be borne by all, according to their respective means. But it surely is absurd to say, that, what a part of us are not only capable of bearing, but do actually bear, cannot be borne by all together; as if addition to, subtracted from our strength.

And after all, what is there wanting, but the disposition, to make some near approach to justice? Is it a task too difficult, or an assumption of authority too great, for those who scrupled not to permit a trading company to issue notes to an unlimited amount, and absolve it from the obligation of discharging them in specie; thus rendering the circulating medium of the country, perpetually liable to a variation and considerable diminution of its value—is it not rather become their duty, now that such flagrant abuses have arisen from their strange experiment, to strive at least to correct them;—for that end to form without delay a scale of the real value of our currency from time to time, posterior to the suspension of cash payments; which might be nearly estimated from the probable quantity

* See Reflections, p. 52. 58.

of coin and bank paper in circulation, the rate of the exchange, the average price of gold and silver, corn and meat (making due allowance for the seasons) and of whatever other commodities may appear best adapted for the purpose as having been least influenced in their price, by other causes ? Such scale as this might easily be applied for the regulation of all recent contracts according to their dates. A novel mode, indeed, but such as the novelty of the case would fully sanction,—though liable to errors, its very errors would prove approaches to justice ; and, however incomplete the approximation, it would still be beneficial.

Both government and private debtors might be thus in great measure, if not entirely, protected from the loss they would otherwise have sustained on the return to cash payments, at the time now limited by law ; while their creditors, though left without recompense for the loss they have already sustained, would be insured from further loss. Some might still, indeed, have reason to complain that, having in their contracts had regard to the existing law, and, consequently, to the future improved value of money, they should thus, by an *ex post facto* law, be deprived the benefit of such improvement. These, however, it is probable, are comparatively few in number.

But if no expedient such as the above, nor any other, shall be adopted by the Legislature, to give protection and relief, on principles of real equity; if it be deemed absolutely requisite that we either return to cash payments, without any special fresh provision for the modification of all recent contracts, or persist in our present system of paper money, excessive and depreciated as it is, and still more so as it is, if left to itself, likely to become; let it be seriously and conscientiously considered, whether it be most fit that he, who knowing well the terms of his engagement, when he enters into it, should be compelled to perform it, though at a heavy loss; or that he, who relying on the faith and honor of individuals and the government, on the sacred authority of the laws, for the protection of his property, should be cruelly betrayed by them, despoiled, and arbitrarily interdicted from the recovery of that to which he is otherwise most justly and indisputably entitled.

April 18th, 1814.

ERRATA.

LETTER.

Page 15 line 17 *for* " six" *read* two.
— 21 *after* " and" *insert* that such notes.

REFLECTIONS.

6—20 *after* " and" *insert* probably.
19 5th col. l. 4. *for* " war" *read* peace.
— —— l. 5. *dele* " peace."—*next space read* war.
— last col. l. 32. *for* 4l. 16s. 2d. *read* 5l. 7s. 0d.
20 3d col. l. 21. *for* 96s. 2d. *read* 107s.
— —— l. 3 from bottom, *dele last* " average."
— 15 *for* " 96s. 2d." *read* 107s.
43 2 *for* " 2s." *read* 1s.
— 3 *for* " 9s. 7½d." *read* 15s.
46 28 *for* " 84s. 7d." *read* 86s. 9d.
48 5 *dele* " now unredeemed."
67 20 *for* " more than" *read* about.

APPENDIX.

Page 20 line 20 *dele* " well."
— 21 *for* " better" *read* more so.

EXAMINATION.

Page 19 11 *for* " thee" *read* our.
51 14 *for* " of" *read* for.
56 3 *for* " fact" *read* facts.
— 6 *for* " But" *read* And.
— 10 *for* " its" *read* Bank.
58 6 *dele* " be milled."
— 7 *for* " basis" *read* bars.
— 21 *for* " scarcity in our shops or our markets, as seldom to be seen," *read* rarity as seldom to be seen in our shops or markets.
60 25 *dele* " as."
66 4 *for* " owner and cultivator" read owners.
90 28 *dele the last comma.*

CONTENTS.

Letter, containing Observations on some of the Effects of our Paper Currency.

Resumption of argument and summary to shew that an excess of currency is the real cause of the increased price of provisions, p. 31.

On the disappearance of the precious metals, p. 33;—unnecessary alacrity of our banks in substituting paper in their stead, p. 35;—their scarcity the natural consequence of the diminution of their value, p. 36;—this occasioned by the enormous issues of paper-money, p. 37. Other assigned causes,—decline of our foreign trade, p. 39;—foreign expenditure and subsidies, p. 40;—reduced supply from South America, and concealment on the continent of Europe, p. 42.

Recent inconvenience of the lack of coin, p. 44. Other more important effects of our excess of paper-money,—reduced provision for widows and younger children, p. 45;—damage to landlords, p. 47;—annuitants, mortgagees, and stockholders, p. 51;—discouragement to industry, p. 53;—supposed accommodation to the agricultural, manufacturing and mercantile classes, p. 54,—and general necessity of increasing the circulating medium, p. 57.

On the extent and duration of the paper-money system, p. 58. Original intent of government in suspending cash payments, and effects of that measure on the pecuniary means of government, p. 59. Folly of the people in voluntarily furthering the paper-money system, p. 62;—rapid and alarming increase of the mischief, p. 66;—its possible extent, p. 67.

On the restoration of our currency to its former value, p. 68;—loss which may thence result to debtors, p. 69,—country bankers and their creditors, p. 70. Method proposed for putting an end to the circulation of country bank-notes, limiting the amount of bank of England notes, and returning to cash payments, p 72. Objections considered, p. 78;—its advantages, p. 81.

Postscript,—on the effects of restoring its former value to the currency on the interests of lessees, p. 1.

Reflections on the possible Existence and supposed Expedience of National Bankruptcy.

Further Observations on the Increase of Population and high Price of Grain.

Comparison of the returns of population in 1801 and 1811, p. 1. Probable increase within the last ten years, p. 3.

On our capability of raising sufficient food at home, p. 5. Cause assigned for the neglect of cultivation, and large importations from abroad;—high profits of manufacturing compared with those of farming capital, p. 7. On the Comparative profits of pasturage and tillage, p. 9. High prices and large importations from abroad no certain proof of the insufficiency of our own produce, still less of our own soil, ib.

Cause of continued high price, notwithstanding our great supplies,—an excess or depreciation of currency operating on the course of the exchange, p. 10. Cause of continued importation,—disproportion between the depreciation of currency and depression of exchange, p. 12;—tendency of this disproportion to encourage the importation of wheat in particular, p. 16.

Principle of the corn trade laws, p. 18. Narrow views of land-owners, p. 19. On the change which has taken place in our corn trade, p. 20. Project of raising the importation price, p. 22;—its mischievous tendency, p. 24;—present importation price already too high for an undepreciated currency, p. 25.

Summary, p. 26.—Conclusion, p. 28.

An account of the quantity of corn, &c. imported into Great Britain from 1775 to 1810.

An Examination of Sir John Sinclair's Observations on the Report of the Bullion Committee, &c.

A LETTER,

CONTAINING OBSERVATIONS ON SOME OF THE EFFECTS OF OUR

PAPER CURRENCY,

AND ON THE MEANS OF

REMEDYING ITS PRESENT,

AND

PREVENTING ITS FUTURE EXCESS.

London:

PRINTED FOR T. CADELL AND W. DAVIES,

STRAND.

By G. SIDNEY, Northumberland-street.

1810.

ADVERTISEMENT.

In offering these few pages to the Public, the writer is influenced by a desire, which he has not the vanity, indeed, to suppose will be gratified much the sooner in consequence of his exertions alone, to remove what he conceives to be a sorely-afflicting, and widely-spreading evil. Facts, however, which seemed to him as clear as the sun at noon-day,—Propositions which he held to be of the nature of truisms—if they have not sometimes been boldly denied, have not always been candidly acknowledged, by men who, in general, are able enough to see and judge right. Whilst, on the other hand, tenets have been avowed, and attempted to be supported, which appear to him utterly subversive of justice, and manifestly tending to the ruin of the nation. He pretends not to novelty of doctrine or argument—though perchance he may have stumbled upon it. His arrows, it is likely, have all been shot before.

It is evident, however, that they have not yet brought low the giant against which they may have been directed. Whether they have been sharpened or blunted—more or less skilfully aimed by the present assailant,—will be better known when their effect has again been tried. It is true, the monster has hitherto borne a charm about it,—but the powers which bestowed the charm, will surely not permit it to prevail for ever against the arms of reason and truth. 'Yet, whether reason and truth do not aid it is first to be determined.' And this is a question within the scope of that, with a view to the determination of which the delegated Council of the Commons has actually been occupied, and that council, it is said, has actually pronounced the propriety of speedily dissolving the charm, of revoking the edict of inviolability, which has so many years been kept in force.

A LETTER,

CONTAINING

Observations on some of the Effects of our Paper Currency.

DEAR * * *

I AM not surprized at seeing once more the threadbare hexameter —

> "Tempora mutantur nos et mutamur in illis,"!!!

which, as long as the world endures, furnished as it is with human beings, will ever be applicable to the time being. The triple note of admiration, however, with which you have adorned the adage, is a mode of punctuation which does not appear to have been adopted by any of the old editors; but is pathetically intended by you, I presume, to apply to this time in particular.

You cast your eyes over your old weekly account book; you notice the entries that were made there, five and twenty, or thirty, years ago, and are too well satisfied of the fact, that the pound note and shilling of 1810, will not procure more than half, or two-thirds, of the provisions which a guinea did in those times. Should your memory have failed you, which, in matters of that nature, is not likely to have been the case, you see it recorded, in your own legible hand writing, what was the condition of things in the days that are passed.—You shrug up your shoulders, deprecate the frequency and long continuance of wars, and their numerous train of evils; the heavy weight of taxes they bring along with and leave behind them. To these you ascribe the distressing change which you know, and feel, has been effected, not only in your household expenditure, but in the aggregate of your comforts and enjoyments.—You had more meat from your butcher—more bread from your baker; you distributed more to the infant and aged poor, well-accustomed to your hospitable threshold; and, notwithstanding you then maintained your children at home, your tradesmen's bills amounted to much less than they amount to at present—your equipage, though not shewy, was respectable—you felt easy in your circumstances, and were happy in the reflection, that you were making a decent future provision for your family. But that recollection must now be painful to you. War and its consequences are indeed severe calamities—many mothers have mourned for their children—many wives for their husbands. Our luxuries and our comforts, (to descend to a less afflicting part of the theme) have been abridged—the annually-allotted savings for our children have increased less rapidly, if we have not positively diminished them—nay, sacrilegiously entrenched upon the very capitals of our ancestors. The taxes are truly burthensome.—But the worst evils of war we have never felt,—and may this country never feel them.

You are wrong, however, to attribute the vast difference, which, with dismay, you behold in comparing your account of seventeen hundred and eighty, or eighty-five, with that of eighteen hundred and ten, solely to the operation of the taxes. You say there can be no doubt as to the duties imposed upon your house, your windows, your horses, and your carriage; and that it is easy enough to perceive, there may be a multitude of taxes affecting the prices of many articles of consumption, besides those which are the immediate objects of taxation.—That of this nature are taxes imposed upon articles of general necessity—upon candles, soap, and leather,—since those who are employed in raising and manufacturing these, or any other commodities, must, (at least in this country) receive such wages as will enable them to procure the former; and if the wages of labour be increased, the price of the articles produced, or worked up by that labour, must also be increased.

I will not dispute with you upon the truth of the last observation, though it might very candidly be questioned, whether an increase in the wages of such as are employed in agriculture does not, in a great measure, if not altogether, fall upon the owner of the land--so as partly, if not wholly, to exonerate the consumer of the article produced. But how does all this affect the point under consideration? What additional taxes have been imposed upon these articles of necessity? Examine the several items in your aforesaid weekly account book—for it affords instances of many articles of necessity, whereon no duties have been imposed, whilst at the same time it affords instances of the vast increase in their price. What has been the additional duty of Excise upon candles and soap, within the period of which I am speaking; and have not other articles of much greater importance, namely, butter, cheese, corn, and butchers' meat, and fuel, continued wholly free from such duty? But have not likewise coarse linen, and woollen cloths, continued so? Has any additional duty been laid on leather used for shoes? 'Tis true, the old duties upon salt, sugar, tea, and malt, have been repealed, and heavier duties are now levied upon them. But how little of these articles is generally consumed by the labourer?*—Enough, I will acknowledge, to make it questionable, whether such duties ought to have been imposed—but too little to raise any reasonable ground for supposing that they have occasioned an increase in the price of the wages of labour, sufficient to account, in any degree worthy of our present notice, for the increase in the price of the other commodities to which I have alluded.

How, then, can it be said, that the taxes have occasioned this difference in price?

* It was supposed, at the time when the additional duty of five shillings per bushel was imposed upon salt, that the additional sum to be annually paid by the labouring class, in consequence of that duty, amounted upon an average to two shillings and sixpence for each family. And if any one will give himself the trouble to calculate the annual sum which is paid by the same class, upon an average in respect of the additional duties upon sugar, tea, and malt,—(not forgetting that the use of malt is very far from being general, even amongst the men, and that of sugar and tea, almost confined to the women) I doubt not he will soon satisfy himself, that it bears but a very trifling proportion to the increase in the wages of labour.

Abandon your prejudices—no longer fancy that to be the consequence of the taxes, which, upon a fair examination, you cannot perceive how the taxes can materially affect. Their direct and indirect perceptible operation is extensive and alarming enough. The circumstances of the times in which we live have called for extraordinary exertions and corresponding sacrifices. It may be worth while, however, to enquire a little further for the cause which has produced this rapid advance in the price of goods in general, that if practicable and prudent so to do, we may remove it.

Does the labourer who is employed in raising or manufacturing these articles of necessity, though his wages be increased, enjoy more of the comforts of life than he formerly did? Is he more capable of maintaining his infant family? Does he make fewer applications for assistance to the overseers of his parish, than in the times when a peck loaf cost him not more than twenty-pence or two shillings?—It cannot be pretended. Neither, then, ought it to be pretended, that this advance in the price of goods proceeded originally from any advance in the wages of labour, which itself must rather have proceeded from an advance in the price of goods.

We have occasionally experienced bad harvests—the usual supplies of tallow and potash were for a time interrupted,—and the prices of grain and candles, and soap, were raised accordingly. The finer sort of wool, from its extreme scarcity, real or pretended, has also of late been greatly enhanced in value, which has led to an increase of demand, and consequently of price, for the coarser sorts; but I speak not of such temporary advances as these, which are sooner or later reduced, and the particular causes of which are sufficiently manifest—but of the continually-growing price of almost all commodities whatsoever.

Has our soil been less cultivated? Has the skill and ingenuity of our engineers and mechanics been cramped or lethargied? Have the labourers stood idle in the vineyard? On the contrary, have not extensive wastes been enclosed, brought into tillage, and their produce abundantly augmented? Where nought but rush and moss, or furze and heath, grew before, are not rich meadows and furrowed fields to be seen, smiling with numerous flocks and herds, or with loaded ears of corn? Have not a variety of bridges, iron rail-ways, turnpike roads and canals, been formed to facilitate the conveyance of the productions of the surface and bowels of the earth, to and fro, throughout all parts of the kingdom? Have not our manufactories been enlarged and multiplied to an extent that is amazing? Our machinery improved to such excellence, that in many instances it has been brought to perform the same quantity of work as formerly, nay, infinitely more, with half the labour, and in half the time? and shall it be maintained, notwithstanding all this, that the supplies of food have been diminished,—that the work of our manufactories has been retarded,—that no encouragement has been afforded to them,—that all things have hence become more valuable, and of greater price? Or, shall it be said, contrary to the reason and experience of mankind, that the very improvements and facilities which we have slightly recounted, have eventually tended only to enable the farmer and manufacturer to impose upon the consumer? Shall it not rather be confessed, that some most powerful cause must have operated to prevent a reduction of price in the common articles of food, and all other articles, the production of which has been so accelerated and multiplied by our agricultural and mechanical improvements, and fresh-acquired means of intercourse?

I leave it to those who are able to shew, what other cause has contributed to the increase in the price of such necessaries as I have mentioned, besides that which, to my mind at least, is nearly adequate to the effect. I mean the enormous increase of money, compared with that of the commodities which it is employed to circulate. —It is a principle admitted, I believe, by all who bestow the least consideration upon the subject, that the quantity of money, whether it be bullion, coin, or paper money, (for they all serve the purpose of a circulating medium) be increased in a greater ratio than the quantity of commodities, which it is employed to circulate, its value will be diminished proportionably. Or, in other words, the nominal, or money-price of things, will be proportionably diminished. For, although it be evident that an increase in the price of divers particular articles may, and often does, take place, notwithstanding the relative quantities of such articles, and the money employed to circulate them, together with other commodities, continue the same; yet that is a circumstance to be ascribed to causes generally, if not always, discoverable,—as in cases of increased demand for those articles, or of taxes newly imposed upon them. But if the money-price of all commodities be increased in any considerable degree, whilst the demand for, and supply of them, appear to continue the same, and no other cause for such increase, than the positive increase of money, can be discovered, it is natural to conclude that it must proceed from this; nay the general increase of price, if not otherwise to be accounted for, justifies a strong presumption, that the relative quantity of money has been increased, though no other proof can be adduced that such has actually been the case.

Had the absolute quantity of money continued stationary, the nominal price of the commodities, which I have above particularly referred to, must doubtless have been diminished, in consequence of the vast increase of the quantity of commodities in general. The trade and commerce of the country would have required it. Had the quantity of money kept pace with that of other commodities in general, but not exceeded it, there should have appeared no alteration in the price, the nominal price, of the latter.—The alteration, however, is most apparent; and whilst we have most positive evidence of the flourishing state of our agriculture, manufactures, and commerce, we have the strongest grounds of proof that the quantity of money has increased in a still greater proportion.

For it is further to be observed, that the troubles which so long agitated the neighbouring country, and the calamitous influence they have had upon the affairs of the continent of Europe in general, must have occasioned the introduction of an abundance of gold and silver, in coin and other articles, by those who, seeking refuge from the storms of revolution and war, from the pillage of public and private property, consigned every thing that was valuable, and, at the same time, portable, to the protection of this. Even the very captures which we have made, of rich vessels laden with bullion, must have contributed in no small degree to augment the stock of money, or what is capable of being used as such. But, above all, it should seem that the very long-continued prosperous state of our trade and commerce, must of itself have provided fresh and mighty means of circulation;—that millions, and tens of millions must, from time to time, have been imported to settle the balance of our foreign trade. So decidedly and so greatly does it appear to be in our favour.*

There are persons, indeed, who habituate themselves to doubt the truth of official statements, or strive to weaken the force of the arguments which are grounded upon them; and whom, therefore, it may be difficult to persuade, that the balance of our

* *Extract from Papers lately laid before the House of Commons.*

	" Official Value of Imports.		Official Value of Exports.	
	From Europe, Africa, and America.	From East Indies and China.	British produce and Manufactures.	Foreign Merchandize.
Yrs. endg.	£.	£.	£.	£.
Jan. 5, 1808	25,453,149	3,401,509	25,171,422	9,395,149
1809	23,780,704	5,848,649	26,691,962	7,862,305
1810	30,406,560	†	35,107,439	15,194,324

The actual value of British produce and Manufactures exported from Great Britain, according to the average prices current, and to the declarations of the exporters, was, in the year ending 1810........................ .. } £. 50,242,761

W. IRVING,
Inspect. Gen. of the Imps. and Exs. of Gt. Br."

† Account of Imports from the East and West Indies, and China, cannot yet be given.

trade has, for many years, been so decidedly and greatly in our favour; that any considerable quantities of bullion have, in consequence, been imported into our country. Yet most persons will probably acquiesce in the truth of those statements, and I do not feel much inclined to spend my time in arguing the matter with those who do not. It will, however, be admitted by all, since it has been confessed by those who are chiefly interested in concealing it, that the amount of promissory notes issued of late years, by the Bank of England, has been great beyond example; and that, according to the report which was lately delivered to the House of Commons, upwards of six and twenty millions of pounds in notes and dollars, of which more than one and twenty millions, four hundred thousand pounds were notes, had been issued by that company, and were actually in circulation, soon after the commencement of the present year; the amount of its issues, previous to the stoppage of payment in specie in 1797, not having exceeded, upon an average, ten or eleven millions.

But the Mint and the Bank of England are not alone possessed of this faculty of making money. As the former has admitted the latter to be its rival, so have they both a multitude of rivals in the country Banks; and it is a circumstance not unworthy of remark, that, amongst many of the lower orders, and, perhaps, amongst some of the higher, the notes of the country Bank are preferred to those of the Bank of England. Whether or not, upon any solid grounds, I will not now venture to determine; it is enough to observe, that both one and the other species are sufficiently abundant to admit a free choice of either to any person who is disposed to give for it its amount in gold or silver. The competition, however, in this, as in every other trade, has tended to reduce the value of the commodity, which is the subject of it; but does not, perhaps, alike tend to the advantage of the public.

That there should be so great an abundance of such money as this, is not at all to be wondered at. With what facility may these promissory notes be generated? To beget such children as these requires no labour or ingenuity; the chief thought is how to dispose of them to advantage, how to change them for the legitimate offspring of the government, and to keep the ragged brood as long from home as possible;—whither, however, they are sometimes doomed to return, to the utter dismay, ruin, and disgrace, of their unfortunate parents.

There are, indeed, different degrees of prudence, if not of honesty, observed by the many who are engaged in this new system of money making, not to say coining. Some there are, I believe but few, who, not venturing much into the field of speculation, and contenting themselves with moderate profits, limit the amount of the notes they issue to the average amount of the sums usually lodged in their hands, and remaining uncalled for; others, less timid, confine them, not very narrowly, to the amount of their credits, their own capital in the public funds, on mortgage, or on land, or wherever else it may happen to be vested; deeming it sufficient, if the aggregate amount of these be equal to that of the notes they put into circulation, and that they have assets, which, in case of failure of payment, may, by course of law, probably answer the demands of their creditors. Some, on the other hand, taking advantage of the easy indolence or credulity of the public, without any funds at all, or such only as exist in speculation, so long as their credit lasts, live upon that which their credit can raise for them, without care for the security of their creditors or themselves; or fondly trust, perhaps, to the success of their speculation for enriching themselves, and at the same time affording some security for the eventual discharge of their engagements. In each of these cases, an additional quantity of money is created, not always, it is to be hoped, in proportion to the inclinations and endeavours of those who create it, but according to their respective well, or ill-deserved credit with the public.

In former times, this practice of paying their own promissory notes as money, when drawn upon by their customer, either such as had money lodged in their hands, or such as was desirous of obtaining a loan from them, did not prevail amongst Bankers. To the former they paid back his own money, or as good; (for it was the common coin of the realm;) and to the latter they advanced part of the surplus, the otherwise unemployed part of the surplus, which had been deposited by the former, but not without taking solid and sufficient security for repayment; and it was from this latter transaction, that the Bankers of those days derived their profits,—large enough for men sitting idle in their shops, excepting that they were guarding the property intrusted to their care, or, at least, providing well that it should be forthcoming when called for. They hazarded little; their gains, therefore, were not, perhaps, always great, but they were certain. The Bankers of the present day, however, (I speak not of many of the old-fashioned Londoners, who abide by the ancient practice, so far as the wisdom of

Parliament permits them) have, in their eagerness to become rich, united the business of money-dealer with that of money-maker, amongst others ; and the consequence is, that, instead of being freely and good-humouredly served with the lawful money of Great Britain, or that which the powers of Parliament have, by a sort of politico-chymical process, more than half converted into it, when we civilly wait before their counter, adorned with the needless furniture of a shovel, (as if to mock their customers) and humbly present them with a draft for a small portion of the money that has been lodged with them, they hand over to us nothing but divers dirty, old, tattered, and patched pieces of paper, called promissory notes, of their own fabrication, which, perhaps, without being naturally very suspicious, we may not feel content to put into our pocket books, but which, it too often, I will not say always, happens, they will not, without extreme reluctance, sometimes coupled with ill language on their part, if not on our own, exchange at last for notes of the Bank of England. To those who have had occasional dealings with country Bankers, (not their own) this observation will not, I am confident, appear overcharged.

Do not, however, suppose that I think there are no exceptions to this practice.—Without doubt there are amongst the class of Bankers, to which I have alluded, men of the highest spirit, and of most exemplary liberality,—who, although, the profits of the business in which they are engaged, depend almost entirely upon the circulation of their promissory notes, (for they deem it no crime to make a profit of that confidence which they know to be well merited; nay, perhaps most conscientiously believe, is, at the same time, employed serviceably for the public, whilst they themselves make a profit of it) would scorn to compromise the character of their House, by meanly endeavouring to evade the due discharge of their engagements.—But the class does not consist of men of this stamp only.

Nay, the practice of issuing promissory

notes, to answer the purpose of ready money, is not confined to bankers properly so called; I mean those who have the *safe* custody of other persons' money, according to the new method;—it extends, also, to attornies, manufacturers, and tradesmen, to the proprietors of waggons and stage coaches, to linen drapers and tea dealers.—These, also, inundate the country with their paper currency.—Not a town, scarce a village, that is not furnished with counting house or desk, whence the floods issue forth; and, as if it were decreed to overwhelm and wash away as much as possible the original coin of the kingdom, pasteboard tokens are forced into the circulating medium, as a substitute for the crown piece, and the workman, who receives any payment at all, is oftentimes under the necessity of receiving it in that form.

I do not by this representation mean to insinuate that there is any greater abuse in the latter practice, than in pressing upon the public notes of a larger amount. The abuse is not so great; and if it be true, as I believe it is, in some degree, that the scarcity of small coin or silver has at times occasioned the necessity for a few manufacturers to employ these tokens in paying the wages of their workmen, such a practice, in such a case, is hardly to be condemned, however we may lament the necessity of adopting it. Yet we must, at the same time, be permitted to observe, that the additional profit arising to the manufacturer is probably, in most instances, alone, and independent of every other consideration, a sufficient inducement for him to resort to it. But, whatever may be the motive, the fact is the same. Notwithstanding the very narrow circulation of these tokens, it is plain they answer the purpose of money. The manufacturer who issues them, does not require the same quantity of coin he would require without them; and may be considered as adding as much or more to the public stock of money than he adds to the demand for it. He keeps at a distance that which he before employed, or stood in need of,—and, by the circulation of his tokens, although extremely limited, he renders the coin more plentiful elsewhere, and thus tends eventually to depreciate it.

Whilst the quantity of paper money is thus made to depend upon the discretion of the persons whose profits are proportional to the share of it which they can keep in circulation, it is rational to suppose that, at least, so much as they expect to keep in circulation they will issue. The obligation which the Bank of England, in common with other Banks, formerly lay under of paying their promissory notes in specie, when called upon to do so, had, by some persons, been considered a sufficient security against too profuse an issue of them;—it was conceived by them, that the quantity of paper money could not long exceed the quantity of specie of which it supplied the place, that is, which was immediately before in circulation; that the depreciation in value, occasioned by the superabundance of paper money, would necessarily occasion its return upon the hands of those who had issued it, and thus speedily restore the circulation to its due level. That such would be the case were paper money at a discount when exchanged for gold or silver, may be true. But why should the superabundance of paper money necessarily occasion its return? If the credit of those by whom it is issued be not dubious, it is freely taken in exchange and circulated; and it is of little importance in the opinion of the farmer, manufacturer, or shopkeeper, whether he holds a bank note or specie, whilst he knows that the same quantity of goods may be procured by means of the one as of the other. As long as the public are content to look upon them as of equal value, for what reason should he endeavour to exchange one for the other?

The case is not the same with respect to money as it is with other commodities. If there be a superabundance of corn, more than the existing number of mouths, and keenness of appetite, can devour, or more houses than there are people to inhabit them, it is true some of the corn, or some of the houses, must remain upon hand. But the superabundance of money, though it lessens its value, does not necessarily lessen the demand for it. The demand for it rather rises as its value diminishes—double the quantity of money, you double the price of other commodities—consequently, you double the demand for the former quantity of money. He who would purchase a quartern loaf, for which he formerly gave but sixpence, must now pay a shilling for it, and a shilling will therefore be requisite where before sixpence only would have been sufficient. Upon the whole, therefore, the superabundance of paper money does not appear necessarily to occasion its return upon the hands of those who issue it.

It may, undoubtedly, be the interest of the banker, or other manufacturer of paper money, whose profits are derived from, or closely and necessarily connected with, the circulation of his own promissory notes, to prevent the circulation of those of other persons, more especially if he can thereby ensure the circulation of his own in their stead. Accordingly, whenever the former happen to come to his hands, either deposited there by customers or otherwise, it is his practice straightway to return them for payment in cash, or in notes of the Bank of

England, which he may invest either in the public funds, in the purchase of land or houses, or in any other less harmless speculation he may think fit, after, perhaps, retaining what he conceives to be sufficient to answer the demands for cash or Bank of England notes, which some of the holders of his own promissory notes, issued in lieu of those which he has thus disposed of, are likely to make upon him. But the quantity of money is but little diminished by this operation ;—it is generally but a small number only in comparison with the whole of the notes that are issued by any company that are speedily thus driven back upon their hands ;—were it otherwise, the profit derived from issuing them would be trivial, and not worth the risk ;—and it is always to be remembered, that, in lieu of the greater part of those which are thus driven back, it is probable that similar notes of other bankers are introduced into circulation. But it is also further to be remembered, that as there is a never-failing call for money on the part of individuals, who, to have it, must borrow it, of whatsoever description, and, as there is also a numerous tribe of tradesmen, who, to obtain or preserve the custom of opulent bankers, are willing to receive, as money, their promissory notes, there are always channels through which they may be brought into circulation.

But the security arising from the obligation of payment in specie, when demanded, if it ever were a security, no longer exists. The Bank of England is freed from that obligation—and great apprehensions are, in consequence, entertained, lest it should have exceeded the capital that is to answer the demands which, at some future period, may be made upon it. If we do not hear complaints against the partial protection originally afforded to it by the legislature, in order to screen it from bankruptcy, we hear complaints against permitting it any longer to issue its notes without restoring its former liability to pay them, when tendered, with cash. It is thought folly to trust any longer to its moderation and prudence; moderation worthy of little praise, if we reflect upon the magnitude of its profits, and the means by which they appear to be acquired—prudence, which has been tried and found wanting. Little apprehension, however, seems to be entertained of any unwarrantable issue from the country banks; their present liability to pay with cash, or the notes of the Bank of England, is considered as an adequate security against any abuse of the credit they enjoy—as the similar liability to pay with cash was against any abuse of the credit formerly enjoyed by the Bank of England.

But though, as a matter of policy not measured strictly by honesty, the Bank of England may with safety, at present, under the restrictions imposed by Parliament, put into circulation any number of its notes without fear of Bankruptcy, whilst the private Banker is liable to that misfortune, should he issue more than he could satisfy, when presented to him for payment; yet the privilege bestowed upon the former is not made permanent; it continues only till the expiration of six months after the termination of the war: and may at any time before that period be withdrawn, should the legislature think fit. It may, therefore, very plausibly, if not properly be questioned, whether, possessing that privilege, liable as it is to such uncertain continuance, it is likely to be much more abused than the confidence reposed in many of those private Banks, whose profits depend chiefly, if not altogether, upon the circulation of their notes.

But however solid or feeble may be the grounds upon which their respective claims to public confidence are founded, the probable effect of the restriction from payment, in specie, by the Bank of England, is to augment the quantity of paper money; for it must, I suppose, be conceded on the one hand, that, under favour of such a regulation, the Bank of England may, with greater safety, and, therefore, probably will issue more of their notes, than when liable to be called upon for payment of them in cash; nay, the very fact proves itself; and, on the other, that the private Banks, not being under the necessity of paying in cash, provided they make a tender of payment with notes of the Bank of England, their own notes being generally in as high credit as the former, are less likely to be returned, in order to be exchanged for them, than they would in order to be exchanged for cash, in case those private Banks were under such necessity. Their promissory notes may, therefore, be increased with less hazard, and, consequently, are in all probability increased more abundantly.

But it is time to ask, whether, under such circumstances as have been enumerated, with such extraordinary sources of supply as have been noticed, there is any reason to doubt what is the real cause of the dearness, or rather the increased money price of provisions. Is it not plainly deducible from an excess of money? Can it seriously be imagined, that when all have a power of fabricating money, such as it is, part being the representative of substantial property, part mere counterfeit,—where so many do, in truth, exercise that power to its fullest extent, that the price of all commodities will be naturally, though enormously increased? Is it necessary to explain, step by step, the whole process by which that effect is produced, or barely refer to the principle which has been stated, generally, above? Is it worth while to shew that he who pays only with the money, which, with a scrawl of his own hand, he can in an instant create, will feel less disposed to haggle about the price of the article of which he stands in need, than if the payment were to be made with money earned with much difficulty, by the sweat of the brow, by toil and labour,—that, where it is the interest of many to lend, many will borrow,—that the greater the number of bidders in the market, all having plenty of money at their command, by whatever means they have it, the higher will the article bidden for be sold,—that the farmer, manufacturer, and merchant, will each, under these circumstances, bid higher in the markets they respectively frequent, than if money were scarce, and obtained only with great difficulty. That hence labour in general,—the stock to be improved by the farmer,—the raw material to be worked up by the manufacturer, and the finished article to be sold by the merchant or trader, and retail dealer, will all be purchased by them at an increased price; but that, having purchased at an increased price, they will also sell at an increased price, or lose their accustomed profit—a case not now to be supposed,—that the price of the necessaries of life being thus enhanced, the price of labour must be enhanced accordingly, and hence tend to a further increase of the price of all commodities whatsoever;—and, lastly, that the longer this system is continued, the more powerful will be its effects, inasmuch as it feeds upon, and is nourished by itself.

Though I would have it fully conceived how many, and how abundant are the sources, whence the circulating medium has been derived; yet I do not mean to insinuate that there still remains, in this country, the total quantity of the precious metals, which, from time to time, have been imported into it in the manner above mentioned; if it had so remained, the price of provisions would have been yet further increased. But it is not to be supposed, that the vast supplies of gold and silver, with which we have been furnished, should be permitted to remain at home, whilst they could be employed so much more profitably abroad. We know, on the contrary, that the scarcity of them here is extreme. Anxious for the increase of the wealth and prosperity of the nation at large, not with any view of private benefit to themselves, it is hence, no doubt, that the Bank of England, and a multitude of other banks, profiting by its good example, have, in the fervour of their patriotism, busied themselves in providing vast supplies of paper money, so as to supersede the necessity of gold and silver coin and bullion, as the medium of circulation at home; and thus to afford to traders the opportunity of trafficking with them abroad—a noble instance of public spirit, and much to be commended. But I can hardly prevail upon myself to think, that the country really required of them such violent exertions on their part, or that any great good is necessarily to arise from scouring the land of all its gold and silver.

But they were fearful of doing too little, and therefore did too much. We could have proceeded very well without the assistance of so much as two or three Banks in every town, to shed their benign influence over such of the adjacent villages as had not one or more already established in them. We could have spared them, and also the Bank of England, the risk they have encountered in putting forth their credit to such an alarming extent for our sakes. We could have spared them those extraordinary expenses which they have incurred, in the heavy salaries to the multiplied tribe of clerks and other officers, employed in the money-forming department, the mere signature of one of whose names upon the notes, issued by the Bank of England, has been considered so laborious, from its frequent repetition, that it has of late been solemnly dispensed with. We could have borne the weight of a few guineas in our pockets, and made room for a few more in our bureaus, without much burthen or inconvenience to ourselves, without much injury to the nation at large, and without materially cramping and disabling its commercial interest in particular. At least, the total dismissal of gold, and almost total dismissal of the silver coin of the realm, was not, in any political view, so desirable an event upon the whole, that the country really required such an inundation of paper money to bring it to pass. Neither do I apprehend, that such an inundation, like the waters of Egypt, will bring along with it the plenty and riches which have been ascribed to its influence—whatever may be its effect in generating, and maintaining, a swarm of caterpillars and locusts, to devour the harvest of the husbandman.

That the diminution, nay, almost total expulsion, of the precious metals, is the natural consequence of constant and unlimited issues of paper money, I had imagined would scarcely have been denied. If the gold and silver coin, and bullion, be of such little value here, that paper, which can be fabricated almost for nothing, is become equally valuable, stands as high in repute, and answers every purpose as well—provided it bears the signature of a man of opulence or credit ?—if the promissory notes of the company of the Bank of England, who are at liberty to issue them to any amount, without being under any present obligation to pay in cash beyond the trifling sum of a few shillings ?—if those of every shopkeeper in England, Scotland, and Wales, who thinks proper to issue them, and is not already a bankrupt, or does not deserve to become one, are to be received as of equal value with gold and silver, and are circulated as freely—of what value are either ? Well, indeed, must it be worth the while of cunning traders to convey the latter, whither they are held in greater esteem than with us. They have found how profitable the traffick is,—and no sooner are the precious metals poured into the country, than they are poured out of it. They have thus become scarce, because they have become comparatively valueless. Even the very weeds themselves, by being constantly eradicated, at last become a curiosity. Here, alas ! the goodly herb is rooted up, and the weed is suffered to remain, and overrun the land.

That the deficiency of gold and silver coin and bullion, and the unfavourable state of the exchange, must have proceeded, if not altogether, at least principally, from the cause here assigned, I had, indeed, imagined would have been generally understood and acknowledged. And, truly, I believe there are but few who do not ascribe them, in some measure, to the enormous issues from the Bank of England. Care, however, seems to have been taken by some persons, to absolve the notes of private bankers and tradesmen, from every imputation of having essentially contributed to the same effect. With what view, or ground of persuasion they have formed an opinion of the inefficacy of the paper, which seems to constitute almost the only currency, at a distance from the metropolis, I am at a loss to discover—especially when I reflect upon the very numerous manufactories and marts with which the country in every direction abounds. They give, however, full credit for the operation of divers other causes, which have been suggested—such as the diminished profit, or rather absolute loss from our foreign trade,—the vast expenditures for the maintenance of our army and navy on foreign stations,—the prodigal subsidies to foreign states,—the slender supply of gold and silver from the mines of South America, and the multitude of pecuniary interments on the Continent of Europe.

There is, however, a degree of boldness in these suggestions, and of simplicity in yielding credit to them, which commands admiration.

That our trade should be on the decline,—that our forces abroad should have exhausted all our stock of specie, that had escaped the capacious net of the princes we have subsidized, unless it were before reduced to a very low state indeed, to such as nothing but the operation of some most powerful cause could have reduced it, I thought, was hardly to be credited by any one who had the common means of judging of what passed before them. If we do not utterly deny the direct conclusions to be drawn from the only documents, to which we can have recourse with any hope of correct information upon the subject, we must admit, that the vast importations of gold and silver, to which I have before alluded, must have proved much more than sufficient to provide, not only for those scanty subsidies which have lately been afforded, but also for those extraordinary supplies, which, from time to time, have been remitted for the maintenance of our army and navy upon foreign stations. It is not, however, to be imagined, that specie alone is employed upon these occasions, or that the specie which is so employed is wholly lost to this country. In furnishing such subsidies and supplies, it is not necessary that any money at all should be actually remitted from hence, provided the balance of trade be in our favor— a circumstance which would soon restore it, even if it were so actually remitted. And can it be doubted, that the present peculiar state of Portugal and Spain, where our troops have of late been chiefly occupied, (for really it is idle to talk of the recent subsidies; and the temporary retention of Walcheren, so far as it rendered necessary any remittance of gold or silver, for the maintenance of our troops, is not much more worthy to be noticed) has necessarily tended to increase our exportations thither to a considerable amount? Desolate and laid waste by a cruel war, their manufactories can hardly have provided, in any sufficient degree, for the necessities of the people. They must have needed assistance from without, and have doubtless received it more particularly from us. The specie, therefore, with which our armies have been supplied for procuring their subsistence in those countries, has thus, probably, been rendered back by our merchants, in exchange for the produce of our manufactories.*

* The passages which have been cited by Sir Philip Francis, (p. 31 and 32 of his Reflections) from the letters of Sir John Moore, may, perhaps, be thought a refutation of what is above stated. Those passages, indeed, shew the difficulty under which that accomplished officer laboured with respect to the obtaining of money, and the probability that ministers here were not well acquainted with the channels through which he might have been supplied, without actual remittances from this country,—the old channels having, I conclude, been disturbed and broken up,—the regular system of commercial credit having

And, with regard to the alleged poverty of the mines of South America, or the failure in remitting their recent produce to Europe--- taking also into account the possibility of hidden treasures on the Continent, I really cannot consider these causes, if viewed within the extent of their probable existence and operation, though co-operating with those which I have just been alluding to, viewed by the same rule, as at all adequate to the effect under contemplation—accompanied as they are with circumstances of a totally opposite tendency, sufficient it should seem at least to negative their effect.

What, indeed, may be the degree of importance intended to be attached to these allegations I know not.—But, unless it can be shewn that the present state of the world requires a greater stock of the precious metals,

been destroyed, or much impaired, by the violent shock which had been given to the Portuguese and Spanish nations. It is pretty plain, however, that specie was at length obtained, and proved so cumbersome to our army, on its retreat to Corunna, that it was absolutely thrown away.

than was required prior to the supposed failure from South America, this latter circumstance should have no effect towards producing any greater absolute scarcity of them than existed before.—But, whatever further supply that state might require, and whatever temporary deficiency may have been occasioned by the sepulture of gold and silver, it is not, perhaps, too much to imagine and presume, that they are well nigh, nay, much more than compensated by other means, when we reflect how great a portion of the accumulated wealth of the ages which have passed since the discovery of the mines in the new world,—what a multitude of ingots, or bars of silver and gold, which, from time to time, had been formed into innumerable articles of ornament and use,—what heaps of sacred utensils, and offerings of richly-endowed churches and monasteries,—what splendid services and appendages, with which the tables of nobles, dignified ecclesiastics, princes, and sovereigns were furnished, have been brought forth, cast into the crucible, and melted down to save them from, or to glut the rapacious hand of, anarchy and conquest

These calamities of revolution and war, which have overspread the greater part of civilized Europe, overturning and destroying, in great measure, the mechanic arts, the trade and commerce of nations, and thus rendering unnecessary so large a share of the money requisite for maintaining them, have, at the same time, in other respects, by injuring or impairing the credit of those nations, excluded it in a manner from their dealings one with another, and thus rendered the use of specie alone almost necessary amongst them; the precious metals, therefore, have thus, from the degraded state of public and private credit upon the Continent, been cherished there, perhaps, as much as they have been despised and rejected by us.

Indeed, it is not till lately, that those who are much listened to, when they raise a complaint, have felt any weighty inconvenience from this almost total expulsion of our gold and silver coin. So steadily was the credit of our paper money, I mean the paper of the Bank of England, supported, even when the holder of it was by law declared incapable of obtaining payment of it in specie, that the same value continued to be attached to it as to the coin itself, in our dealings amongst each other; and so long as a pound note could procure as much bread or beef as could be procured with twenty shillings in silver, it seemed immaterial to the holder, which he was master of. And so, perhaps, it was. But now that we begin to open our eyes a little, and to see what those around us have been doing;—that the country has been so drained that it is hardly possible to get a sufficiency of silver, excepting in dollars, to answer the common purposes of buying and selling in a meat or a fish market,—when we are astonished at the production of a guinea, we think of inquiring how it has all happened, and apprehend some dreadful public calamity.

And it is well if, by this lack of specie, we are roused not only to inquire into the cause which has led to it; but, also, to reflect, and seriously too, upon a few other effects, which have been wrought by the same cause.

Those of our forefathers, who were so lucky as to be possessed of real estates, in adopting the practice of settling upon their wives and younger children, certain yearly incomes, or gross sums of money to be paid out of the lands, which they gave or permitted to descend to their eldest sons, did no more than what was just and reasonable; they considered the value of that land, and laid proportionate charges upon it, for the above praiseworthy purposes. In our days, I speak of a period of thirty or forty years, provisions of this nature answer, but in a small degree, the end proposed; that of a reasonable jointure for the widow, and portions for the younger children. In consequence of the depreciation of money, and of the great addition to the taxes, a thousand pounds will not now purchase more than a half or a third of the commodities they would then. But the land, which is charged with the payment of that sum, yields double, or three times, the rent it then did. The eldest of the children is thus apparently enriched, (it is true) but at the expense of the rest, and their widowed mother, who are in reality despoiled.

But how great soever may be the additional rental which the man of landed property may boast of, with whatsoever satisfaction he may compare the fresh with the faded rent-roll, and imagine that, because the nominal amount of income has increased so enormously since the days of his grandfather, his powers have increased accordingly ;—yet, if he examine the relics of his grandmother's account book, he will find that he entertains not so hospitably, that he is obliged to dismiss the servants and the horses of his acquaintance, his friends, and his relations, from his board and his stables,—to look narrowly to his consumption ; or if not, to take heed of the sheriff's officers.

" But all this proceeds from the pressure of the taxes ;" the greater part, I will allow, but not all.—For if the gentleman of landed property will give himself the trouble to reflect a little, he will find that his income does not keep exact pace with the price even of such provisions as the taxes do not affect; and he may be well satisfied that he will, in the long run, be a loser in consequence of this depreciation of money.

Let him suppose only the case, which has actually happened to himself, of a lease for the term of twenty-one years, granted fifteen or sixteen years ago, at a rent fixed upon what was then considered a fair valuation, being estimated at the value of the produce of the land upon the average of a few years preceding, when the price of meat, of grain, and hay, and of all the necessaries, as well as luxuries of life, were much lower than they have been of later years.

The average produce has continued nearly the same, or perhaps increased; but the price at which it has been sold has advanced prodigiously, so that if the lease were now expired, the landlord would be justified in demanding, and would be paid, at least a third more rent than he has hitherto received for it.—But as the price of the produce of the land which he has let has risen, so has that of all other commodities, for which he has had occasion; insomuch that he has deemed it prudent to abstain from so large a consumption of them as formerly, rather than exceed his income; and thus from time to time he is compelled to lessen his enjoyments, till, by the expiration of the lease which he has granted, he is enabled to lay on an additional rent, in proportion to the depreciation of money, which has gradually taken place; and the further depreciation of which must subject him to the repetition of the like inconvenience and loss; whereas, had the relative quantity or value of money, and the taxes, continued the same, his income, though stationary, would, without the influence of any other cause, have afforded him a continuance of the enjoyments to which he had been accustomed.

I have here adduced only the instance of a farm, let upon lease for one and twenty years.

Where leases are granted for a greater number of years, or upon lives, the loss to the landlord, it is evident, must be proportionably greater.

Neither is it permitted to a landlord, in fixing the rent to be paid for his land, to calculate upon the probability of a future depreciation of money.—The average of the crops, and the price they have obtained at market, for the few years last past, are the only criterion by which a farmer will admit the value of the land, for which he is in treaty, and consequently what rent he ought to pay to be estimated. As he is not on his side allowed to stipulate for the contingency of any additional taxes, which may happen to be imposed upon the house he is to inhabit, its windows, or the increased rates for the maintenance of the poor of the parish; neither will he allow any thing for the contingent depreciation of money; and the utmost a landlord can provide for himself, is an earlier determination of the lease, manifestly tending to check the improvement of the land, and thus eventually the solid improvement of his own income.

It is plain, however, that the injury sustained by the land owner, in consequence of this depreciation of money, is but trifling, compared with that sustained by others, who have merely annuities, or gross sums of money charged upon land.—It is the fate of these, together with the stock-holder, to see and feel their property sink yearly in value, without the means of preventing it.

Since the vast accumulation of national debt, the number of persons whose sole, or chief property consists of stock in the public funds, must be very considerable; if we add to them the number of those whose sole, or chief property consists of annuities, mortgages, or other charges upon land, the amount will probably appear not very insignificant, compared with the land-owners themselves.

But, whatever be the privations which the former two may suffer from the value of money being thus lowered, we shall be told, that the nation at large has been benefitted by it; that it matters little how reduced in circumstances those may be who add nothing to the stock of the nation,—those idle drones who, without toiling, consume the fruits of others' industry.—Conditioned, however, as society now is, this is dangerous language to employ. If the interest of the stock-holder, or man possessed merely of personal capital, is so little to be regarded, what regard is it likely, or is it reasonable, that he should pay to the interests of others? Or why should the land-owner enjoy advantages which the former does not? Does the utility of the country gentleman, busied as he is with the ordinary occupations and pleasures of that class, appear so pre-eminent, that he is peculiarly entitled to our regard? But let us consider a little further, who are the idle drones here spoken of. Are they not the representatives of, if not the identical persons, who, in their time, toiled, ere they enriched themselves; who, whilst they laboured to acquire independence and ease to themselves, and those most dear to them, at the same time laboured, in effect at least, to acquire wealth to their country; and, having laboured successfully, supplied others with the means of enriching themselves and their country in their turn, or accommodated them in their distress? Are they not men who, in times of public exigency, have come forward, not without self-interested views I will acknowledge, but at the same time, with real advantage to the community, (and what would we more) to tender the wealth, which their industry had accumulated, for the defence and service of the nation? Is it for the private, or the public debtor to upbraid them, or those who represent them, as idle drones, who consume the harvest they have not sowed, — who deserve no pity, and no redress?

Discouraging, indeed, it is to the exertions of the industrious, pressed hard as he is with taxes, to find that the wealth acquired with labour and difficulty, is rendered yearly less availing; that the income, arising from the funds wherein the earnings of a toilsome, frugal life, had been invested, is, together with the capital itself, constantly and rapidly diminishing in value; that income, which he relied upon as a resource for the support and comfort of himself and his widow, in their declining years; and for the maintenance and education of his children in their youth; and that capital which he had cherished, as the means of their eventual establishment in the world, By this exorbitant increase of money, the aged, the widow, and the orphan, are effectually despoiled of the full benefit of the provisions intended for them; the income and capital reserved for them continue stationary;—the fruit and the trunk of the tree, do not extend or enlarge themselves; they grow not with the growth of price, of all the necessaries and comforts of life; they are overshadowed, and not only rendered comparatively insignificant, but they positively lose their former efficacy.

But let us now examine a little, how far the nation has been really benefitted by this depreciation of money. We have heard much of the advantages arising from a free circulation; that the accommodation afforded to the agricultural, manufacturing, and mercantile classes, by the Bank of England, and the numerous private Banks, which, from time to time, have been opened in all parts of the country, has contributed largely to the wealth and prosperity of the nation.

That a nation, such as ours, should thrive as it does, were it confined and straitened in its means of circulation, no one perhaps will be found to assert; that it is necessary such wide and unbounded means should exist, as do at present, no one, perhaps, will more readily be found to assert. The money that is borrowed of a Banker, or any other individual, for the purpose of employing it in the cultivation of land, the establishment, enlargement, or improvement of a manufactory, or in extending the commerce of the country, supposing there are hands enough to be engaged in these new undertakings, as it conduces to the productive labour of the country, is certainly employed to greater advantage, than whilst sleeping in the drawer or closet. But it is not the great absolute numerical quantity of money, or the facility with which it may be obtained, that are alone to be considered; the quantity of additional productive labour that it can purchase, should also be taken into the account. The loan or command of a pound, in the early part of Elizabeth's reign, would have been as serviceable in the latter point of view, as of eight or nine pounds in these days. The effect of multiplying the quantity of money beyond a certain demand for it, beyond what is requisite for the improved state of the country, is to diminish the value, to increase the number of figures in the column for pounds in our account books, and leave that for pence, a mere blank, as it often is,—it can serve no good purpose whatsoever. That the plough, the loom, and the wheel, should stand still for want of money to pay the wages of workmen; that goods should rot in a warehouse, because none have money wherewith to purchase them, would, indeed, be a serious evil; but not one which need at present be much apprehended; our fears should lie rather in the opposite direction.

From the circumstances which have been alluded to, from the improved state of agriculture, and the arts in general, our trade and commerce have been swelled to such unprecedented magnitude, that it was necessary there should be a proportional addition to the means of circulation, or that the relative value of money should be increased. The condition of Great Britain, at the commencement of the nineteenth, differs so widely in these respects from what it was at the commencement of the eighteenth century, that its trade and commerce could not be carried on by the same quantity of circulating medium, without greatly enhancing the value of that medium.—An evil to be avoided as much as the directly opposite. But, in consequence of the establishment of numerous Banks, and a regular system of correspondence throughout all parts of the kingdom, not only has much of the money which before remained idle been brought into action, but Bills of Exchange and Orders have superseded the use of money upon many occasions, where it before was absolutely necessary.—And hence, as well as from the vast additions which have been made to the circulating medium, from the many and extraordinary sources which have been above noticed, it has increased much more than the exigency of the case required; as the prodigious advance in the price of the necessaries of life, as well as of almost all other commodities whatsoever, and the absence of gold and silver money, most clearly testify. The nation, however, seems smitten with the magnificence of its ideal riches, with the shew of the many millions worth produce of its industry, its amazing commerce, gigantic revenue, and extended power.—She smiles in the embraces of the deity, I will not say the deity which she worships, approaching her not like a shower of gold; neither will I say, in a flimsy tattered garb of paper, but with the superior glory and effulgence of unbounded universal credit. It is to be hoped, she will not, like Semele, expire under those embraces.

Injurious as this practice of putting into

circulation such vast quantities of paper-money is to the land-holder, the stock-holder, and others of fixed incomes, to what length is it decreed that it shall extend? What limit is proposed to be assigned to it? Shall the Bank of England, year after year, be allowed to add millions to millions of the currency, merely in order to give larger dividends to the proprietors of Bank stock? Is it not enough that it should be excused the pain, if not the disgrace, of having disappointed the public confidence, in refusing payment of its promissory notes,—without being allowed to accumulate and distribute amongst its members fresh and unheard-of profits, by means of the unlimited multiplication of those notes unblushingly intruded into circulation?

The Parliament hath in its wisdom effectually upheld the Bank of England in this practice.—Yet, no doubt, originally with views of high consideration.---But is it pretended, that the necessities of government have of late required such large supplies of gold and silver, as to render it expedient that the Bank of England, in order to furnish them, should continue to avail itself of the act for restriction from payment in specie to its creditors, and to augment its promissory notes to the amount of one and twenty millions and a half? Does not this very restriction operate to the exclusion of all other means whereby specie might be obtained by government? Is it not in consequence of this restriction, that little or nothing else but paper money is brought into the treasury—that the taxes are all paid with notes of the Bank of England, or such as are finally exchanged for them? And is it not, therefore, in consequence of this restriction, that the government is obliged to have recourse to the Bank of England for such specie, as it may stand in need of for the public service? It is true we are in the front of the stage, and cannot see well what is passing behind the scenes; but, after what has passed before them, it is a serious responsibility which the government would take upon itself, if it were, without absolute necessity, to involve the Bank of England in its former difficulties;

or, on the other hand, to support and abet it in its schemes of unfair gain. Many years have elapsed since the act alluded to first shielded it from the peril with which it was environed—the effect of unforeseen accident, patriotic zeal, its own avarice, or want of prudence. If the intervening time has been honestly and well employed, that peril should have been removed long ago, and its coffers should now be opened to satisfy the claims of its creditors. Is it wise, is it conduct worthy of Statesmen, to rest the credit of a government upon that of a mercantile body such as the Bank of England, important and magnified as it is? Suppose the case of its failure,—(which no one will now be bold enough to say is out of the sphere of possibility,) are there not many who do not scruple to affirm, that the government itself would in such a case become bankrupt? And with such an enormous debt as at present incumbers it—relying as it does at present upon the Bank of England for every supply of specie—making the promissory notes of the same company equivalent to a legal tender for satisfaction of all claims on the part of government, for taxes, and other dues from individuals; and on the part of individuals for debts from government, how can it be well denied? But is it, I ask, the measure of Statesmen to rest the credit of a government upon such a prop as this—to make its honour, its power, nay, its very existence, depend upon the prudence, and the integrity of a mercantile company? Does it not become them, with all possible speed, to rescue the government from such a degraded and alarming state?

For us, the people, it is left only to lament the enormous amount of paper money, which has of late years been issued by this Bank of England—it is hardly in our option not to assist in the circulation of it. But, complaining so bitterly as we are of the heavy taxes, tithes, and rates, which we pay of necessity in support of the government, the clergy, and the poor—it is somewhat strange, that we should voluntarily subject ourselves to the payment of an additional imposition to the several private companies of bankers, and other makers of money, resident in all parts of the kingdom. How long will the folly of the nation, thus already oppressed from the fullness of its circulating medium, permit it to be still further increased by the overwhelming tide from country Banks, Factories, and all the curious variety of other rival offices, sources, countless and exhaustless? What ground or pretence have the proprietors of these, for expelling the good and lawful coin of the realm, and pouring forth in lieu of it the uncalled-for engagements of their own partnership and individual persons—many of them mean persons, of doubtful wealth, and little consideration in the country; whose joint and several securities for a hundred, or a thousand pounds, no prudent man would trust to? Of what estimation are they, in the scale of public utility, that they should be allowed to detract from the honest gains, the fair inheritance of the people? What obligations to them do we lie under? On what, but a short lived precedent, do they ground their title to this eleemosynary tribute—this share of our daily bread? There are some amongst us, I am aware, whose interest it is to keep well with them, who occasionally have need for a loan of such money as they can obtain—to wit, these promissory notes, which oftentimes come thus into circulation. But the great body of the people is not, I trust, in circumstances so depressed—notwithstanding the pressure of the times, and this sad feature of them—to be subject to the controul of creditors; more especially of such as are fattening upon the blindness and folly of those whom they pretend to serve.

Why any gentleman of moderate fortune, and in his senses, who has no desire to throw away his money, or render it less valuable than it ought to be, should seek to do any further service to the bankers with whom he intrusts his money, than to allow them the use of so much of it, as, from time to time he himself does not stand in immediate need of;—why, instead of insisting upon payment in cash when he draws upon them, he should be content to put up with their flimsy fetid promissory notes, and thus countenance and contribute to the depreciation of the currency of the kingdom, contrary to his own interest and feelings, I am quite at a loss to discover. There may be still, indeed, a little mystery in the business—and good-natured neighbours, and old women, who do not thoroughly understand it, although they would not wittingly throw away a counterfeit halfpenny, or pay a farthing more than the common assize price for a peck loaf, will indulge their banker most readily in his fancy of paying them his own promissory notes instead of coin, doubting not that they will pass as readily, and procure as much corn or meat in each of the neighbouring markets—for the banker is rich, and has acquired great landed property in the country.

That great and small gains are acquired by these means, there can be no doubt at all—the number, character, and situation in life, of those who employ them, sufficiently prove it. But the folly of those, who do not profit by, but encourage it, is amazing. They are blind to the consequences which are so ruinous to themselves—so long as they fancy, that the persons whose name is subscribed to these notes are not in jail, or likely to be there, they are willing to accept them as readily as cash—not considering that in the very next article which they purchase, they pay a tribute to the maker of the note,—or, if they do consider it, they imagine that the tribute is so small as to be unworthy of consideration,—they forget what a few years since would have been paid for the same article, or fondly impute the difference in price altogether to the operation of other causes.

But the mischief increases so rapidly, that it is high time to put some check to it—if we do not resolve and endeavour to put down this craft of money making, it will effectually put us down, unless, indeed, it first ruin and destroy itself. For it is no longer the mystery it was thought to be—the knowledge of it is widely disseminated. No more is it sought after in vain in the laboratory of the alchymist---the art of conversion is now easily acquired, and practised in every corner of the kingdom. The school master in every village---the clerk in every counting house, with his "Easy method of Arithmetic" before him, is well instructed how to calculate the compound interest upon a pound, or a penny, with sufficient accuracy to show how much may be made in process of time, by means of the circulation of promissory notes---and the attorney, or linen draper, at the next door, who has credit enough in the neighbourhood to get them into circulation, will have boldness enough to try the experiment of fabricating them, fear ess of the explosion that may ensue.

It is putting an extreme case, and I do not despair that the eyes of the public will be opened long before such an event will happen. But, suppose that every one who is not in a state of insolvency, who has property in land, or the funds, or any where else, should set about to circulate his promissory notes to the full amount of the value of that property, that these notes should be generally received as money, being considered as the representative of such property—I ask, what would then be the real value of a guinea, or a guinea note?—Would it buy us a pair of shoes, or even a string to tie them with? The real case before us is different only in degree, and the effect, therefore, is less violent. Comparatively, a few only pledge their property in this manner; but it is to be feared, that some of those few, instead of confining the amount of their pledges to the value of their property, considerably exceed it, as many innocent persons can testify, to their irreparable loss. But the effect, however small it may be in the view of those who are rolling in affluence, is sufficiently alarming and distressing to the multitudes who have difficulties to encounter, who suffer many privations of former comforts, and are unable to maintain their birth-place, and rightful situation in society.

It is on account of these, and many others who depend upon the same fountains for support, that humanity and policy require even those who are not individually interested in the restoration of the former value of money, to exert themselves in promoting it. No arguments need be employed to stimulate such as are so interested; it is sufficient to shew them plainly, what is their real situation, and leave them to judge how much worse it is soon likely to become, if this pernicious system of money-making be much more generally adopted, as it is likely to be, unless proper means be speedily devised and employed to prevent it.

It is not to be denied, that the sudden restoration of the circulating medium to its proper level, may prove prejudicial to certain interests of those who lie under engagements for the payment of such sums as may have been advanced to them, or for which they have received the consideration, since this depreciation of money has taken place. And, no doubt, the difficulty of providing that perfect justice shall be done, in every case, is great. But the number of those, who may be thus injuriously affected by such an event, bears but a small proportion to the number of those who have long suffered, and are yet suffering, under the present system and, if it be continued, will continue to suffer from it still more and more; and who, whilst they are the more numerous, are not the less estimable class of individuals. But it is further to be considered, that the present system cannot last for ever; it must sooner or later destroy itself. The time must come, and that shortly, if it has not come already, when the promissory notes of the Bank of England, and other Banks, will be viewed with jealousy, and accepted with reluctance. The competition has been already commenced; new companies are perpetually obtruding themselves, to the detriment of those already established; they glean in the same field, and interfere with, and press upon each other, in their eagerness to pluck, with unsparing hands, from the harvest of the public. Is it not the wisest conduct, therefore, to check the growing evil, and with all reasonable promptitude to correct it? Long delay can serve no good purpose; it manifestly tends to ill.

But humanity again steps forward and exclaims, " Would you ruin a multitude of respectable gentlemen, who, trusting to a continuance of the present system, have ventured their fortunes in the speculation of Country Banking, which you are invidiously pleased to call the craft of money-making; who, if you insist upon the payment of their notes in cash, or notes of the Bank of England, must inevitably become Bankrupts, and whose Bankruptcy will assuredly effect the ruin of many persons, who have kindly confided in their solvency."

That their boldness in speculation might terminate unfavourably, ought to have been previously well weighed by these gentlemen who have engaged in it. If they mounted upon the wings of Icarus, they should expect his fate. If any have voluntarily trusted their fortunes on board a rotten vessel, or foolishly depended upon the solidity of a bubble for support, they have little else to accuse than their own blindness and folly. But I do not desire any wide calamity. Let those who have soared upon false wings drop, but drop gently. With prudence they may ease themselves in their descent. Take from them, however, no more of their paper money. They have profited, and we have suffered from it, enough already. But do not press clamorously and all at once for payment of all that is now in circulation, for that would speedily end in a refusal of payment altogether.

If resolutions were publicly entered into by men of consideration, in every county, giving notice that they would not receive in payment the promissory notes of any private Bankers whatsoever, beyond a limited period, suppose it were twelve or fifteen months, such an expedient, at the same time that it would give a caution to the customers of those bankers, not to take from them any more of their notes, would be a caution also to the latter to call in their securities, and provide for the discharge of such notes as they have now in circulation; and thus might the evil, so far as it proceeds from them, be remedied without any serious distress to any persons engaged in Banking, except those who would experience it in consequence of their own rash, not to say dishonest, speculations; and to whose distress, therefore, it need not be the care of the public to pay much regard.

But that the aid of the legislature may not be wanting to render more effectual the endeavours of individuals, to redress the whole evil complained of, it is desirable that its authority should be employed, not only for restoring, as speedily as is consistent with public security, the liability of the Bank of England to make its payment in cash; but, also, for immediately limiting the amount of its promissory notes, a measure of itself highly conducive to the speedy reproduction of the precious metals; from the want of which so much inconvenience has been suffered. Without such a precaution as this, on the part of the legislature, the reduction, or total destruction of the notes of private Banks, would tend only to the further increase of those of the Bank of England, which would negative the desired effect of diminishing, and keeping within due bounds, the quantity of circulating medium.

Enjoying the privilege from payment of their promissory notes, it cannot be thought unreasonable that the Bank of England should be prohibited from issuing them beyond a limited amount; but no such privilege being allowed to private Bankers, the people themselves, without the legislature, having full power to suppress *their* promissory notes, the same reason or necessity does not appear to prevail for its interference in respect to them. If the people themselves think it not worth while to make any exertions for that purpose, it is a work of supererogation, perhaps, in the opinion of some persons, for the legislature to make them. Nay it may, perhaps, be considered as an exercise of power, somewhat incompatible with the principles of a free and commercial people, to restrain any set of men from employing the credit they enjoy in any manner they shall deem most profitable to themselves, provided they do no other injury to the community than such as is voluntarily courted and submitted to by individuals. But here the injury is done to a multitude of individuals who have no power of avoiding it. But though it were not so, had it not frequently been found requisite and necessary, however, to interfere with the acts of divers sets of men, and of public bodies, when individuals are thus injuriously, though voluntarily, affected by those acts? Most assuredly it has;—and the occasion, perhaps, has not often been more pressing than that afforded at present. If the effects, resulting from the system of money-making, now so commonly adopted, be in reality so baneful as I have represented, and believe them to be, it is surely high time for the legislature to interfere and put a stop to them.

"But it is the excess of paper money, not the moderate issue of it, that is injurious." Yet more, its utility is most apparent; nay, I am willing to confess, notwithstanding all that has been said, that the total suppression and prohibition of promissory notes, (those I mean which are intended to answer the purpose of money,) would be attended with great inconvenience to the public. The facility with which they may be remitted from place to place, render them more useful in that respect than specie; and if means were devised for keeping the issue of them within due bounds, that is, to limit the amount of them, together with the specie remaining in the country, to the amount of the specie which, from time to time, would be employed there, in case there were no paper money, little but what is good would result from such a mixed medium of circulation.

But what are the means to which we can have recourse, in order to accomplish this end? Suppose it were permitted to the Bank of England, country Bankers, and others, to issue their promissory notes to a limited amount. What are the proportions which ought to be assigned to the various Banks, that are already or may hereafter be established throughout the country? Who are the persons to compose the Board of Control in this department, to arrange and assign those proportions? and what is the security which ought to be required against the issue of notes to a larger amount than may be authorized? The difficulties and objections, which must necessarily attach to any scheme founded upon a general license to issue them, subject to such provisions as would be expedient, must be extreme.

Were the practice of issuing promissory notes payable without interest, by private Bankers, tradesmen, and all others, except the national Bank, altogether prohibited by law, and the national Bank permitted to issue them to a limited amount only, from time to time, to be regulated by the legislature, according to the exigency of the trade and commerce of the country, which might be discovered with sufficient accuracy from the price of necessaries, a fair comparison of our Exports and Imports, and the state of the exchange, due regard being always paid to such other occasional causes, as may affect the price of necessaries, our trade, and the exchange, independent of the quantity of money; and if such notes were in no case made a legal tender, but were faithfully to be paid with specie, whenever demanded, all the convenience of a paper circulation might be obtained free from the inconvenience, nay, the positive ill, now attending it. But another and great advantage might also be derived from this exclusive privilege of issuing paper money. The public would be justified in requiring, whilst the company possessing that privilege would, doubtless, gladly render a fair compensation for it, even under the regulations adverted to.

But what an alarming innovation is this! What a dreadful monopoly of paper-money! What total ruin to our trade!—What a sudden, what a paralysing shock to our manufactures and agriculture!—What a death-blow to the industry of the people! Stupendously grand, indeed, are the ideas of the all-pervading beneficial influence of promissory notes, as if heaven itself, in the fulness of its bounty, had showered down this blessing upon us, to vivify, invigorate, and multiply, every herb and every beast of the field that are food and raiment for man—and it is natural there should be correspondent ideas of the mighty mischief which would ensue, if any considerable check were put to the issue of them; but I have touched upon this string before, and, therefore, need not now dwell upon it. Let it, however, always be remembered, that neither the relative, nor the absolute increase of money constitutes, or necessarily contributes to the absolute increase of food or raiment. Our trade, our manufactures, and our agriculture, may live and flourish, the industry of the people may be exerted to its utmost extent; though half the money now in the kingdom were absolutely annihilated; and when we are told that commerce cannot exist without money, that our merchants have oftentimes stood in need of more than they could command or procure,—that our goods have hence remained upon the hands of our manufacturers, and the people sat idle for want of employ,—let it be clearly understood, that all this affords no proof whatsoever, that half the money, half the number of pounds, shillings, and pence, to which the gold and silver coin, and bullion, and promissory notes of Bankers and others are current, would not answer every requisite purpose of trade and commerce, and afford every requisite encouragement to national industry, as well as the present total, provided the price of things in general were, as they soon would be, reduced to half their present price. Nor that the same lack of money, of which our merchants have complained, might not be experienced, though twice the present quantity of money were in circulation.

It was partly to the practice of our merchants that I attributed the present deficiency of gold and silver; I meant not any thing, however, to their prejudice. If there be any real calamity arising from this deficiency, let the blame fall where it ought. To trade with gold and silver, as with other commodities, deserves no condemnation. It would be folly to prohibit it. Here they were to be purchased cheap. Here, therefore, it was rational to purchase them and to carry them elsewhere, where they bore a higher price, there to be exchanged for raw or manufactured produce; and to return hither with that produce to be disposed of here with advantage to the merchant; and, by so disposing of it, to enable him again to carry out gold and silver with the same object and success as before; and every attempt to prevent this practice, so long as there is an excess of circulating medium, is not merely idle and absurd, but it is mischievous and earnestly to be deprecated.

By the adoption of such a measure as I have proposed, enough of the precious metals would, ere long, return, the balance of trade continuing, as of late, in our favour; but it were well to ensure their return more speedily. It were well if the merchant, instead of exporting our gold and silver, and importing the consumable articles of luxury, furnished to him by other nations, were to export the produce of our own land and labour, and import the gold and silver of other nations.—No danger of future deficiency need be apprehended, (except from such accidental causes as can be provided against, if at all, only as they occur.) However more remote may be the event, which our patriotic purveyors of promissory notes have been so active in their efforts (with other views, no doubt) to bring to pass—I mean the emigration of public and private creditors—that injured multitude who, in consequence of the excessive price of all the necessaries and comforts of life in this country, would seek to enjoy them in another, who would either dispose of their capital in the public funds, on mortgage, or elsewhere, and flee with the amount in silver and gold ; or, from time to time, obtain remittances of the dividends and annual produce of that capital in the same form. A consummation devoutly to be wished by our inveterate and jealous enemy.

That these evils may beeffectually prevented, that the *Golden Age* may speedily return, and that we may enjoy that plenty which, I trust, we should, without murmur, manfully resign for the real service of the state, when fairly called upon ; but which we cannot be expected, with cheerfulness, childishly, yet knowingly, to surrender, for the mere benefit of a tribe of men who have no solid claims whatever, either upon our gratitude or our bounty, is the earnest wish of,

Dear ***,

Your's, &c.

June 1, 1810.

ERRATA.

Page.	Line.	
8,	21,	For the last " Has," read " Have."
9,	15,	for " Our machinery," read " Has not our machinery been."
10,	21,	dele " that of."
12,	19,	for " the latter," read " those particularly referred to."
13,	11,	after " thing," insert " they had."
14,	5,	for " weaken," read " lessen."
16,	9,	for " Bank," read " Banks."
27,	1,	after " in," insert " government securities."
28,	5,	for " they," read " these."
39,	22,	for " them," read " him."
42,	9,	for " alluding to," read " examining."
44,	9,	dele " or impairing."
46,	8,	for " lands," read " land."
47,	16,	for " that he," read " he."
48,	15,	for " price," read " prices."
51,	11,	for " preventing," read " ever occasionally restoring."
64,	17,	for " his money," read " it."
65,	last,	for " name is," read " names are."
66,	5,	for " maker of the note," read " makers of the notes."
75,	2,	for " had," read " has."
—	3,	dele " however."
76,	17,	after " Banks," insert " and offices."
80,	5,	for " they," read " it."

POSTCRIPT.

You, perhaps, will think that I have not sufficiently anticipated and discussed the various objections that may be raised against the restoration of the circulating medium, to what may be considered its natural level. I did not, indeed, conceive it necessary to bring before you, for the purpose of refutation, all that might be made to bear upon the subject. Those persons, (and you, I now presume to be amongst them,) who will keep in mind the probable, I had almost said, the inevitable, and alarming consequences of persevering in the present system, will not feel much inclined to listen to the many frivolous pretexts which may be employed in its defence, however ready they may be to examine candidly what wears the semblance of reason and argument, in points of magnitude and importance;—but, you will possibly say that, even with this impression, I ought to have noticed how the interests of the lessees of land might be protected in the event first referred to, having already noticed how those of the landlord are affected, under the present system.

That you may not think I have neglected the consideration of the former point, it may be as well to observe, that the tenants whose leases have been of many years duration, would cease to enjoy so large a share of profit as they have of late enjoyed:—whilst, on the other hand, those whose leases have lately been granted, would probably pay higher rent than the annual value of the land. With regard to the first, therefore, that only would happen to them which ought to happen—and with regard to the last, it surely is not too much to suppose, that they would experience the good sense, if not the favour or justice of their landlords, by a remittance of a reasonable part of the rent—for the landlords themselves would ill consult their own interest if they denied it. In all likelihood their rent would run into arrear—their lands would be deserted, and returned untenanted upon their hands. Cases, indeed, might occur where the rent could not so easily and conclusively be remitted without the aid of Parliament,—but with its aid they might easily be provided for, and no doubt would be so. It seems needless to press this point further;—I shall, therefore, only hope that your patience is equal to mine,—not having the modesty to doubt, that it will bring you to the same conclusion as I have long continued to embrace.

REFLECTIONS

ON THE

POSSIBLE EXISTENCE

AND

SUPPOSED EXPEDIENCE

OF

NATIONAL BANKRUPTCY.

By PETER RICHARD HOARE, Esq.

London:

PRINTED FOR T. CADELL AND W. DAVIES, IN THE STRAND; HATCHARD, PICCADILLY; AND RICHARDSON, ROYAL - EXCHANGE.

By G. SIDNEY, Northumberland-street.

1811.

ADVERTISEMENT.

IT may be proper to advertise the reader, that in some of the following pages he will meet with a course of reasoning not very different from what may be found in an anonymous publication of last year ;* wherein it is attempted, amongst other things, to be shewn, that the high prices of the necessaries of life have proceeded chiefly, if not altogether, from the excess of our currency.—A notion which, however prevalent it may be amongst certain individuals, either as resulting

* Entitled, " *A Letter, containing observations on some of the effects of our paper currency ; and on the means of remedying its present, and preventing its future effects.* In two points the author, it seems, was ill informed.---viz. in respect to the amount of dollars circulated by the Bank of England, and the scarcity of the precious metals---as appears from the subsequent publication of the report of the bullion committee, and the evidence on which that report was founded.

from examination or from prejudice, is yet not so general as, perhaps, they may suppose.—The author of that publication, however, could hardly have expected that what he had assumed as fact in regard to the advance of prices, would have been so boldly and publicly contradicted; or even that more proof was necessary to be brought forward in support of some of the conclusions which he had drawn from that assumed fact. This, however, seems to be the case. It is a point of the utmost importance; and being so, it must stand as an apology for introducing the subject so much at length, but with so little novelty of principle, into the present publication.

REFLECTIONS

&c.

The lawful money of Great Britain is metal,—copper, silver, and gold,—each piece being coined, and that of gold remaining with little variation of standard weight and fineness. He that becomes fairly indebted to another in any sum of this money, does not legally or equitably repay his debt, if he pay with other money of whatsoever denomination, unless the amount of the money so paid be equal in value to the former; or in other words, enable the holder to purchase the same quantity of commodities, supposing the supply of, and demand for these, to have continued relatively unaltered.—It is the same thing, in effect, whether he pay with metal debased by alloy, or reduced in weight, or with paper which is not convertible, without loss, into money of weight and fineness or value equal to that in which he became indebted. Though his creditor may acknowledge payment and satisfaction of the debt; yet, in neither case does he actually receive full payment and satisfaction. And the debtor, who is unable to discharge his debts but with such debased, light, or paper money, and without making due allowance for its depreciation, is, in reality, bankrupt and insolvent.* So, although the government of a country may enact laws raising the denomination of the old coin, or authorizing the mixture of base metal with new coin of the same denomination as the former; or may declare paper, wood, or stone, or any other substance which it may be pleased to issue, or allow to be issued, in all respects, the same as coined metal money, to be current for such sums as may be specifically inscribed thereon, and legally to be tendered as such money, but which cannot be converted into it without loss—although, I say, the government of a country may, in the decline of its credit and its resources, or in the

* I am aware of the objection, which may be, and I believe has been, set up to the doctrine here attempted to be maintained, on the ground of law and of general practice. The diminution of weight, which the coin necessarily, from its very use, undergoes, does not always, in a legal sense, reduce its value; nor is the creditor, who is paid with light coin, if legally current, in any worse condition, than he who is paid with weighty coin just issued from the mint. But the objection is, for the most part, frivolous and unimportant. It is to small payments only that our silver coin is usually applied, and such as are made soon after the debt has been contracted; so that little diminution in the value of the coin can have taken place, in consequence of its reasonable wear in the mean time. If, however, taking advantage of the law, which enables a debtor to discharge his debt in silver coin of reduced weight, he does so to the full extent which that law allows, and cannot otherwise discharge it, shall we say, that he is equitably solvent? Shall we say that he is altogether legally so, when we consider by what means he would probably enable himself to make such payment?

plenitude of its power and its profligacy, do all this, yet it alters not the real nature of the transaction. The government itself, however, which is reduced to the necessity, or is unnecessarily guilty of having recourse to any of these practices, in order to answer nominally the demands of its creditors; but to evade, in reality, the satisfaction of them, becomes, in like manner, bankrupt and insolvent, or, morally, what is worse.

Cases, indeed, may sometimes occur, when so large a portion of the precious metals may be withdrawn from the circulation of a country, that the stock remaining in it may, for a time, become more valuable. Thus the extensive practice of hoarding—the payment of heavy tribute, or subsidy to foreign powers—large remittances for the maintenance of fleets and armies on foreign stations—or for the settlement of unfavourable balances of trade, might, in process of time, well nigh exhaust a country of its circulating medium, when composed of the precious metals, if no counteracting causes should exist. But as the natural tendency of a scarcity of the precious metals, when they form the circulating medium, is to lower the nominal, or money price of goods; and it is the interest of the merchants to purchase at the low, rather than the high market—to bring gold from those countries where it is plentiful to that where it is scarce, in exchange for the produce of the land and labour of the latter;—the natural consequence of such drain of the precious metals, as has been noticed, is their reflux, sooner or later, into the same channels from whence they have been withdrawn.

Still, however, as much inconvenience may be supposed to arise from such a reduction in the price of goods as would insure the immediate return of the precious metals; it may, perhaps, be deemed advisable to prevent that reduction by such means as are harmless, and seem best adapted to the case. And, in countries where public confidence and credit run high, none, it must be admitted, appear more harmless, or better adapted, than the substitution of paper money in lieu of the precious metals, which may have been withdrawn. But, if it be thought important that these should gradually, yet at no very distant period, be restored, it is important that the amount of paper money so substituted, should be somewhat less, instead of more, than the former; so that the money price of goods might be in some degree reduced, and, consequently, a greater number of purchasers be attracted from abroad. But, at all events, it is carefully to be provided, that the means employed for the prevention of an inconvenient reduction of prices should not operate too powerfully in raising them, and thus produce an evil as great as, or greater, than that which is sought to be prevented—that they should not work an injury to the private and public creditor—prove violatory of the faith of individuals, and the government,—and doom the nation not only to the disgrace of courting, or voluntarily submitting to a bankruptcy unprincipled and fraudulent, but to the danger of a rapid overthrow and ruin.

For it would be waste of time to set about to shew what has so often been shewn before, and what all who have a fair measure of understanding, and will make proper use of it, must clearly see, that the greater the quantity of money employed in the circulation of a given quantity of goods, and with a given rapidity of circulation, the less must be its value. A proposition, indeed, which seems to be almost identical. Any specific quantity of money, therefore, may become more or less valuable according to the less or greater total quantity which may happen to be brought into circulation. And hence it follows, that, by means of an excessive increase, each piece may be depreciated, exactly in the same degree as if it were debased by alloy, or reduced in weight to the half, or the hundredth part of the value of such piece, or any other of similar denomination, before any depreciation had taken place.

And it is the same thing, in effect, whether the money consist of paper alone, or partly of paper and partly of the precious metals. It is, however, a redundancy of the former only, when unexchangeable for the latter, that can long exist in a country,—a redundancy of the latter would quickly be reduced, by reason of the more profitable employment which would be found for it else where; and hence it is, that the former ought always to be limited narrowly in its amount, unless at all times exchangeable for the latter.

A Strange notion, the upset notion of other days, has, indeed, again been put afloat in ours, of the innocence of issuing any quantity of paper, provided those who issue it have property equal in amount to the quantity of paper so issued. But how, I would ask, is it possible, if every one were to issue promissory notes to the full amount of his property, all could provide for the payment of them? If it be said, that it is not intended that actual payment should be made, the notion is absurd from its very condition; and it is equally absurd if it be grounded upon the supposition, that the payments could actually be made, or would not be demanded,—as the experience of latter years has abundantly proved.

Gold, from its durability, divisibility, and rarity, is the article appointed by civilized nations as the common measure and representative of the value of other commodities; and though, in many countries, where confidence and credit run high, the paper of government, of companies, and individuals, may circulate as freely as Gold; yet it is with the belief, or trust, that that paper entitles the holder to receive the same quantity of gold as that for which it purports to be current, or the value of that quantity in other commodities. The amount of the paper circulated, together with the gold and other metal in circulation, ought, therefore, never to be so great as to exceed, in a considerable degree, the quantity of gold and other metal which would circulate in case there were no paper at all,—and never would, if paper were always, as it ought to be, convertible into gold without loss.

It is in vain to attempt to determine, with accuracy, what may have been the amount of money in circulation previous to the restriction of cash payments by the Bank in 1797, or what it is at present. We know not the amount of the promissory notes issued by country banks, nor the amount of coin, at the former, or the present, period. The number of country banks which were, as well as those which are, established, might, indeed, enable us to form some loose judgment of the amount of their respective issues; but from the amount of the coinages which have taken place, we could form no just estimate of the quantity of coin which remained. Nay, the frequency of those coinages might, perhaps, be adduced as a proof, that much of the gold and silver coined was continually withdrawn from the circulation.

But, whatever might have been the amount of species which remained at the period of the restriction, it is probable that the quantity of gold coin, lying in the coffers of the Bank of England, and of private banks, is not less now than it then was. It probably is more. The amount of that *actually employed in circulation* is, no doubt, much diminished. It is become quite insignificant, compared with what it then was. But its amount, even at that time, could have borne but a very small proportion to the aggregate amount of country bank, and Bank of England paper. For, supposing the total weekly payments to labourers, artificers, and workmen in general, (who, from the enumeration taken in 1801, do not appear to have exceeded 4,215,531 persons throughout England, Wales, and Scotland;) supposing, I say, such payments to have amounted, upon an average, to three millions in gold and silver; (which, when it is considered that many of those persons received no weekly payments at all,—that those employed in husbandry, equal nearly to one half of the whole number, who did receive them, earned only from 3 to 10 shillings per week,—and that some of the payments were made in the pound or guinea notes of country banks,) will not, I conceive, be deemed much below the truth,—how small does the quantity of gold coin requisite for these purposes, appear? Let us say, however, that *two millions* of gold were requisite,—and that *two millions* more, besides other metal and paper, were requisite for the use of all other classes of individuals for the purchase of the various commodities of which they stood in need.—A sum which, however small it may at first sight seem, will not, perhaps, upon reflection, seem at all unreasonably so;—since it appears that the produce of the income tax itself, for the year ending the 5th of April, 1800, did not exceed 5,801,624*l.* and, for the succeeding year, not three and twenty thousand pounds beyond that sum. And though it be admitted that the assessments were, in a material degree, defective; yet, making ample allowance on that account, the sum of two millions, in gold, will still appear considerable, and, probably, not insufficient for the purposes which I have specified, when compared with so large a portion of the assessed income of the people. But it may not be amiss further to observe, that, from what appears to have been the average amount of *one* and *two* pound notes issued by the Bank of England, during the two or three years immediately subsequent to the suspension of cash payments, (with the view of supplying the deficiency of the gold which had been withdrawn from the circulation,) we may reasonably conclude that previously to that suspension, the quantity of gold employed for other purposes, than such weekly payments as are mentioned above, did not exceed the sum which I have stated, since the average amount of those notes did not so much as nearly equal it.* Neither is that statement rendered less probable, notwithstanding it appears, by the returns officially made, that within those two years, the quantity of gold money coined, amounted nearly to five millions; for it is,

* The average amount of the years 1797-8, and 9, computed from the Accomptant-general's account, dated 15th Dec. 1800, was 1,502,736*l.*

at the same time to be recollected, that the Bank of England had need of large supplies, with the view of providing for cash payments; which, towards the close of 1799, it declared itself well prepared to make. And, in addition to all this, it should further be recollected, what was the average proportion which the amount of gold usually bore to the amount of paper, in payments previous to the issue of the low notes of the Bank of England; which, when we come to inquire what was the amount of the paper at that time in circulation, may serve yet more to confirm the statement which I have ventured to offer.

Let us suppose, therefore, that two millions in gold was the sum employed in weekly payments to workmen in general, and two millions more for the use of all other classes of individuals, as specified above, making a total of four millions of gold actually employed in circulation; that the average amount of gold so employed did not exceed this sum; and that the remainder of the circulating medium actually employed, consisted merely of silver and paper : and then let us enquire what, probably, was the amount of paper,—an inquiry which need not long detain us. For of the paper of country banks little approaching to certainty can be known, and therefore no proof shall be attempted. But, in regard to the notes of the Bank of England, of those we can speak with more accuracy. And for our present purpose, I trust there is, upon the whole, full enough to shew, most satisfactorily, that, by means of the one and the other, considerable additions have been made to the total circulating medium since the period of the supension, or restriction to which I have alluded.

We learn, in short, from the Report of the committee of the Lords in 1797, that the number of country banks then established was about 230, and that the average amount of Bank of England notes, including post bills, for some years immediately previous, was *between ten and eleven millions.* If, therefore, we add to this the *four millions* actually employed in circulation, and allow *five* or *six millions* more as the amount of the gold lying inactive in the coffers of the Bank of England and other banks, &c. and *seven millions* as the amount of the paper issued by the country banks, the total would not exceed *seven or eight and twenty millions.*

Again, from the report of the Committee appointed by the House of Commons in 1810, we learn, that the Country Banks then established was about 721, and that the average amount of Bank of England notes, including post bills, in circulation in the preceding year, was upwards of *nineteen millions,* which, it seems, has since been increased to more than *three and twenty.* Add, therefore, to this sum the notes of 721 country banks, or now, probably, of still more, amounting, perhaps, to *twenty, or five and twenty, or thirty millions,** and the quantity of coin at present in circulation, and in the coffers of the Bank of England and other banks;—and it will appear that the present total circulating medium is not much less, if it be not much more, than *twice its average amount for some years previous to the restriction of cash payments.*

Has not then our circulating medium become excessive?

---

* See Mr. Tritton's evidence before the Committee, p. 214 of Minutes, and Mr. Richardson's, p. 230.

Has not its quantity been augmented much beyond what it ought to be in order to the preservation of its just value ? Or has the value of the precious metals been so diminished, or the produce of the land and labour of the country been so increased of late, as otherwise to account, in any reasonable manner, for this vast addition ? The almost total absence of the gold coin, the extreme scarcity of the silver coin, even of that which is greatly below the standard mint weight,* the high money price of gold and silver bullion, and the very depressed state of the foreign exchanges,† are circumstances notorious, and such as cannot be denied; all tending to prove that the value of the precious metals is not diminished, in proportion to the increase of the quantity of our circulating medium; if they do not further tend to prove that the produce of our land and labour likewise, is not increased in that proportion.

But, it is asserted, that the great increase of our taxes has rendered necessary this increased quantity of the circulating medium. It is well if, through the operation of taxes, an increased quantity of wealth may be obtained; if, spurring us on to industry, they tend thus to insure to us its fruits, or, in other words, an

* Our shillings are about one fifth, and our sixpences about one half below their proper weight. Shillings and sixpences, I call them, though for the most part they do not bear the marks of the legal coin of those denominations, and, perhaps, never did.

† Portugal gold coin 4l. 15s. Silver bars, standard 6s. 0½d. Hamb. Ex. 25s. 6g. July 12, 1811. See Wettenhall's Table.

augmented produce, for the circulation of which, an augmented quantity of the circulating medium may be fit and requisite. That such may be their operation, in some degree, cannot, with justice, be denied; though, on the other hand, it is not with any greater justice to be denied, that they tend, in some degree, to prevent the accumulation of wealth, and to divert it from productive into unproductive channels of employment. Yet, neither effect will serve to shew the necessity or utility of creating any additional medium of circulation, to answer the increased taxes; or that these can have any necessary tendency to create it. On the contrary, such increased medium, if formed by means of the issue of paper, not representing or standing in the place of the precious metals, which would otherwise be in circulation, render the imposition of additional taxes, both expedient and just.

For, if we consider the nature of taxes, and what is the fair intention and sound principle in imposing them, we shall easily perceive how fallacious is the notion, that any addition which may be made to them, can require any great correspondent addition to be made to the circulating medium in which they are to be paid. In imposing a tax, the fair intention and sound principle is to acquire a portion of the income, or capital of the people, for the service of the state. If the amount of the annual income of the people be 100 millions, and 10 millions be annually requisite for the public service, upon the supposition that the value of money continues the same as it is at present,—should you lessen that value by increasing the quantity of money, say one-fourth, instead of 10 millions, 12 and ½ millions would be requisite; so that no advantage would be derived from such a practice, either to the government or the people. Whether the tax be imposed upon the commodities which we consume, or upon the income which we derive from our labour, or our capital—whether in land or in buildings, in money, machinery, or merchandize,—it is intended, or ought to be, that so much as we pay to the government, should be paid out of that income—that the full use of so much should be transferred from ourselves to the government. The total income of the people is not increased by the tax; but a deduction is made from the income of such individuals as are subject to it,—and what is so deducted is to be applied to public purposes. What then can be more absurd than to suppose, that, by putting into circulation vast quantities of paper, and thus diminishing the value of the circulating medium, the means of discharging the taxes are facilitated? I mean those taxes which are raised for the maintenance and support of government,—for the necessary salaries to its several officers,—for the manning and provisioning its fleets and armies. The smaller the quantity, the greater is the relative value of the money which circulates in a country; and the lower, therefore, will be the nominal amount of the taxes necessary for the support of its government.

It may, upon a different principle, indeed, be maintained, as it has been, and not upon contemptible authority, that if great additions have been made to the taxes, some addition to the circulating medium is requisite, by reason of the greater number of payments which are then required to be performed. But what, in this country, are the payments necessary to be performed in consequence of the increased taxes? They are those which are made to the collectors of taxes,—by them to the receivers,—by the receivers to the exchequer,—from the exchequer to the bank,—and from the bank to the orders of the several officers or boards, authorized to direct such payment. But, does not this accumulation of large sums of money, in the hands of the bankers, employed by the several collectors and receivers, or in the hands of the collectors and receivers themselves, but more especially of the Bank of England itself, and the subsequent application of the money by way of loan, instead of impeding the circulation, tend rather to quicken it, and render it more active, than if the money lay dormant in the drawers of individuals, as in some, if not in great, measure it would, had not such taxes been imposed? But, whatever delay in the circulation, these increased payments might have occasioned under other circumstances, it surely is not too much to suppose, that the great improvements in Banking, (as they have not unusually been termed, but, under the present system, little worthy of the title,) and the great multitude of negotiable bills which are set afloat, have rendered any further increase of the circulating medium wholly unnecessary, on the score of such delay. The necessity of such increase, if any necessity there were, would be seen in the rise, not in the fall of the value of the circulating medium,—in the low, not in the high price of bullion and almost all other commodities whatsoever.

Well then, it is next said, the multiplied improvements in our manufacturing, agricultural, and other arts, and the great increase of our national produce, the consequence of those improvements, have manifestly required great additions to the medium of circulation; and such additions, therefore, have from time to time been made to it. Surely, however, it was beyond, much beyond the ken of the directors of the Bank of England, and of country Bankers too, to apportion the just quantity—so much as, and no more than our circumstances, from time to time, required. Had things indeed been left entirely to themselves to find their proper level, without any interference on the part of these gentlemen, all had then perhaps, been well. An increased produce would naturally, and without their aid, have attracted a due proportion of the precious metals;—for which they might have substituted their paper if they pleased. But, in taking on themselves to judge how much was fit, it seems they judged amiss;—amiss for the country, though rightly for themselves. The additions they have made, it is plain, have been excessive; it is plain, from the facts which have been already mentioned,—the almost total absence of gold coin; the extreme scarcity of silver coin, even in its debased state; the high price of bullion, and the depressed state of the exchange. But we have other direct and indisputable proof in the known fact of the enormously increased price of almost every article produced;—and it is upon this fact that I wish the attention of the reader to be more particularly fixed, the rather because endeavours have been made to do away the strong impression which it naturally is calculated to make.

For, whilst it is contended that the quantity of the circulating medium has not been increased beyond what the improved state of our agriculture, manufacture, and commerce, have reasonably required, it should, at least, be shewn that that increase has not occasioned any increase in the price of goods. Had the additional quantity of the former been proportionate only to the additional quantity of the latter, which it is employed to circulate, the price of goods, in general, would have remained stationary; unless other causes, indeed, should have operated to affect their price. It remains, therefore, for those who would say, that other causes have so operated, explicitly to point out what they really are.

If it be said, as I believe it often has been, that long, previous to the restriction of cash payments, the price of things in general had been progressively advancing in this country, and that the further advance which has since been made, has, probably, proceeded from the same cause; though we should admit the former part of the assertion to be true, (which, perhaps, we all do not;) yet we might still desire something more to be said, by way of proving the latter to be true also. For, although it should be admitted that the constant influx of the precious metals from the mines of South America, may, for a long course of years, have in some measure tended gradually to raise the price of things in general, as well in this as other countries; yet, that there should have been any extraordinary influx of late years, (whatever the real fact may be) can hardly be contended by those who are disposed to account for the high price of bullion, and low state of the exchange, from a cause directly opposite. If, however, the supply of the precious metals has, notwithstanding, been so great, that their value is diminished—how happens it that their money-price is so increased; unless the value of that money is yet more diminished, by excess or otherwise—though here, not otherwise, it seems, than by excess, the consequence of an unlimited issue of Bank Paper, unexchangeable for gold?

True, indeed, it is, that divers commodities may be enumerated, the nominal or money prices of which, since the period of the restriction of cash payments, have either remained nearly stationary, or increased much less than others, or been more or less diminished. The mere improvements, however, which have taken place in various branches of our machinery and arts, may have enabled some of our manufacturers to furnish their goods, at a rate lower, in reality, than they formerly could. The abundant importations from our own colonies, and those which we have wrested from the enemy, have glutted our markets at home with the produce of each—whilst the system adopted for the exclusion of such produce, as well as that of our manufactories, from the markets on the continent, having considerably lessened the demand for, must also have tended in no small degree to reduce the real price of both. Such commodities, therefore, as these here described, may, notwithstanding the depreciation of our currency, be sold at a nominal or money price, the same as, or perhaps, somewhat lower than heretofore they were. Whilst on the other hand, taxation, direct and indirect, may have increased the price of sundry others, much beyond the rate of the depreciation. In our attempt, therefore, to ascertain whether any depreciation at all has really taken place, let all commodities, of the former, as well as of the latter description, be placed wholly out of the question, and let us consider some few, only, on which the taxes imposed since the period of the restriction, have had, or at least ought to have had, little or no effect whatsoever.

An Account of the Market price of Wheat, from 1700 *to* 1810, *inclusive.*

	Years.	Annual price per quarter.				Years.	Annual price per quarter.		
		l.	*s.*	*d.*			*l.*	*s.*	*d.*
	1700	1	15	6		23	1	10	9
	1	1	13	5		24	1	12	10
War.	2	1	6	2		25	2	3	1
	3	1	12	0	War.	26	2	0	10
	4	2	0	10	Peace.	27	1	15	6
	5	1	6	8		28	2	8	0
	6	1	3	1		29	2	1	7
	7	1	5	4		1730	1	12	5
	8	1	16	1		31	1	9	2
	9	3	9	9		32	1	3	8
	1710	3	9	4		33	1	5	2
	11	2	8	0		34	1	14	0
	12	2	1	2		35	1	18	2
Peace of	13	2	5	4		36	1	15	10
Utretcht.	14	2	4	8		37	1	13	9
	15	1	18	2		38	1	11	6
	16	2	2	8	War.	39	1	14	2
	17	2	0	7		1740	2	5	0
War.	18	1	14	6		41	2	1	5
Peace.	19	1	11	1		42	1	10	2
	1720	1	12	10		43	1	2	0
	21	1	13	4		44	1	2	0
	22	1	12	0		45	1	4	5

	Year	£	s.	d.
	46	1	14	8
	47	1	10	11
Peace of	48	1	12	10
Aix-la-Cha-	49	1	12	10
pelle.	1750	1	8	10
	51	1	14	2
	52	1	17	2
	53	1	19	8
	54	1	10	9
War.	55	1	10	0
	56	2	0	2
	57	2	13	4
	58	2	4	5
	59	1	15	4
	1760	1	12	5
	61	1	6	10
	62	1	14	8
Peace of	63	1	16	2
Paris.	64	2	1	6
	65	2	8	0
	66	2	3	1
	67	—	—	—
	68	—	—	—
	69	—	—	—
	1770	—	—	—
	71	2	7	2
	72	2	10	8
	73	2	11	0
	74	2	12	8
War.	75	2	8	4
	76	1	18	2
	77	2	5	6
	78	2	2	0
	79	1	13	8
	1780	1	15	8
	81	2	4	8
	82	2	7	10
Peace of	83	2	12	8
Versailles.	84	2	8	10
	85	2	11	10
	86	1	18	10
	87	2	1	2
	88	2	5	0
	89	2	11	2
	1790	2	13	2
	91	2	7	0
	92	2	2	11
War.	93	2	8	11
	94	2	11	8
	95	3	14	2
	96	3	17	1
	97	2	13	1
	98	2	10	3
	99	3	7	6
	1800	5	13	7
War.	1	5	18	3
Peace.	2	3	7	5
	3	2	16	6
	4	3	0	1
	5	4	7	10
	6	3	19	0
	7	3	13	3
	8	3	19	0
	9	4	15	7
	1810	4	16	2

The account down to the year 1766, inclusive, is taken from the table of prices at Windsor market as given in 14th vol. of Mr. Young's Annals of Agriculture—from 1771 to 1809, inclusive, from the account transmitted by Mr. Catherwood to the Committee for inquiring into the high price of Bullion—and for the year and a half succeeding from the monthly returns. The price of wheat at Windsor is supposed by Mr. Young, to be 2d. per quarter higher than the general average of the kingdom, for which, therefore, allowance may be made.

*Average Prices of Meat at Smithfield, sinking the offal, per stone of 8lb.**

	Average amount of Bank of Engl. notes, (post bills included.)*	Average price of Wheat. per quarter.		Beef.				Mutton.				Veal.				Pork.			
				lowest.		highest.		lowest.		highest.		lowest.		highest.		lowest.		highest.	
	£.	s.	d.	s.	d.	s.	d.	s.	d.	s.	d.	s.	d.	s.	d.	s.	d.	s.	d.
1795		74	2	2	$0\frac{1}{3}$	3	8	3	8	4	$4\frac{2}{3}$	3	$5\frac{1}{3}$	5	$2\frac{2}{3}$	4	$1\frac{1}{3}$	5	$2\frac{2}{3}$
6		77	1	3	$3\frac{3}{12}$	4	$4\frac{4}{12}$	3	$10\frac{2}{12}$	4	$8\frac{2}{12}$	3	$11\frac{9}{12}$	5	6	4	7	5	5
7	11,356,996	53	1	3	$6\frac{2}{12}$	4	$5\frac{2}{12}$	3	$11\frac{3}{12}$	4	$5\frac{8}{12}$	4	$4\frac{4}{12}$	5	$7\frac{4}{12}$	3	$10\frac{8}{12}$	4	$8\frac{10}{12}$
8	13,334,752	50	3	2	$11\frac{10}{12}$	3	$9\frac{10}{12}$	3	$0\frac{11}{12}$	3	$9\frac{4}{12}$	3	$9\frac{2}{12}$	4	$10\frac{6}{12}$	2	$8\frac{5}{12}$	3	$6\frac{8}{12}$
9	14,062,327	67	6	3	3	4	$5\frac{8}{12}$	3	$6\frac{8}{12}$	4	$6\frac{10}{12}$	3	$10\frac{10}{12}$	5	$1\frac{10}{12}$	3	6	4	5
1800	15,841,932	113	7	3	$8\frac{8}{12}$	5	4	4	$5\frac{6}{12}$	5	$5\frac{8}{12}$	4	$5\frac{10}{12}$	6	4	4	11	5	10
1	16,169,594	118	3	4	$4\frac{10}{12}$	5	$8\frac{4}{12}$	5	$2\frac{4}{12}$	6	$3\frac{8}{12}$	4	$11\frac{6}{12}$	6	$8\frac{2}{12}$	5	$8\frac{8}{12}$	6	$9\frac{2}{12}$
2	17,054,454	67	5	4	$2\frac{8}{12}$	5	$5\frac{2}{12}$	5	$1\frac{6}{12}$	6	1	4	$10\frac{6}{12}$	6	$3\frac{6}{12}$	4	7	5	$6\frac{7}{12}$
3	16,847,522	56	6	4	$3\frac{10}{12}$	5	6	4	$5\frac{6}{12}$	5	11	4	3	6	$7\frac{4}{12}$	4	1	5	$1\frac{8}{12}$
4	17,345,020	60	1	4	$4\frac{4}{12}$	5	$5\frac{4}{12}$	4	6	5	$3\frac{10}{12}$	5	$0\frac{4}{12}$	6	$5\frac{8}{12}$	3	$11\frac{4}{12}$	4	$11\frac{4}{12}$
5	17,241,932	87	10	3	$11\frac{6}{12}$	5	$0\frac{8}{12}$	4	2	5	$1\frac{2}{12}$	4	$7\frac{8}{12}$	5	$11\frac{2}{12}$	4	4	5	3
6	17,135,40[illegible]	79	0	4	$3\frac{1}{12}$	5	$3\frac{4}{12}$	4	$7\frac{4}{12}$	5	5	4	$7\frac{4}{12}$	5	$11\frac{4}{12}$	4	10	4	$9\frac{4}{12}$
7	17;405,001	73	3	3	$11\frac{4}{12}$	6	$0\frac{8}{12}$	4	$1\frac{10}{12}$	5	$1\frac{2}{12}$	4	$3\frac{10}{12}$	5	$9\frac{10}{12}$	4	$5\frac{10}{12}$	5	$4\frac{8}{12}$
8	17,534,580	79	0	4	$0\frac{10}{12}$	5	$2\frac{10}{12}$	4	4	5	$5\frac{6}{12}$	4	$8\frac{8}{12}$	6	$3\frac{2}{12}$	4	$9\frac{8}{12}$	5	10
9	19,001,890	95	7	4	6	5	$9\frac{6}{12}$	4	9	5	$10\frac{9}{12}$	5	$0\frac{4}{12}$	6	8	5	7	6	$8\frac{8}{12}$
1810	†22,266,970	96	2	4	$6\frac{11}{12}$	5	$11\frac{1}{12}$	5	$1\frac{8}{12}$	6	$1\frac{11}{12}$	5	$3\frac{10}{12}$	6	11	5	$9\frac{2}{12}$	6	$9\frac{6}{12}$
1	‡23,441,866	91	3	4	$10\frac{4}{6}$	6	2	5	2	6	2	5	10	7	$5\frac{4}{6}$	5	7	6	8

* From the Report of the Bullion Committee.

* These yearly average prices are computed from the monthly average prices as given in the Gentleman's Magazine.

† The average computed from the amount on the 7th and 12th days of each month.

‡ The average computed from the amount on the 25th day of each of the first six months.

I know not, but it may be thought, that the demand for the several articles of human sustenance which are specified in the preceding tables, has of late years been so materially increased, that there has been no correspondent increase of supply; and that the great rise in their price, is to be referred to that cause. Yet, what foundation is there for the supposition, that the demand has been increased in any extraordinary degree at all? 'Tis true, we are wont to hear of the consumption and waste attendant upon the maintenance of our seamen and our soldiers. But then it ought at the same time to be recollected, that much of their supplies is drawn, not only from other countries, in which, or in the neighbourhood of which they may happen to be stationed, but from those also which, are remote, yet not so far remote as this;—on which last, for their maintenance in time of peace, they must chiefly, if not wholly depend. And it may, moreover, be observed, that if the effect of war were certainly to raise the prices of commodities, in any great degree, it should have been apparent, not only in the present and preceding, but in all former wars. From the table first presented, that, however, does not prove to have been the case.

Has the condition of the country labourer been improved? Is his consumption enlarged? Do his increased wages enable him to indulge more freely in any of these articles of subsistence?—Is their high price occasioned by the increased demand, and increased expense of cultivation, the consequence of such increased wages? Look into the cottage of the labourer, and see if his comforts have been thus multiplied; listen to his tale of other times, and hear him lament the change which he has experienced. Go to the overseers of his parish, and compare the accounts of the present and few preceding, with former years; satisfy yourself, whether in this class of people poverty has diminished, as the price of necessaries has increased; whether it is to the increased wages of labour, that this increased price is in the least degree to be ascribed.

Nor, does it appear that the increase of demand arises from any extraordinary increase of our population. That our population has increased, I will readily admit. But, what proof has been offered, that, within the last twelve years, it has increased extraordinarily? Already it has been intimated how little the condition of country labourers has been improved.—And how much more has that of others been improved? What probability, of any extraordinary increase of our population in general, arises from the general situation of the great mass of the people---straitened, for the most part, as they are in the means of maintaining an infant family? What from the want of fresh inducements held out to them for marriage,—what from the state of war in which we have been so much engaged with little intermission,—by which lives have been prematurely destroyed, and the intercourse of the sexes has been in some degree diminished?*

But, though our population had increased in such extraordinary degree, since the suspension of cash payments

---

* The enumeration of 1801 was avowedly defective; the present is likely to be more correct, and will probably be higher.

at the Bank,—nay, though its increase had been effected, (as some persons, it should seem from their language, are inclined to believe,) by means of that suspension; in what manner would this increase have operated in raising the price of corn, unless an excess of currency had accompanied it? Do those who attend open-mouthed in our markets, but, without money in their pockets, enhance the price of corn and meat? Does not the price depend a little on the means of those who come to buy? Besides, the mere increase of population without a proportionate increase of the necessaries of life, (if such a supposition be not in itself absurd, or nearly so,) would naturally operate in reducing the wages of labour;—there would be a greater number of competitors for employment, and their services might be obtained at a lower rate. Hence, the expense of cultivation would be diminished. And though the poor's rates for a time, might fall more heavily upon the farmer; yet, upon the renewal of his lease, he would stipulate for a proportionate abatement of rent, in case the increase of those rates exceeded the reduction which had taken place in the expense of cultivation. But what abatement of rent,—what reduction in the wages of labour, has of late taken place? In what district have not the nominal rents and wages of labour been enormously increased;—though not, perhaps, every where, or any where, in proportion to the depreciation of money? But after all, is not the increase of population the sure sign of increased means of subsistence, and nearly in the same ratio? But if those means have so increased, what is the pretence for saying that the increase of population is the cause of this enormous increase of price?

Has the supply then been diminished? Years of scarcity we have occasionally experienced, and large importations of grain have been requisite to relieve the public want. But years of scarcity have been experienced in former times, and the price of grain has risen accordingly; but no such continued rise as has of late years been experienced resulted from them. The price soon fell to its former average level;—and it was not till fresh years of scarcity again enhanced the value, that the price rose to any extraordinary height,—and then, soon again to fall.

Of a long series of years which preceded the suspension of cash payments by the bank, the two immediately preceding it, seem to have been those in which wheat obtained the highest price. Whether at this period the quantity of money circulating in the country exceeded its due amount, and thus contributed to raise the price of corn beyond what the real scarcity of that article could warrant,—or whether the scarcity was so great as alone to justify that high price, it is difficult to ascertain. True, however, it is, that the people were under the necessity of resorting to new expedients for supplying the deficiency of food, and serious apprehensions of famine were entertained. Yet, whether any greater actual scarcity has prevailed since the two years immediately succeeding the suspension of cash payments, than occasionally at other times prevailed during the course of the last century, is not to be discovered by a comparison of the respective prices only which the principal articles of subsistence have, from time to time, obtained in this country; nor of the respective quantities of grain which may, from time to time, have been imported into it. Had our currency continued stationary in value, a fair criterion would, perhaps, have been afforded by the former, as well as by the latter. But, as the excess of currency must naturally tend to increase the price of grain, as well as that of all other commodities—so the high price of grain naturally tends to increase the quantity imported from abroad; though, I fear, it must be allowed on grounds which shall presently be noticed, to diminish that which is grown at home.

Let us, then, argue from the nature of things, and judge whether the improvements which have within these fourteen years been made in our systems of agriculture—whether the wide-extended tracts of land, which have, within the same period, been brought into cultivation from a state comparatively barren, must not, or might not, if more of it had been applied to the growth of grain, have furnished us with great additional, nay, sufficient supplies of food,—of grain, if not of meat of every description, which our habits require, and our climate can afford---whether they do not enable us amply to provide for all that additional population which we have, and which generally succeeds, but seldom can exist, without an abundance of the common necessaries of life, —for which, in part, however, we have of late been indebted to other nations.

But, though thus indebted, let us not suppose, that the supplies of food, in proportion to the number of those who must be fed, cannot be raised at home. Since sometimes, nay, oftentimes, there has been an excess of our own produce beyond our own consumption,—the consequence in some degree, perhaps, of bounties upon export. And though now, it seems, that our consumption far exceeds our produce,—at least, that our export is exceeded by our import,—yet, that is not as some would say, because the bounties are withdrawn,—for at so high a price as corn has been, none would claim them; but rather, as I apprehend, in consequence of the excess of currency which has occasioned that high price. For, I think, it will not be denied by those who say, that the growth of grain has been diminished in this country, or not increased in proportion to the increase of our population, (notwithstanding the high price which may be obtained for it,) that such diminution, or want of increase, has been occasioned by the greatly augmented nominal expense attending its cultivation—that hence the farmer is induced to graze rather than to till his land, a practice to which the scarcity of corn has often been ascribed. But from what cause has this augmented expense, and, therefore, this consequent practice, proceeded? Whence is this vast increase in the cost of horses, and of the implements of agriculture—and in the price of labour? Is it not all the sure natural effect of the augmented price of the produce of the land itself, of oats and fodder, of wheat and the common necessaries of life,--an effect which the excess of currency has most manifestly produced?

What then can be more manifest than that hence, too, proceeds the reduction in the quantity of grain which, of late years, has been exported, and the great augmentation in the amount of that which has been imported? Even with the bounties which, under the old regulations were allowed upon the export, the profit could hardly have been so great to the merchant then employed in that trade, as is now the profit attending the import from other countries.* It is idle to talk of general inclosures, of a free corn trade,---nay, of bounties upon its exportation. Where in Europe, where, on the surface of the globe, is a market to be found, in which corn bears so high a price as in ours? Add to that price the costs of freightage and insurance, and the trader will make but a sorry voyage homewards with his corn on hand, who would venture out in such a trade as this.

Did the high price of wheat, in reality, proceed only from the small quantity which is grown compared with the demand---could it be doubted, that more and would speedily be put into tillage, and render the supply sufficient? Again, if so much land, as it is contended, has been converted from the purpose of tillage to that of pasturage—has the price of wool, of leather,‡ and of meat, been proportionally lowered? If the high price of wheat be the effect of diminished tillage—the effect of increased pasturage, should be to lower the price of those articles—of which the quantity must be multiplied by means of that increase. But, notwithstanding their multiplication, their price has been enormously advanced, as the second table clearly shews.

That the price of meat must, in some measure, depend upon the seasons, it would be absurd to deny—since it is upon the seasons that the supply of grass and

---

* See p. 42, infrà.

† I mean, no doubt, British leather.

other herbs, must depend,—and hence the quantity of young which are reared, and of the stock rendered fit for use. No such sudden and violent variations are here, however, to be expected as in the price of grain, and more especially of wheat, which constitutes the principal article of food for the great mass of people; and from a real or supposed scarcity of which, it naturally follows that the increase of price must be rapid, and may be almost unlimited, except by the want of means wherewith to purchase it. But, is it pretended, that during the course of twelve years, our seasons have been invariably unfavourable to the production and maintenance of cattle and sheep,—that the propagation of the several species has been retarded,—that the herbs of the field have been checked and blasted in their growth year after year? It is childish to imagine and assert it. Whereas it is most reasonable to conclude, that from the regard which has been paid to the breed of animals, their qualities have been generally improved—whilst, from the improved system of husbandry which has been adopted, not only has the quantity of food, fit for their support, been greatly augmented, but greater economy has likewise been observed in its consumption. So that the very animals themselves are thus not only maintained in greater numbers, but are rendered fit food for man at an earlier age than formerly they were.

Neither can it with much shew of reason be said, that the additional taxes, which have been imposed since the restriction of cash payments, have occasioned this extraordinary rise in the prices of almost all articles whatsoever. That the prices of some articles have been raised, and greatly too, in consequence of these taxes acting directly or indirectly upon them, is certainly true.---But upon the prices of a variety of others (such as those specified in the preceding tables;) they ought to have little or no operation at all, whatever they do have:---For, though we admit that a tax upon the necessaries of life must operate as a tax upon all articles whatsoever; yet we do not admit that a tax, imposed upon such articles as are not of that description, should attach to those which are---or, in other words, that the price of corn, or of meat, or the wages of agricultural labour, should be increased by a tax upon spirits, or hair-powder, or upon incomes, exceeding what the necessities of those employed in agriculture absolutely require.

It long, indeed, had been the policy of the legislature of this country, as it ought always to be, to abstain from the imposition of such taxes as appear likely in any considerable degree to affect the wages of agricultural, if not of manufacturing, labour,---well knowing how prejudicial they are to the real interests of the nation:---and although I fear it may be gradually deviating from this policy, yet, since the period of the restriction of cash payments, it seems to have imposed no fresh duties of that nature, to such an amount as ought to have produced much effect on the price of the necessaries of life. The additional duties of 5s. per bushel each, which were laid upon salt, in 1798, and 1805, should be considered as in part negatived by the reduction of $\frac{1}{3}$ of the duty upon candles in 1803. And, together with the increased duties on horses employed in husbandry, now perhaps operating merely as a tax upon the high profits of farming capital or of land, would scarcely have been perceptible in the reasonable consequent increase of the price of agricultural produce, even though those profits had remained stationary, and the duties been thrown altogether upon the consumer.*

If, then, since he restriction of cash payments no material taxes have been imposed upon the necessaries of life, none, at least, the tendency of which, towards raising the price of those necessaries and of other agricultural produce, is not greatly counteracted by the partial abatement of other taxes—with what reason can it be said that the price of all things has been increased by means of the increased taxes ?

I do not, indeed, intend to argue, that if there had been no increase of taxes, the prices of things in general would have been increased to their present amount;—but, that if there had been no increase of the circulating medium, they would not have been materially increased, notwithstanding the heavy taxes, which

---

* The annual sums payable in respect of these duties may be upon an average about 3*s*. for each person.

* With regard to the additional duties upon sugar, tea, and malt, these are not justly to be deemed necessaries, since in the families of country labourers they are not generally used, and no increase in their wages seems to have taken place in consequence of those duties,—But see p. 44.

I will not, however, therefore say, they have not proved oppressive to the lower classes of the community, in depriving them in great measure of their almost only luxuries, if luxuries they can be called.—It can hardly be doubted that very many who, before the additional heavy duties were imposed upon tea and malt, indulged themselves in, are now, in consequence of those duties, precluded from the use of them,—perhaps to the detriment of the community. But as to the increased

of late years have been imposed. For, it is not at all improbable that much of our paper money has been put into circulation, for the purpose of providing for the discharge of them. Those, who by raising the price of the commodities which they sell can acquire to themselves sufficient to discharge, either partly or wholly, the taxes which are imposed either upon themselves, or upon the articles they consume, be they articles of necessity or luxury, will naturally so raise them. And as the greater the plenty of money, and the greater the facility of obtaining it, the greater is the price which a purchaser is willing to give for the commodity of which he may stand in need; so the less is the difficulty of obtaining that which the seller may think fit to ask;---and without much offence to his conscience, he will ask so much as will insure to himself his accustomed enjoyments. Whereas, had the quantity of money remained stationary, the purchaser would be no better able than before, to pay an advanced price for the commodity: which, therefore, must, probably, continue to be sold at the same.

For it is not only what the seller may demand, but what

---

duty upon sugar,—the large supplies which have been thrown into our market, since the numerous captures of sugar islands from our enemies, and the exclusion of the produce, as well as that of our own colonies, from the greater part of the continent of Europe, have rendered this article so plentiful, as to counteract, for the present, the tendency of the new duty, to increase its price to the consumer.

the buyer also can give, that fixes the price. Is he, then, who pays 10 per cent. on his income, or is subject to an additional per centage upon the old duties on his house and his windows, better able to pay an advanced price for his shoes or his coat, than before those additional duties were charged upon him? As a purchaser he will contend against any increase of price, as much as the vender will contend for it; and on the score of taxes, there would, in general, be no better reason for the latter to increase than for the former to abate from it. The consequence of all which would be, that the taxes would be paid by those who it was rightly intended, should pay them, and not be thrown, unjustly, upon others who may not now have the power of avoiding them.

And these observations, perhaps, cannot be applied more properly than to the case of those commodities which are particularly specified in the tables. In regard, indeed, to the class of farmers, (such as the majority of them were in this country not long ago,) few are the taxes which affect them in any material degree, if we except the duties upon income, sugar, tea, spirits, malt, and hops, all but the first, reducible at will. The taxes upon houses and windows, though in most cases trifling, being considered in the adjustment of their rent,—and those on horses being properly chargeable on others. Now, whatever may be urged in favour of this, or of any other useful class of individuals, it surely will not be maintained, that this or any other ought to be exempt from the charge of contributing equally (according to their respective abilities) to the service of the state; unless it can satisfactorily be shewn that such exemption is conducive to the general welfare and prosperity.

How, then, does the exemption of the class alluded to conduce to these ends? How speeds the public, that this, above all other classes, should exclusively enjoy its wonted luxuries and comforts without abatement---that out of the clear profits of farming stock alone (as profitable perhaps as any other) nothing, or but little should be deducted? Admit the principle but for a moment. Would the landlord, when the lease which he had granted should expire, so far neglect his own interest as not lay on an additional rent in proportion to the advantage which his tenant derived from such a privilege? It would not be the farmer, then, but the landlord, who would be exempted. And what claims has the landlord---the idle capitalist---the owner of the soil---from whence, if not above, at least in full as great a degree as all other funds, the taxes must be drawn?

But, however small the claims of both may be,—when we come to consider, as we shall, the average prices which the produce of land has attained, within these few years—we may be satisfied that not only has the farmer been enabled entirely to reimburse himself for the payment of such additional taxes, as have been imposed since the period of the suspension of cash payments, but has also acquired such extraordinary profits as might, if applied to the service of the public, have been productive of most essential, and important benefits.

Enough, however, has now, I trust, been said in opposition to the arguments which have been brought forward with the intent to shew that the high prices which have prevailed since the suspension of cash payments, have in a material degree proceeded from any other cause than an excessive paper currency; which simply, and alone, is fully capable of accounting for them. So that if any reasonable man had considered, fourteen years ago, what effect such an increase of the circulating medium, as, since that period, appears to have taken place, would probably have, in the augmentation of the prices of commodities, it is not too much to presume, that he would have judged that augmentation to be greater, instead of less, than it has actually proved to be. For our great and unforeseen improvements in machinery and other arts, and the extension of our agriculture, must, no doubt, have had a tendency to reduce them in some, and that no small degree.

It is curious, indeed, to see to what shifts men who are intent only upon supporting a favourite, and as they believe to themselves most profitable doctrine, will sometimes have recourse. The high price of bullion, say they, is no proof of the depreciation of paper, but of the increased value of Gold and Silver.---But when it is shewn that the value of these has not been increased abroad, and that their value, at home, compared with the generality of other articles, is relatively diminished; that an ounce of gold will not now buy as much corn, or meat, as it would have done before the restriction of cash payments, when the market price of bullion was below its mint price;* that the value of gold, in the

* If the price of wheat were 50s. per quarter, an ounce

form of bullion, is reduced, and greatly too, in consequence of the excessive issue of paper money—they will tell you that it is the scarcity of those articles—of corn, and meat, compared with silver and gold—that has occasioned their high price—thus almost in the same breath denying the very assertion which they themselves had made. And, though they would argue that the increase of taxes has a tendency to render a larger supply of the circulating medium necessary for effecting payments in general, yet we hear them on the other hand, contending that the natural and requisite consequence of taxes, whatever they may be, is the increase of the price of all articles whatsoever, whether taxed or untaxed.—Thus affording an argument for the expediency or justice of reducing instead of increasing the quantity of that medium.

In truth, more full and convincing proof of an excessive currency can hardly be desired by those who are anxious only to obtain the truth. What other proof will the nature of the case admit? The vast issue of paper money; the almost total absence of gold, and great scarcity of silver, coin; the depressed state of the exchanges; the increased nominal price of bullion; but the still more increased price of all other commodities whatsoever—excepting those only whose prices have either been reduced or held in check, or stationary, from peculiar circumstances of increased supply, diminished

---

of gold at the mint price, would have purchased 1½ quarter of wheat and upwards. Supposing wheat at 85s. the quarter, and gold at 4l. 15s. the ounce, the ounce of gold will not purchase so much as 1⅛ quarter of wheat.

demand, or fresh facilities of production—all combine powerfully and irresistibly.

It has been said, indeed, that Bank Notes are not at discount. But that has been denied on the authority of facts, proved and proclaimed in court of law. It was, moreover, amongst the last acts of the legislature itself, to provide against it by prohibiting them from being received for any smaller sum than the sum therein specified.* It was not, however, necessary to prove the depre-

---

* A measure, supported by those very persons, who, a few weeks before, had supported the resolutions proposed by Mr. Vansittart, declaratory of the undepreciated state of the paper of the Bank of England.—A measure, however, which, (alarming as it is, from the apparently acknowledged tendency of that paper to depreciation) may seem at first sight wise and prudent; and would, perhaps, be so, if effectual steps had at the same time been resolved upon, and taken for the gradual, yet speedy reduction of the quantity now in circulation (such steps as those recommended by the committee appointed to inquire into the cause of the high price of bullion)—but which, otherwise, will probably fail of its intended object,—and fail too, it probably would, though it had been backed by the enactment of Earl Stanhope's Bill auxiliary thereto, if bereft of the clause of limitation, as to the amount of notes to be issued—the only clause in the bill which has been passed, and in that which has been rejected, which seemed at all calculated to restore things to their pristine state of fair and reasonable price, and to keep them in it,—for it is much to be doubted, whether the establishment of provincial offices would have any great effect in reducing the quantity of the notes of country banks, on the solvency of which, the surrounding inhabitants seem

ciation of the currency in general, that bank notes alone should be at discount. A well-founded confidence in the resources of the bank, and a general anxiety to support its credit, prevented, a long while, the depreciation of its notes below the legal coin,— which rather was itself depreciated by the abundance of paper money, purporting to represent it. Both the coin and the paper were thus depreciated below the value of the metal, of which the former consisted. But now, since the practice of receiving in exchange for gold more than its nominal amount in paper, became, though rare perhaps, yet so notorious, and undeniably confirmed---since a peer of the

---

now to depend more confidently, than on that of the Bank of England itself. But what Earl Stanhope's final views and schemes may be, 'tis not yet quite easy to develope—What, indeed, is his principle ? Is it the real reformation of the currency,—the restitution of their due to all men ? I trust it is. To gold, however, he objects as a standard,—as a measure of that due; and yet, how else would he determine it ? By a standard, properly so called, forsooth—by a standard whose value is not liable to change. Where will he find it ? In wool or in wheat ? Not in paper, though limited in amount ; still less, if unlimited—for he will not find it in the discretion of the directors of the Bank of England, nor yet of country bankers, nay, not of the minister himself for the time being. The relative value of a given quantity of paper money, like gold, may rise or fall. But it may fall so low, as to be good for nothing. Let Earl Stanhope beware, lest he place in the hands of men an engine, which will shatter still deeper the foundations of all property whatsoever.

realm publicly avowed his determination not to accept notes of the Bank of England, but at a discount equal to 20 per cent.---a determination founded upon principles to which no reasonable man can object, however alarmed he may be at the probable consequence of the practice*---it became the labour of the legislature to bolster up the declining value of those notes, by the means to which I have alluded. The next step, it is probable, will be to make them a legal tender for the payment of a debt. And thus, it seems, are we to run the vile and wretched course of unprincipled and needy bankrupt states.†

* "What!" say his opponents, "receive gold in payment of rent, but pay your coach-maker with paper!" And where, good reasoners, is the injustice though he do? You surely have not considered all his lordship's terms. He did not say (whatever the new law may compel him now to say) "I will have nothing but the lawful coin;" but "I will take the lawful coin, or paper, at a reasonable discount; I will take the latter for so much gold as it will purchase; and I do not demand a greater quantity of gold than at the time of our contract I could have purchased with the amount of my stipulated rent, if paid in paper." The coach maker has increased his charge in consequence of the depreciation of that paper; and thus he indemnifies himself. Why should not others be allowed to do the same?

† Could our fathers, could we ourselves, till we had witnessed it, have believed, that in a British House of Commons, the prime minister of the day would hazard even an insinuation, still less a threat, that under any circumstances, the

Grievous, indeed, it is, yet not unprofitable, I trust, here to pause awhile, and to contemplate the circumstances which present themselves to our observation.

It appears from the first of the preceding tables, that the average price of wheat for ten years, immediately preceding 1797, the year of the suspension of cash payments by the Bank of England, did not amount to 53s. 3d. the quarter, notwithstanding the two last of those years were years of distressing scarcity; the average price of those two years was 75s. $7\frac{1}{2}$d. In the year of the suspension, the average price fell to 53s. 1d. and in the following year to 50s. 3d. the average price of both being less than that of the ten years immediately preceding the suspension. Since the year 1798, the average price, it will be perceived, has in no year been so low, but has in most years been much higher than that of 1798.---But it is peculiarly worthy of remark, that in the years 1800 and 1801, though they must be admitted to have been years of great scarcity, the respective average prices were 113s. 7d. and 118s. 3d. the quarter, far exceeding those of any former, or even subsequent year, not excepting the years 1809 and 1810. I say this is peculiarly worthy of remark, because it is also remarkable, that the increase in the amount of bank notes in 1800 and 1801, was

---

paper of the Bank of England should be made a legal tender? Mr. Perceval seems to have said, that "as to the measure of making bank notes a legal tender, he hoped it would not be necessary; he trusted that the seasonable adoption of the present bill would prevent it." Notice intelligible enough.

likewise very great; the average amount in 1799, being only 14,062,327*l.* but in 1800, 15,841,932*l.* and in 1801, 16,169,594*l.* between which latter period, and the year 1808 inclusive, it appears that the yearly average amount of Bank of England notes rose (the amount of one year, however, being sometimes somewhat less than that of the preceding year) to 17,534,580*l.* which is an increase of only 1,364,986*l.* in the course of eight years.* In 1809 they were increased rapidly to 19,001,890*l.* an increase exceeding the total increase during the whole course of the eight preceding years, and in 1810 still further, to the enormous sum of 22,700,000*l.* whilst the price of wheat rose, upon an average of the former year, to 95s. 7d. the quarter, and of the latter, to 96s. 2d.

Can it really be doubted, then, that the extraordinary and unprecedented prices of 1800 and 1801 proceeded from the extraordinary and unprecedented amount of Bank paper put into circulation, as well as from the scanty supply of wheat which our harvests afforded---and that the high prices of 1809 and 1810, and even of the present year, must have proceeded, if not altogether, at least principally from the former cause? How far the promise of the present year may be blasted, I know not. If plenty

---

* Though the average amount of Bank Notes appears to have been less in 1805 than in 1804, the average price of wheat was greater than in that year or 1806, probably owing to the deficient crops of 1804, for it will, upon enquiry, be found, that the rise in the price of wheat commenced in the middle of that year, and continued to increase throughout it.

should abound, it must, in spite of our excessive currency itself, have some effect, though small I fear, upon the prices---nay some it already has.

Again, if we consider the advances which have, from time to time, been made in the price of butchers' meat, we shall, perhaps, observe a still stronger correspondence between those advances, and the amount of Bank Notes which, from time to time, have been in circulation. For, let us even suppose the average price of the years 1797 and 1798, (remembering, however, that the former immediately succeeded a year of scarcity and would, therefore, naturally be somewhat dear) to be the average price at which meat would have been sold, in case there were no depreciation of money.---The price of 1799, it will be seen by the table, differed little from that of 1797; for it was not till the close of 1799, that the currency (if we judge from the amount of Bank of England Notes then in circulation) appears to have materially exceeded its due level. The average price of 1800 and 1801, and of every succeeding year up to the present, has, however, greatly exceeded that of 1799.

That the high prices of meat as well as corn in 1800 and 1801, were in part occasioned by the deficiency of the supply of food in general, in proportion to the demand, ought certainly to be admitted. When that cause, therefore, ceased, the prices fell, as in the next ensuing year, but not to the level of preceding years,—neither till the year 1809, do they seem to have risen so high as in either of the two years, 1800 and 1801, notwithstanding the gradual increase in the amount of Bank Notes. In

1809, however, the prices rose above those of 1800, if not of 1801, and in 1810, above both, except in one article, the probably increased supply of which, from some of the causes I have mentioned, may account for the lowness of its price.---But by this time the excess of paper money alone seems to have effected (as might have been observed in regard to the price of wheat) what a smaller excess of paper money, co-operating with a real scarcity of the chief articles of subsistence had effected in 1800 and 1801---the augmentation of their price to the extent of 40 per cent. or upwards, beyond their average price in preceding common years.

Looking, then, to the established high prices of our markets, it is not to be wondered that we should receive from foreign countries such large supplies of the necessaries of life. It is no proof of the present, though it may be the cause of the future deficiency of our own produce, that such great importations of grain have taken place.

From the Report of the committee of the House of Commons, 6th March, 1800, it appears that at that time 33s. per quarter was held sufficient to cover the expense of insurance, freight, and other merchants' charges of conveying wheat from the Mediterranean or America, to this country---so that supposing the price of that commodity to be even the same in the countries bordering upon the Mediterranean, and in America, as the average price at which it was sold here for ten years previous to the suspension of cash payments, (including two years of scarcity,) the price at which it might be sold in our markets, need not exceed 86s. 3d. which is about 2s. more than the average price of the last eleven years, but 9s. 7½d. less than that of the last two. To what a state of calamity and distress, then, may this country be reduced, if the prime article of subsistence cannot be produced at home at so cheap a rate as it can be furnished to us from abroad;---if the native farmer shall be undersold in his own market; if we shall for ever be dependent upon foreign countries for supply! Yet as we surely shall, should all our corn fields be thus converted into pastures. In times like the present---with a foe so powerful in arms, and so inveterate in spirit, what dreadful affliction may we not expect? We have seen his policy extended against our manufactures;---he has excluded them from the limits of his wide-extended sway.---A different policy, suggested by the same spirit, may prompt him to interdict wholly, as he has already, partially, interdicted our supply of corn from the countries lying within those limits,---and the powers which are without them, may yet adopt his policy.

Let us now, however, consider a little further the effects of these high prices. Although I would adopt it as a principle, both of justice and of policy, that no peculiar class of individuals ought to be exempted from contributing an equal share, according to their respective abilities, for the service of the state, unless such exemption be manifestly beneficial to the general interests of the community; yet I am not disposed to urge any thing against the practice, or the principle of improving the condition of our agricultural labourers;—still less would I urge any thing against the continuance of those comforts, or innocent enjoyments, which they have at any time heretofore experienced. I would admit, therefore, that in consequence of the fresh duties which were (improvidently, I think) levied upon malt, a proportionate rise ought in justice to have taken place in the wages of such labourers as were, before the imposition of such duties, accustomed to the constant use of that article; and that those farmers, who themselves immediately supplied their labourers with drink, ought to have incurred a proportionately greater expense on that account?

Supposing, then, that either way the cultivators of land had been fully justified in laying on an additional charge upon its produce---what probably would be the amount?---Taking the number of persons employed in agriculture to be about 2,080,000, which exceeds, in a small degree, the number stated in the returns of 1801, and estimating that half that number was accustomed to the constant use of beer,---the additional duties which, since the restriction of cash payments, have been imposed on hops and malt, and such ought to have been defrayed, in the first instance, by the farmers, by way of increased wages or expenses, could hardly have amounted to the sum of *eighteen hundred thousand pounds.**

But did such rise in the rate of wages actually take place---or was such additional expense actually incurred on this account? Has not the labourer been compelled rather to abandon altogether, except perhaps in harvest

* This is allowing for each person more than 8lb. of malt, and 4lb. of hops per annum.

time, the use of his accustomed beverage if made of malt, or to put up with such as is of far inferior quality ?* If not, tis highly fit, on grounds of public policy, that these heavy duties upon malt should cease. But so they should, in either case.

What, however, is the amount of the additional sums which are paid to our farmers for the produce of their land, or rather not only to our farmers, but to those traders also, whom the high prices of our markets have enticed to import the corn of other countries, and enabled to undersell our farmers ?

In supposing that the average price of the quarter of wheat would not in common years have much exceeded 50s. in case there had been no excess of currency; I am aware, that I hazard objections from many quarters. The objections, however, I have endeavoured to anticipate and remove,---though not with the expectation that all those who would advance, are well disposed to retract them, even though they should be convinced of their futility. But it matters little what those who are intent upon supporting a particular dogma, rather than in searching out the truth, may either assert or contradict. Facts manifest themselves. Look, then, at the foregoing tables, and let it be shewn, if it can be, what other cause than the depreciation of our money, has produced the extraordinary increase in the price of the several articles of sustenance comprized in them. We will,

* In many districts, cider, if not water, is the common beverage of labourers employed in agriculture.

in the mean time, proceed in endeavouring to ascertain, in some degree, the aggregate amount of the vast surplus which the prices of the present day yield over and above those which would probably be obtained under a well-regulated currency.

It appears, then, from the first of the tables, that excepting in the two years immediately preceding that in which the cash payments were suspended, the average price of wheat for every five years since the year 1770, was always something, and occasionally greatly, below the standard I have chosen. The two years which form the exception, viz. 1795 and 1796, were (as I have more than once observed) years of scarcity; but the average price even of the ten years ending with 1796, and, therefore, including both those years of scarcity, amounted to less than 53s. 3d. The quantity of land which, merely in consequence of that scarcity, had been brought into tillage, and the general economy which was also the consequence of it, (though no extraordinary inclosures of wastes had since been made), would have contributed much, both to multiply the produce and to diminish the consumption of this chief article of subsistence. The improvements and extension of our agriculture, it is reasonable to think, would, under all our circumstances, excepting the depreciation of our money, have kept its price upon the level of former years, if it had not positively lowered it. But what appears to have been the average price for the last five years? No less than 84s. 7d.;—a sum, however, much below the present and two preceding years,—for the quantity of paper money has, within that interval, been greatly increased. Admitting, however, that even in the present state of the currency, the price of common years did not exceed 85s. the quarter—the amount of the difference between this sum and 50s. calculated upon the total amount of wheat consumed in Great Britain, (supposing that consumption to be, upon an average, equal to one quarter only for each person per annum, and reckoning the whole population according to the returns to parliament,* in 1801) would of course be equal to 18,842,369*l.*†

But this is not all---the difference which the table points out between the prices at the period of the restriction of cash payments, and subsequent thereto, is not confined, to the article of wheat, but extends also to the several sorts of butchers' meat—and supposing the average consumption to be at the rate of one pound per day for one-fourth part only of the inhabitants of Great Britain, the total difference between the average price of the years 1797 and 1798, and that of last year being estimated at 3d. per pound, would amount to 12,281,186*l.*

And thus if the grounds, on which the above calculations rest, are as fair as the nature of the case will permit us to employ, it seems that the additional sums which are paid for the maintenance of the inhabitants of this country, in consequence of the depreciation of the currency, over and above the sums paid for the like purpose previous to that depreciation, even supposing our numbers not to have increased since the last enumeration, and that no other sort of provisions than those above noticed were consumed; [and that after making full allowance for the

* Exclusive of seamen, soldiers, and convicts, the number appears to be 10,767,068.

† At 91s. 3d. the average of the first six months of the present year, the difference would be 22,211,577*l*, 13*s*.

operation of the additional duties upon hops and malt, as already estimated,] amount nearly to the enormous sum of *eight and twenty millions* !---an aggregate sufficient to discharge the entire interest payable on the national debt now unredeemed.

But, in addition to this enormous annual sum arising only from the increased prices of the articles specified in the table—we ought further to take into the account the difference in the price of every other species of produce of our soil—of butter, cheese, barley, oats, hay, straw, and whatever else our farmers, and our gardeners too, may bring to market, which would altogether not only discharge the interest on the debt but probably also, in the course of a few years, the capital on which such interest, computed at the rate of 5*l.* per cent. is payable. It would form a total astonishing to many of those who would rashly say, and ignorantly think, that the additional taxes have wrought those high prices which are the subject of our present observation.

But do the cultivators of land, then, receive as clear gain and profit, the total of this vast surplus, arising from the difference of prices? Most assuredly not—and though they did, it is to be remembered, that the surplus is to be reckoned in a depreciated currency. But still it would be considerable, notwithstanding that depreciation. The cultivators, however, in consequence of the increased prices of the necessaries of life, the produce of their own farms, must pay higher prices for their implements of agriculture—higher wages to their labourers—higher rates for the maintenance of the poor,---and (if not the owners of the land and their leases should have been granted since the depreciation of the currency,) higher, perhaps, much higher, rent to their landlords. Still, however, gain and profit enough they enjoy—immense capitals have been realized by our farmers—they have become great purchasers of land—they indulge in luxuries which their forefathers knew not;---their children are instructed in new sciences and arts---new habits of life are induced amongst them---they are not what they were. That their wealth should be disposed of after this manner, we do not complain. But we complain, as well we may, that a system should have been adopted, which has overturned the fortunes of many without any real benefit to the community at large. It would have been no injury to those whose expectations and hopes were bounded by the limits of their experience, that these expectations and hopes should not be prodigiously exceeded. But it is an injury, and a serious one, to others, who, confiding in the honour and integrity of the government to which they were subjected, doubted not, that the property, which they rightfully possessed, would be effectually secured to them;—but who, on the contrary, are cruelly abandoned by that government,—and year after year, without the means or hope of redress, are reduced to the hard necessity of yielding up their rights, and submitting to the abridgment of their wonted comforts and enjoyments.

Had it been at any time proposed, that an annual sum, far exceeding the interest now payable on the public debt, should be raised by a permanent tax upon the land---what wailings and complaints should we have heard of the injustice and impolicy of the measure. But what greater injustice or impolicy would attend it, than attends that of permitting the currency to be so depreciated, that the price of the common necessaries of life, the produce of that land, should be augmented to such an extent, as to yield a surplus beyond the former price, equal on the whole to the amount of such a tax? The impolicy is as great;---but the injustice is above comparison greater. Had such a tax been levied, the price of commodities would have risen as they have now risen; but we should, at least, have had the satisfaction of knowing, that the public at large was not without benefit---that it would be relieved from many of the taxes now imposed, and, perhaps, from the necessity of being burthened with others, which, sooner or later, we must now expect.

Without attempting any nearer approach to accuracy, than what I have already made, in calculating the average amount of the circulating medium, for some years previous to the restriction of cash payments, and what it is at present,---we may reasonably suppose that from the improvements in our agriculture and manufacture, and their augmented produce, a larger quantity of circulating medium than we possessed at the former period, even if it consisted of the precious metals alone, might now be current, without suffering any diminution of its relative value. We will, therefore, say, that only two fifth parts of its present amount ought to be withdrawn, in order to restore it to its due level.

Nor is the degree of depreciation here supposed, altogether without proof, as may be seen upon a comparison of the present with the former prices of the several articles specified in the tables which have been submitted to the reader. And though, perhaps, it may be urged as an objection to this hypothesis, that the market price of bullion does not exceed the mint price, nearly in the proportion which we have assigned for the depreciation,---yet, whatever the true proportion may be, the market price of bullion can hardly, in the present state of things, be admitted as a just criterion. For, notwithstanding that, in former times, the price of gold could never long remain much below the mint price, by reason of the greater profit which it would afford in the shape of coin; yet now, since that chief purpose for which there was then in this country a demand for gold has ceased to operate upon its real price, this naturally falls,---and hence its nominal price is not so high as it would be, had not the demand been thus diminished. The chief demand must now indeed arise from abroad; and much, it seems, has been exported,---in part no doubt, because our home demand is small, whilst the supply is much increased by means of our direct and indirect intercourse with the Portuguese and Spanish settlements. But, were the Bank of England to return to its cash payments, and it were possible, notwithstanding, (which it would not be) to retain the present quantity of paper money in circulation, it is probable the price of gold would rise rapidly to a level, with that of other commodities. It is not, therefore, on the whole, I apprehend, too much to say, that, notwithstanding the market price of gold, does not exceed the mint price above 20 or 25 per cent. the currency is depreciated in a still greater ratio, even to the extent of 40 per cent.

What then is a further consequence of this depreciation? Is not the amount of our public expenditure, exclusive of the interest payable on the debt, two-fifths more than it ought to be? And is it a small matter that we should annually pay from *fifty* to *sixty millions* for supplies and services which, if the money were undepreciated, might be obtained for *thirty* or for *thirty-six?* Is it of no importance that loans should be required to an enormous amount, and a debt fixed upon the country for which we receive not an equivalent, but what is equal in value to no more than three-fifth parts of the amount of debt incurred---that taxes should be levied upon those of fixed incomes, as well as others, to defray this vast expenditure, or to discharge the interest of that debt, and, in time, the principal? I know there are some temporary advantages, (if such they should be called) derived from this depreciation.---I know that serious abatement is virtually thus made from the pay of our naval, military, and other officers, as well as pensioners of government. I know that the public creditors, those who were so from of old, receive much less than what is owing to them. But who would not be ashamed of such advantages as these, disgraceful as they are? If salaries or pensions have been bestowed to an excess, or lavished on unworthy objects, let them at once be curtailed, or totally abolished ---But let not the meritorious servants and fair creditors of the public be abridged of one tittle of their due, so long as we have wherewithal to pay them.

The rapid rise of rents, has been another consequence of this depreciation of our currency, and reasonably enough. But a further consequence, I fear, has been the adoption of a notion amongst our landlords, as well as tenants, that the latter could not provide for the payment of those rents, if the quantity of currency were reduced, and therefore that no reduction should be made. As if all leases had been granted since the depreciation of the currency---as if no means could be devised for the establishment of an equitable arrangement in each possible case, either by the parties themselves, or by the legislature, establishing a fair scale whereby to regulate the amount of rent to be paid, according to the depreciation at the period of entering into the contact,* or by enabling the tenant, at his option, to rescind it---and, above all, as if a system, fraught with such glaring and extensive mischief, as is the present, should be upheld upon so trifling a pretence as this.

Yet what other and better pretence is there? Where, let us ask, is the necessity for continuing—what views and notions have they who would urge us to continue this destructive course?

Some there are, and those well meaning, honest men, who deny not the existence of the evil, even in its utmost extent; but they despair of the possibility of removing it. "Would you," say they, "compel the Bank to pay in cash? It has not gold sufficient in its coffers." But we do not require the immediate resumption of cash pay-

* As Lord King, it seems, would have done in respect to his own tenants, had not the legislature interfered to prevent him.

ments. We admit, that suddenly to reduce the quantity of the circulating medium in any very great degree, would be attended with mischievous effects. The committee appointed to inquire into the cause of the high price of bullion, did not recommend it. It is the prohibition of any further increase of notes of the Bank of England; it is the gradual diminution of the quantity of those now in circulation—the narrowing of its discounts, and lessening its advances to the government which we require of the Bank of England. We require also the gradual diminution of the notes of country banks, now in circulation, the prohibition of any further issue of new notes to succeed them when no longer legally re-issuable. So that the former value of the currency may be at length restored.

But then there is a notion entertained by some, that if the amount of the circulating medium were greatly reduced, there would be much difficulty in providing for the quarterly payments of interest on the public debt.---But when we call to mind what was the amount of interest actually payable on that account in 1799, when the currency was but little, if at all, depreciated, the average amount of Bank of England notes being then only about fourteen millions,--- it will appear plain that the additional interest now payable, cannot require such an addition to the circulating medium as has since been made. The amount of interest on the debt, then unredeemed, being 17,019,399*l.* 9*s.* 1¼*d.* and on that unredeemed last year 21,555,401*l.* 4*s.* 0¾*d.* making a difference, therefore, of 1,138,000*l.* 8*s.* 8¾*d.* only in the average amount of the quarterly payments, whilst he difference in that of the currency is apparently not much less than *five and twenty millions.* But I would contend, though the former difference were much greater, and the latter much less than they appear to be, that the currency ought not to be materially depreciated throughout the year, or for any considerable part of it, for the purpose of facilitating these quarterly payments. It clearly is not necessary. The times of payment may be multiplied, and the subsequent issue of paper delayed, till the return of that which may have been put into circulation for the due discharge of the interest.

"But wait," say others, (who would do well to consider a little more what they are about to say) "wait," say they "till the arrival of peace, and all will then be well. We shall then be enabled to return to cash payments without difficulty or danger." Because forsooth, I guess, we can perpetuate the war taxes. But may not the evil be then so aggravated---so deeply rooted and confirmed, that no effectual remedy can be applied? May not the public debt be swelled to such enormous magnitude, that no sufficient means can be devised, not even with the aid of the income tax itself, to discharge the total interest?

It is true, our commerce may be restored to us,---and there may be those who fondly imagine, that so favourable a balance of trade will be the consequence, that it will speedily furnish us with ample supplies of the precious metals,—or at least that these may then be obtained in any quantity like other articles in exchange for our commodities. But what is to occasion this extraordinary balance in our favour- -these vast supplies of gold and silver?---The high prices of our commodities,---

operating almost as a prohibition of their sale in foreign markets? Whence the probability, that the precious metals will then abound so greatly, as at present, in this country---the channel through which alone or chiefly they at present take their course to the greater part of Europe, and the rest of the Old World---this country---now the sole ally of the Portuguese and Spanish nations---the only friendly power which they have, or with which they seem to hold commercial intercourse? And after all, supposing by those means, or any other, short of a discovery of new mines, that gold and silver were with peace to be imported, and that to a considerable amount,---will the price so materially fall as to enable the Bank of England to purchase them at the mint price? Most surely not—if (as is pretended) our present market price be not below the continental price. Nor even if it be,---for as the drain from other countries will make them scarcer there as they become more plentiful here, the fall will surely not exceed the expense of re-conveyance to the former. Perhaps it may not fall at all. But, on the contrary, may rise,---as probably, nay, almost certainly it would, in consequence of the increased demand which would be made, with the view of providing for the supposed cash payments;---unless, indeed, a stop were put to the further increase of the currency. And so, if this were now considerably reduced, the price of gold would fall. No fall, in short, is otherwise in reason to be expected.

What solid ground, then, have we for conceiving, that the currency ought to be reduced in time of peace rather than in that of war? Have we not been told (with what degree of reason I leave others to determine) that it is by means of the great issue of its notes, by way of discount, that the Bank of England renders such service to our merchants, thus enabling them to extend the commerce of our country? Would the time of peace, then, when so many markets would probably be open to the speculation of our merchants, be more fit for narrowing Bank discounts, and consequently the issue of Bank paper, than the time of war, and of such a war as this, when almost the whole civilized world is shut against our commerce---when our goods are rotting in the warehouse for want of markets, and the machinery of our manufactories is standing still and rusting for want of use?

Why, then, any longer delay to remedy so great an evil? Were prompt and decisive measures adopted for such a purpose we should hear complaints no doubt, from a variety of quarters as we have already heard them. The interested few would strive their utmost to set the public face against them. They would tell us that our manufacturers and merchants would be ruined---as if it really were a matter of importance to these what may be the nominal or money price at which they sell their goods, provided the real price be the same---whether they sell this or that lot at a *hundred* pounds in a currency depreciated two-fifths, or at *sixty* in a currency not depreciated at all---enabled, as they would be, to purchase the same quantity of commodities with the one as well as with the other; or, as if justice herself should be sacrificed at the altar of mercantile, or manufacturing speculation. They would tell us, that our exertions against the enemy would be relaxed---

as if our strength were derived from the abundance of our paper, its enormous nominal amount---and not from our real and substantial wealth, and capital---our persevering industry and courage. Lastly, they would tell us, that the public creditor cannot be paid with such facility---that the revenue would be diminished, and prove insufficient for the discharge of the interest on his debt.---The very point to which I would now turn the attention of the reader.

I will not suppose, that at the period when the law was first enacted for suspending cash payments at the Bank of England, the government of this country deliberately intended to defraud its creditors. And I would fain suppose, it does not now intend to defraud them by continuing that suspension; but that it deems such suspension expedient and necessary to preserve itself from bankruptcy. Yet, if the very measure itself under the existing circumstances be an act of bankruptcy, what boots it? If in effect it be equivalent to the establishment of part, instead of entire payment, and satisfaction of the debt; what is it but bankruptcy manifest and decided?

But why is it to be feared, that sufficient taxes cannot be raised, except in a depreciated currency,—that they would prove inadequate to the discharge of the interest on the public debt, and of the ordinary, and extraordinary expences of the government? What, though the present taxes should prove so? what, I ask, is the reason which any honest man will venture to put forth, that should prevent the imposition of additional taxes to make good the deficiency? Is the private debtor, who has the means of paying all his debt, allowed to pay but half of it, and stand acquitted of the rest? Does the law permit him then to go at large---roll at ease in his carriage, and feast in luxury and splendour, whilst the poor half-starved creditor must be content to receive as a boon from his hands just so much as his bounty, or his conscience can afford? No, no, it does not. But, too surely, I fear it will. The same spirit will extend the same law, and the same law will sanction the act in one case as well as in the other;—but the same justice will cry loudly against both.

It is true that with a blindness, I could almost say wilful and criminal, this excess of currency has been permitted gradually to grow up, from time to time, during the course of many years, so that the loans which have latterly been advanced, have proved much less effective for the service of the state than they would have been, had the currency maintained its former value. We have, in consequence, a larger annual sum to provide for the discharge of the stipulated interest, than we should otherwise have had. But I know not with what semblance of consistency, the legislature, after having solemnly proclaimed the undepreciated state of the currency, can now turn round and say (unless it first acknowledges its error) that, henceforth, should the currency be duly regulated, an abatement must be made in the amouut of interest, payable to persons whose claims may happen to be derived from those whose loans were advanced during the depreciation. I fear, however, it will rather still persist in maintaining, that none at all has taken place; notwithstanding, that by the laws which it enacts, it goes well nigh to prove directly the reverse to be the fact.

Besides, upon an equitable view, the present owners of the stock allowed for the sums originally advanced to government, may, perhaps, be those whose property before was vested in mortgage or annuity secured on land, or otherwise; or which was the accumulation of rents under old leases, or of interest on other stock acquired long ago; persons who, already, have been grievously oppressed. Could perfect justice be insured, indeed, by apportioning such quantities of capital with interest, payable in a more valuable currency, as should equal the value of the capital, advanced at the time it was originally acquired by the present owners of the stock, they would have no reason to complain. But a measure such as this, is now, no doubt, impracticable. Moreover, the sum which might be thereby saved, though, certainly, not inconsiderable, would not, I apprehend, be so great as many persons may conceive---for the loans which have of late years, since the great depreciation, been advanced, have been comparatively small. And it should, also, further be observed, that if justice were completely done, each public creditor should be indemnified for the injury which he has already so patiently endured.

But whatever line of distinction, it may be thought fit, should here be drawn, it is, plainly, the government which has, in its power, if not in its wisdom adopted, those measures which have led to the depreciation of the currency.

It is likewise as plainly one of the chief ends of every good government to establish justice amongst the people—to protect the property of all, alike,—moreover, to deal justly by its own creditors,—a sacred and inviolable charge, which nothing but necessity should ever compel it to abandon.

If there be amongst us those who have unfairly profited of the confidence reposed in them, and turned to their own emolument what should rather have been for that of the community at at large---it might be well, perhaps, were restitution to be made. But let the Bank of England, and the country bankers, retain their past gains, enormous as they are; let public and private creditors abide by their past loss, more enormous than than those gains. But, no longer, let the government stand aloof in this scene of iniquity,—no longer countenance and applaud it,—still less participate in, and support it by the arm of law. If the government be not too weak and degraded to perform its just engagements, and I trust it is not, let it faithfully perform them. For the discharge of the interest stipulated to be paid on the millions which have, from time to time, been advanced to it,—its honour,—the honour and property of the people have been pledged; they have been pledged for the full, true, and faithful,—not the partial, fictitious, and fraudulent, discharge of that interest. So long as there is taxable property in the nation, it is liable, in justice, to satisfy the claims of the public creditor. I do not say those claims are to be preferred to the immediate necessities of the state,—but this I say, that the interests of individuals, or of peculiar bodies, or orders of men, ought not to be preferred, but ought to be postponed to them.

Look around then, and see whether the country is so destitute of resources, as to be utterly incapable of affording to the government, the means of discharging the interest of the public debt, except in a depreciated currency. Are our nobles, our clergy, our country gentlemen, our farmers, manufacturers, tradesmen, bankers, and merchants,—all—all of them so pinched withal in this long struggle, against the common enemy, that nothing further can be wrung from them for the creditors of the state? Has the land ceased to yield its harvests, its accustomed rents, its tithes and its profits, to their necessitous proprietors? Do none of our manufacturers, tradesmen, bankers, and merchants, any longer derive gain, or even common interest from their enormous capitals, as well real as fictitious? Or must we be compelled to abandon the principles which we have dared to maintain, and confess that it is reasonable?—is it right, that peculiar orders of men and individuals should be privileged, and exempt from all further contribution, though the public creditors be left unpaid,—or paid, at least, not honestly, unequivocally, and without abatement? We hope not.

Be not alarmed, my countrymen, for it is not expedient that any vast and intolerable sacrifice should be made. Though great and sorely distressing, the loss which public and private creditors, landlords and others, sustain, in consequence of the depreciation of the currency; yet, by means even of additional taxes, or the additional pressure of those already levied, to make good the future payments to the first, in a currency free from depreciation, it seems that not more than one-fifth part of the taxable income of the people would be requisite; since no more, it seems, would, probably, be requisite to make good the deficiency in the revenue, applicable to the discharge of the interest and other sums payable on account of the public debt; though the quantity of currency were reduced within its proper limits, and the nominal amount of the revenue reduced in the same ratio---a sacrifice which, I fain would hope, the people would for such a purpose most willingly undergo.

For, supposing that the annual sums payable on account of the public funded debt, amount to *four and thirty millions and a half*; and that we have been right in assigning two-fifth parts of the circulating medium as the amount of its excess---and allowing that those sources of revenue which are now sufficient for the discharge of those annual sums, would, upon the restoration of the circulating medium to its due level, yield only *three-fifth* parts of their amount---it follows that there would be a deficiency of 13,800,000*l*. only,* to be raised by additional taxes. But instead of such an actual deficiency, and correspondent levy of fresh taxes, the pressure of some of those which are at present levied, would be increased. The effect would, notwithstanding, be to certain individuals the same. Should the depreciation, however,

*Not very much more, it seems, than *two-fifth* parts of the additional expenditure occasioned by the depreciation of the currency. See p. 52, supra.

here assigned, be overrated, the less would be the sum required, the less the sacrifice in doing justice to the public and the private creditor.

Now, upon the presumption, that *twelve millions* are the amount of one-tenth part of the taxable income of the people, reckoned in the present depreciated currency, but over and above all abatements and exemptions which are allowed, under the present income or property tax (and it probably is not much less) this deficiency of 13,800,000*l.* might be supplied by an additional tax of *less than one-fifth part* of the taxable income of the people, subject to proportionate abatement when reckoned in an undepreciated currency, taking, according to our supposition, the present currency to be depreciated two-fifth parts, and, consequently, that income to amount only to three-fifth parts of the present.* For, if a

* Presuming that so much of the public debt as has been created subsequent to the year 1799, was on account of advances made in a depreciated currency, and that the depreciation was, upon an average, in the proportion of one-fifth of their whole amount, which is in the ratio of one-half of the assigned present depreciation, (a proportion, I conceive, not very wide of the probability;) then it follows, that the annual interest payable in respect of these advances, over and above what in strict justice, perhaps, the public ought to pay, may amount to 2,000,000*l.* for the discharge of which, it should seem that about 2*l.* 15*s.* 6*d.* per cent. upon the taxable income of the people, reckoned in an undepreciated currency, would suffice. But again, if justice were strictly to be pursued, the public creditor, as before has been observed,

tax of one-tenth of the present income, now produces 12,000,000*l.* it necessarily follows, that supposing that income to be reduced two fifths, the like tax would produce only 7,200,000*l.** which being doubled, amounts to 14,400,000*l.* a sum exceeding the supposed deficiency, by 600,000l.†

And what is such a tax as this, of which a large proportion would be paid (no doubt, most cheerfully) by landlords, who may, some time since, have granted leases for long terms,---by mortgages,---by stockholders and annuitants---what, I say, is such a tax as this (let it affect other persons as it may) compared with that enormous sum, arising from the difference of price of the common articles of subsistence, which we so long have been content to pay?—What, when that enormous sum is further magnified, if it were possible to calculate it, by the difference of price of other articles,---and what

should receive complete indemnity for the loss he has hitherto sustained, in receiving payment of his dividends in a depreciated currency, during the last eleven years.

* It is not unworthy of remark, that this sum amounts nearly to 1,400,000*l.* beyond the produce of the income tax, for the year ending the 5th April, 1800. A circumstance somewhat corroborating the assumed extent of the depreciation. The substantial revenue, and the mode of assessment, are both, probably, improved; the abatements too are less; and hence, no doubt, in part, it is that the present produce is so great.

† Which probably would nearly meet the amount of the depreciation in the sum requisite to discharge the interest on the unfunded debt.

compared with the real deprivations to which so many of us have in consequence so long submitted?*

Profiting, as many of us are by the system at present pursued, such an expedient as this, I fear, will not be generally countenanced. They, however, who can feel for others wrongs, should cast a thought at least upon those whom that system so heavily oppresses—upon the multitudes who have fixed incomes only for their support,---who, in effect, suffer a loss not of *one-fifth*, but of *two-fifths*, not of *twenty*, but of *forty per cent.* upon the amount of those incomes. It is by distributing the burthen equally amongst us all, according to our abilities to sustain it, that we should alleviate those who have already so much more than their due share of it.

If, however, this sacrifice to justice be thought too great to endure; if we have not the prudence and resolution to submit to it—it may, with equal advantage to the public creditor (though not perhaps to the public, if we consider as well the future as the present) be mitigated to an extent not inconsiderable, by providing such additional tax as may meet the deficiency in the amount of, or by submitting to the additional pressure of the taxes producing so much of the revenue only as may be applicable to the discharge of the interest actually payable to the public creditors—not to that which is made to accumulate for

---

* For I would not have it understood, that persons of every description are materially affected by the increase of prices; but what multitudes are?

the gradual reduction of the debt. But if even this—if an additional tax of about *one-eighth* part only of our incomes be deemed intolerable---(shame upon our selfishness and folly!) if we be averse to draw an additional shilling from our pockets in such a righteous cause, still are we possessed of resources which, without distressing ourselves, in any material degree, we may apply upon an occasion of such importance—an occasion, to meet which, if no other sufficient means can be devised and approved, must surely justify us in having recourse to these. I allude to the discontinuance of the payments to the commissioners for the reduction of the national debt---*the suspension of the operation of the sinking fund*---by means of which alone, without the imposition of any additional tax whatsoever, the public creditor might, though the currency were free from depreciation, receive the full amount, both nominal and real, of what is due to him.---The annual sums now applicable to the redemption of the national debt, amounting to more than *thirteen millions*---and being, therefore, much more than adequate to the amount of any probable deficiency in the revenue, whence the interest, and other sums payable on account of the debt, both funded and unfunded, are now, or may be proposed hereafter to be, discharged.

Nor care I for the clamours of those who would oppose such a measure as this, yet leave the public creditor without redress. For what can be more absurd, if it be not somewhat worse, to make a show of redeeming the principal of a debt, of which we do not fairly even pay the interest? But the nation depends upon the inviolability of the sinking fund. It is the darling theme of our statesmen and financiers. Now, alas! a poor subject of boast—a sorry symptom of prosperity---A richer subject of boast,---a surer symptom of prosperity it is, for a nation to deal honestly with its creditors,---to abandon a system fraught with so much injustice as the present.

What is it, but insulting to our understandings, if not to their own, nay, to their own integrity, that those who have the guidance of our affairs, whilst they are so loudly proclaiming the financial prosperity of the state, the unprecedented magnitude of our public revenue, they should practically acknowledge its real insufficiency---its inadequacy to the expenditure and just discharge of the engagements of the government---by virtually compelling its creditors to accept payment of their demands in a currency which is depreciated? If our prosperity be so great as is pretended---if our means of executing justice be so abundant, (as, I trust, they are,) why submit we any longer to the disgrace of doing that which fits only the insolvent bankrupt?

Whichsoever of the measures here proposed, or whatsoever other be thought preferable, to make good the deficiency of revenue which would probably attend the restoration of the value of the circulating medium to its proper level, by means of a reasonable diminution of its quantity; it does not appear necessary, that it should continue in its present depreciated state, in consequence of any supposed inability to satisfy really, as well as nominally, the demands of the public creditor---which may, without serious difficulty, be both nominally and really satisfied, though the medium of payment were not depreciated at all. And, in regard to any deficiency in the duties applicable to the other ordinary and extraordinary purposes of the government, which would result from such reasonable diminution of the quantity of the circulating medium, it is evident, that the same cause would operate in reducing the necessary expenditure of the government, but probably in a much greater proportion. So also it is evident, that the apprehensions which some persons would entertain, lest the government should be unable to obtain supplies upon the security of their navy and exchequer bills, are, for the most part, groundless and absurd. The sums requisite would be proportionate only to the whole quantity of money in circulation---and the government securities would be purchased by the means of a real, instead of a fictitious capital, at the same rate of interest as they are at present,* or rather at a lower rate in consequence of the increased confidence which then probably would be placed in them.

I know expedients have been suggested very different from the above.---We have heard it said, that the denomi-

---

* In *An Examination of Sir John Sinclair's Observations on the report of the Bullion Committee,* I have entered more fully into the discussion of these points, p. 69. 79, et seq. 84, et seq.

nation of the coin may be altered,*--that the interest payable to the public creditor may be reduced,---and that if the Bank of England should resume cash payments, some such measure must surely be adopted. Abominable doctrines!

But better---the latter better far, than that by which it is attempted to support our present system,---for by the former the evil, vast as it is, might be limited to its present extent, and by the latter not only so limited in respect to some, but in respect to others totally removed. And of what greater advantage to the public creditor, or to the public, is this pretended payment of the whole interest, but in a depreciated medium of circulation, than the real payment of such part of that interest in a medium that is undepreciated, as is equal in value to the former? It would be dealing at least as honestly with him and with ourselves, if the latter course were to be adopted.

---

* Is it without astonishment, without indignation, that any one can hear the doctrine of the King's right to alter the denomination of the coin, if not openly maintained, yet insinuated, not merely by men of no consideration or significance, but by senators themselves, even by men of high authority in the state.---A doctrine which ought not to be endured in such a country as this. What! arbitrarily invade the property of individuals! Cancel debts, and reduce all creditors—all money claimants on land and personal securities to beggary, by the edict of a monarch! Shame! shame! 'Tis enough, if we acknowledge the right in parliament itself.

Reduce the quantity of the circulating medium, then, to its proper level; and though you be unwilling or unable to satisfy the just claims of the public creditor, (miserable nation!) you may enable the landlord, or other money claimant upon land, and the private creditor in general henceforth to obtain theirs. You will still relieve many a widow and many an orphan---many struggling with poverty and in sore distress;---the victims of this sad system of finance begun, perhaps, in innocence, but terminating in wickedness and ruin.

It seems, in short, that the grounds and reasons upon which it has been inferred, that it is expedient to uphold the Bank of England and country banks, in their excessive issue of paper, meaning, in other words, to countenance the depreciation of the currency in general, when fairly, candidly, and thoroughly examined, fail utterly and altogether. And, therefore, that to persist in the present course is not only grievously to injure creditors in general, both private and public, but to subject the government and the country to the imputation of bankruptcy unprincipled, fraudulent, and disgraceful.

A hard return, indeed, it is, and most ungrateful to those, who in their ready compliance with measures which were intended to shield the Bank of England, for a while, from the pressing demands which, in time of great alarm, were made upon it, were content to take its notes in payment of their due, till full provision could be made to answer such demands. In their liberal confidence they harboured not a thought that they were nursing a viper in their breast, that, in time to come, would suck their vital blood, and utterly destroy them. Little did they think, in the hour of its distress, when supplicating for mercy, it would rise paramount to justice, and crush the rights of others. And little did they think that the superintending guardians of those rights, would abet and support it in its iniquity.

And what is to be the event of all this? Shall we permit the interests of a mercantile body, such as the Bank of England, great as it is, and of the scattered companies of country banks, numerous as they are, to stand in the way of private and of public justice? Shall we, year after year, creep on in a vile course of iniquity and fraud, faithless to our national engagements, and sanctioning unjust dealings in our several transactions, one with another?---or shall we boldly break up the fountains of justice and honour, and at once dissolve all confidence and credit between man and man? Shall we legally set at defiance the claims of right, or in the pulpits of anarchy and revolution preach up the wild prerogatives of plunder---and, by public and private example, proclaim equity but a name, a mere sound,---which we and our children are no longer to respect? Wide is the mischief, long wasting the evil, which such precept and example must inevitably produce.

You have permitted the issue of paper money to such an excess as to depreciate the currency of the country,---to set a premium upon the melting down our coin, and selling it as bullion, and thus almost wholly to exclude it from the circulation. You may pass laws, as you have lately done, for inflicting penalties on those who would take the paper of the Bank of England only at a discount; you may go further, as I fear it is probable you will do, and declare that paper, to all intents and purposes, a legal tender for the discharge of every debt; you may even forbid all difference between cash and paper-money prices; nay, you may establish an odious maximum in regard to price, throughout the country,---and all this under the pretence of affording facility to the government in raising its supplies, and of upholding the interest of the public creditor. Go on---go on---nor heed the dreadful responsibility which awaits you and your country. There will be a day of rejoicing to the debtor---yet only to the dishonest debtor; he will praise you for your goodly work,—but a night of wretchedness will close in upon him. The creditor, public as well as private, will curse you. Waiting, in sullen inactivity, till the tide shall overwhelm him and his family; he will feel no interest for the safety of the state; no love of his country, or the institutions of his forefathers;—or, urged on by the madness of despair, by the blind, or the watchful spirit of revenge, by the vain or well-founded hope of executing justice for himself, he will seek to re-establish himself on the ruin of those who shall have brought ruin on himself,--nor will stop, perhaps, till the nation itself shall, with rivers of blood, have atoned for the iniquity it shall have permitted,—whilst surrounding states, amazed at our career, checked neither by admonition nor example, will lament or rejoice at our fall from the proud and mighty pre-eminence we had attained.

For, whatever may be the present confidence of the creditors of the public in the government, the time, perhaps, will come, and that shortly, when their confidence will cease. Do they not hold the property of the nation to be pledged to them? Have they not as fair a claim as the landholders themselves? Is it not the duty of the government to protect the property of all alike? Why shrink from the glory of the task? Are no means of doing justice to be found?---Yes, ample. Check the further, and reduce within due bounds, the present issue of paper money.* And though you bring not the Bank of England, nor the country banks, to an account---Though you let not the laws of bankruptcy at once be put in force against them---Though you allow remuneration to all those who merit it,---and that without parsimony,---Though you abolish not all unnecessary places and pensions---Yet may you lay fresh taxes on those who still are well able to bear them,---or you may suspend the operation of the sinking fund. But tell us not that the means of the country are exhausted,---that there are no longer funds from

---

* And this, it seems, may be done without any serious injury to trade, by subjecting every new promissory note, and bill payable without interest, (excepting those of the Bank of England) to so heavy a stamp duty, as to render it unprofitable to issue them. The notes and bills of the Bank of England may be gradually reduced, and their amount expressly limited. And a considerably larger sum than now is paid by that body to the government may be exacted, for the privilege of issuing them payable without interest. This accords with the plan proposed in the "*Letter containing observations on some of the effects of our Paper Currency,*" *&c.* p. 73, and seq.

which can be drawn supplies to discharge the interest of our debt,---so long as our manufacturers, tradesmen, bankers, and merchants, still derive vast revenues from their capitals, of whatsoever description, so long as our farmers are greatly increasing in opulence.---Tell us not so, whilst there is such abundant, not to say superfluous, provision for our clergy---whilst we have such wealthy commoners, and still more wealthy noblemen, possessed of extensive domains, with rent rolls beyond all precedent in amount---heightened no doubt, apparently, by means of our excessive currency, but yet substantially sufficient to allow of great abatement. For why, I ask, are these, or any of these to be exempt, in any degree, from contributing to the full and honest discharge of the interest on the public debt? On what better foundation is built their right of property, than that of others? Lay on the public creditor himself his full and equal share of the burthen, how heavy so ever it may be, but do not lay on him more than that share. At all events, *whilst there is property, let there be justice.*

With such resources as, notwithstanding our adversities, are still in store---with so large a proportion of the property of public bodies and of individuals which may yet be made applicable to the service of the state,—and with so vast a surplus revenue beyond our necessary real expenditure, it is astonishing that any one should be so timid, or so bold as to persevere in our present system. How miserably weak the policy of awaiting patiently the approach of unnecessary bankruptcy! How daringly profligate to court and embrace it! Our taxes press hard,---Without pressing harder, except on those from whom the burthen is now unjustly shifted upon others, they may be effectually increased, and greatly too, if evenly imposed.

Let not, then, the *expedience of national bankruptcy* be avowed in principle---still less in practice. An avowal, dangerous and alarming to ourselves, but pleasing to the ears of our jealous enemy,--flattering his schemes, and encouraging, if not in part realizing, his hopes. Our resources are as yet unexhausted,---and so may they long remain. The stream, flowing, perhaps, through different channels, but from the same plentiful springs,---if these be kept but free and unincumbered---

Labitur et labetur in omne volubilis ævum.

FURTHER OBSERVATIONS

ON THE

INCREASE OF POPULATION,

AND

HIGH PRICE OF GRAIN.

BEING AN APPENDIX TO

REFLECTIONS ON THE POSSIBLE EXISTENCE, AND SUPPOSED EXPEDIENCE, OF NATIONAL BANKRUPTCY.

By PETER RICHARD HOARE, Esq.

LONDON:

PRINTED FOR T. CADELL AND W. DAVIES STRAND;

AND J. HATCHARD, PICCADILLY;

By G. SIDNEY, 1, Northumberland-street, Strand.

1812.

FURTHER OBSERVATIONS

ON THE

INCREASE OF POPULATION,

AND

HIGH PRICE OF GRAIN.

" Let us not be deluded by this phantom of an excessive population, set up against the reality of an excessive currency." P. 28.

SINCE the first publication of the foregoing reflections, new light has been thrown on the subject of our population, by the returns lately made to Parliament; which, as they may possibly seem to contradict the opinions I have ventured to offer, induces me to make some few further observations on this interesting branch of political enquiry, as well as on that which is supposed to be somewhat intimately connected with it; namely, the late high price and large importations of grain.

In regard, then, to the enumeration returns of 1801, on which, together with those of 1811, the notion of an extraordinary increase of population rests, I believe they have generally been considered as greatly defective. Not only were whole parishes avowedly omitted—but it is reasonable to think from the suspicion which prevailed respecting the real end and intent of that enumeration, that the numbers actually returned were much below the truth, though far exceeding the little better than arbitrary estimates of calculating individuals in former periods. The enumeration of 1811, taken under more favourable circumstances, confirms that supposition; for it is quite preposterous to imagine, that within so short a space of time as had elapsed since 1801, so large an addition as 1,629,498 persons should have been made to the population of that period; affected, as it must have been, by causes in their nature operating most powerfully to diminish, rather than increase it.

With the particular official details of baptisms and burials, registered since 1800, we have not indeed yet been furnished. In estimating their probable amount, we must therefore argue upon grounds furnished by the experience of the last century. In 1801, the population of Great Britain, as stated in the returns of that year, consisted of 10,942,646 persons. It is from this stock therefore, we are called upon to infer that an additional population of 1,629,498 persons has arisen within the space of ten years. Now the number of registered baptisms in England and Wales for *ten* years, ending with 1800, being only 2,538,434, and that of burials, 1,989,574, there was, according to these data, within the like period, an increase of 548,860 only on a population of 8,994,718; these two latter sums being together equal to the total population of England and Wales in 1801. The probable increase during the *ten* subsequent years, estimated in like manner from the excess of registered baptisms above the registered burials, would, consequently, by the same ratio, amount to less than 600,000,* upon the population of Great

* The exact proportion would be 594,410, which, if it approach near to the excess of baptisms above burials returned in 1811, (being but a small part indeed of the additional number of persons actually returned) and these returns, as well as those of 1801, be admitted to be correct, would naturally lead us to consider from what cause the registry of so few baptisms can have proceeded. Whe-

Britain in 1801. With every reasonable allowance, therefore, for the excess of births beyond the registered baptisms, and of deaths beyond registered burials, as well as for the influx of foreigners and emigrations from Great Britain; it cannot, with any degree of probability, be assumed, or without tolerably strict proof admitted, that in the course of ten years, ending with 1810, the increase can have been so great, as a mere comparison of the returns of 1801 and 1811, might induce us to conclude; even supposing the same encouragement to marriage, the same facility of providing for an infant family, had prevailed during the one period as the other; still less, then, under the circumstances which have actually taken place, and strongly marked the latter with features of alarming embarrassment and distress.

Taking, indeed, into account, the diminution which must be supposed necessarily to result from a state of war, and the still further diminution, probably, if not also necessarily, resulting from the nature of our present war in particular, in consequence of the unusually heavy blow which it has inflicted on our commerce and manufactures, together with the rapid advance which has been effected in the price of the common necessaries of life, far exceeding the advance in the wages of labour, we should be led to think, that the greater part of the *last ten* years would have proved peculiarly unfavourable to the increase of population; at least, that the increase would not have been

ther from the great secession which appears to have taken place from the established church, or from any other, and what cause. If from such secession—how great must be the majority of Dissenters over the members of that church! For even many who dissent in other points, do not dissent in regard to the ceremony of baptism. The considerations to which this question leads, are of the utmost moment in the present times; the spirit is gone forth, and it is not by a decision of the few that it is likely to be put to rest.

proportionally so great as during the *ten* immediately preceding, and, in all probability, it has not. It is, however, to be remembered, that the almost general introduction of vaccination in lieu of inoculation, by the small pox, has considerably reduced the number of those who perish by the latter disease; insomuch, that supposing the mortality occasioned by it throughout Great Britain generally, compared with the places lying within the bills of mortality, to be as *one* to *two* upon the population of each, respectively; it should seem that the total number of lives saved by means of vaccination throughout Great Britain in ten years, ending with 1810, amount to somewhat more than 28,400;* and thus far, therefore, it is but fair to presume, the ratio of progressive increase would have been greater of late years than formerly, had not the causes to which I have alluded altogether countervailed this beneficial effect of vaccination, and at least prevented any extraordinary increase beyond the average proportion of preceding similar periods.

It is truly amusing to see the mighty parade which is made upon ushering in this new enumeration of 1811; as if new powers of propagation had been bestowed on us latter race of men; or as if some long-lost antediluvian *nostrum* had been recently discovered to stretch the span of human life beyond its wonted extent; and this, forsooth, notwithstanding the

* The population of Great Britain being taken as above, at 10,942,646, and that within the bills of mortality at 747,043, (See Population Abstract of 1801) and the deaths from small pox, in proportion to the total number of deaths appearing from the bills of mortality from the year 1791 to 1800, both inclusive, (when vaccination was but little practised) as less than 1 to $10\frac{1}{2}$, and from 1801 to 1802, both inclusive, as something more than 1 to 15. Throughout Great Britain, therefore, I have supposed them to be in the former period, as 1 to 21, and in the latter, as 1 to 30; consequently, the diminution of deaths from small pox, appears to be nearly in the proportion of one-third.

continued scarcity of food for human sustenance, which the disciples of such doctrines do not fail at the same time strenuously to allege. It, no doubt, follows in the common course of nature, that if in a given number of years there be any material increase of population, there will, in the next succeeding equal number of years, (supposing the same degree of prosperity to attend them) be a still greater increase. The increase being in such case always in a geometric, rather than an arithmetic ratio—as the first increase will naturally itself occasion another proportionate to itself; but in all this there is nothing any ways extraordinary—nothing beyond the mere ordinary progress of all thriving communities.

But as the enumeration returns are attempted to be set up as an authoritative proof of an extraordinary augmentation of our numbers, so are the Custom House returns of the quantity of grain imported, advanced as a further argument in support of the same position; and at the same time as evincing that the produce of our own soil is insufficient for our maintenance. Nay, some will even go the length to say, it is *incapable*, from its limited extent, and untoward nature, of yielding a sufficiency; and accordingly begin to talk of the absolute necessity of obtaining supplies from abroad, encouraging the establishment of fisheries, or hitting on some new expedient for better economising our provisions, even though the seasons should constantly be favourable for their production. But what absurdity it is to go this length, whilst to the eye of the most superficial observer, so much land capable of cultivation yet remains uncultivated. Almost on the very verge of the metropolis, how much do we still see in that condition—in parts further remote, how much more? And though we shall be told, that in many instances the power of converting wastes into fertile corn fields, is checked by the variety of claims to rights of common, and difficulty of reconciling them; yet, does not the Lords' privilege of improving wastes still enable them, if so inclined, to bring thousands of acres into cultivation, which now yield but comparatively scanty pasture for a few straggling sheep ?

Besides, if the redundancy of our population were really so great as is pretended, can there be a doubt that all impediments to the improvement of our soil, would speedily be removed ? Would the legislature hesitate by one act, to authorize the partition and inclosure of every acre in Great Britain, if it judged that the whole island were unable to produce sufficient ?* But 'tis plain the legislature itself is well satisfied that such is not the case. Its acts most plainly prove that it considers not the land inadequate to the population, but rather that the land owner still needs encouragement to cultivate it.

For, whether well or ill-founded the opinion, that it is good policy to encourage the growth of grain at home, by prohibiting its importation from abroad, except in times of real deficiency ; yet, without doubt, it must be acknowledged that the imposition of the heavy duty of 24s. 3d. per quarter, on the importation of wheat, the market price being below 63s. and other intended proportional duties on the importation of various other kinds of grain which were laid in 1804, was an absurd and most pernicious regulation, if our own soil were not, assuredly, alone fully capable of supplying us ; in which case, encouragement ought, on the contrary, to have been bestowed on the importation of foreign grain, to make up the deficiency. Indeed, one can hardly entertain so mean, so despicable an opinion of the understandings of our legislators, as to believe, that when they imposed those heavy duties on importation, they were

* Such act, it seems, is now in contemplation, but we shall see whether, as soon as it becomes effective, another will not be passed to regulate the trade in corn, so as to meet in some degree the effects of our depreciated currency (See p. 22, infra.)

not well satisfied that we had ample means of raising a sufficiency at home. What folly, what infatuation, to prohibit or discourage, either by heavy duties or otherwise, those supplies which we ourselves cannot, by possibility, so raise; but which yet are absolutely indispensable for our subsistence! What gross, palpable absurdity, thus to enhance the price of the necessaries of life, of labour, and, consequently, of all commodities whatsoever! We surely, therefore, must presume, that in laying these heavy duties, the legislature proposed only to guard the interests of the land owner, or the farmer, by securing to him exclusively, the home market, so long as the price yielded only a reasonable profit, such as he was accustomed to in common seasons; and hence that our corn laws are a standing argument of the conviction entertained by the legislature, that the land is yet adequate to the maintenance of its inhabitants; a conviction, the justice of which, there are but few, perhaps, who will not candidly acknowledge.

But if it be not from the scantiness of our own soil, that our home supplies have been so limited, or at least, that we have been induced to derive so much from foreign countries, whence is it that we have permitted our population to outrun our actual domestic means of providing for its maintenance? Will it be said, that our additional population has, for the most part, been employed in the augmentation of our manufactures; and that the cultivation of our lands has been comparatively neglected? It surely, then, should seem, that the profits attending the employment of capital, in the latter speculation, had of late years been less than when employed in the former. Now, without stopping to enquire into the pernicious causes which may heretofore have led to the encouragement of a transitive, rather than the solid improvement of a country, or the remedies which sooner or later present themselves as a corrective to such a system, is it not notorious, that within these few years our manufactories have been deserted, and multitudes of mechanics been compelled to seek employment elsewhere ? Or rather we may say, have they not in divers parts of England risen riotously demanding it; whilst, on the other hand, extensive wastes have been inclosed, and fresh hands perpetually required to improve them ? Has not much of the produce of our manufactories been left on hand uncalled for, without a market in Europe to receive it, and been at last transported to distant quarters of the globe with little profit, if not absolute loss to the manufacturers and merchants, at a time when the demand for agricultural produce has continued quite undiminished, excepting, perhaps, so far as the high price may have tended to lessen it, and the supply of our fleets and troops abroad may have been drawn from other countries?

It might, at other times, perhaps, with justice have been questioned, whether the farmer is not generally less ready than the manufacturer to advance the wages of his workmen. It is not now, however, to be forgotten, that these are oftentimes maintained with food and drink by their employers, a practice which, under the circumstances of the present times, operates as beneficially to husbandmen as though their wages were nominally increased when paid in money only. But after all, if we bear in mind the amazingly increased price of the produce of land itself, more than adequate to the increased expence of labour; that, in most instances, it has added greatly to the real profit of the farmer, (his rent remaining stationary during the existence of his lease) can we doubt that he should be as ready as any other to obtain labour adequate to his purpose, though nominally at an advanced rate? It seems, indeed, that at old rents no production whatever is better able to defray the increased expence of labour than that of grain, and other productions of the farm. The price of wheat on an average, of the last two or three years, being more than double its average price, prior to the suspension of cash payments, (if we except only the two years of scarcity 1795 and 1796,) the price of few other commodities being increased in as great proportion. But the great rise of rents throughout the kingdom, wherever leases have expired, is alone a sufficiently clear demonstration that the profits of the farmer, even after providing for every necessary expence, have of late been much greater than formerly they were.

Why, then, it may still be asked, is not more land put into tillage? Why have we such large supplies from foreign countries? But is it not manifest, that unless the profit to be derived from tillage be greater than from pasturage, no preference will be given to the former? That, on the contrary, if greater profit arise from abandoning the tillage of land, and converting it to pasture, it will at length be so converted? Whether much has yet actually been so, I am not well prepared to assert; though it is highly probable, if not morally certain, that less must have been broken up, less waste improved, with the view of growing grain in preference to grass,* than there would have been, had not the circumstances of the times enabled the foreign to undersell the British grower, in respect to the former, though not, perhaps, the latter, or rather that for which the latter is principally raised.

The mere fact of high prices and large importations from abroad, as has been observed,† ought not, therefore, of itself alone to be admitted as complete evidence of the insufficiency of our own produce, still less of our own soil, (how naturally soever,

* Accordingly we perceive, that the price of butchers' meat has not increased in the same ratio as that of wheat. Though doubtless the price of the necessaries of life (of which corn is the chief), must regulate, in a great measure, that of butchers' meat, and almost all other commodities.

† Pp. 24, 25—*Supra*.

an insufficiency of the former may speedily result from it) unless it can be shewn, that those high prices have proceeded *merely* from the smallness of the home supply, compared with the demand. But it seems that the price of wheat in 1808 was 79s. the quarter, when the quantity imported exceeded not 81,466 quarters; which (excepting the three years 1786, 1787, and 1792, when the average prices were respectively as 38s. 10d. 41s. 3d. and 42s. 11d. per quarter†) is less than the quantity imported annually, during a series of *sixteen* years from 1783 to 1798 both inclusive; in none of which, excepting the two years of scarcity 1795 and 1796, did the average price exceed 53s. 2d.; the yearly average of the series (including those years of scarcity) not exceeding 51s. 8d. Neither does the total quantity of grain, imported during the twelve years, ending with 1810, (notwithstanding the high prices) appear to have exceeded the total quantity imported during the twelve preceding years so much as 290,000 quarters, or about 23,400 annually;* though it must not be denied, that the importation of wheat, compared with that of other grain, has latterly been much increased; a circumstance which shall presently be more particularly noticed.

But as the natural consequence of excessive prices is not only the encouragement of the growth of grain at home, but importation from abroad, both tending to reduce them to the lowest limit at which it is profitable to import; it is not unreasonable to ask of those who deny depreciation, what other cause can have prevented such effect arising from the large importations of wheat which of late years have taken place. It is true, the means of affording fresh supplies to any great extent from abroad, do not always immediately present themselves; and, as at home, can be only gradually enlarged,—whence the price as

* See "An account of the quantity of corn, &c. imported into Great Britain;" ordered by the House of Commons to be printed, 17th Jan. 1812.

† See the Table of Prices, p. 17, 18, of Reflections.

gradually diminishes. But here, notwithstanding the increased supplies, the price continues to increase. To suppose that this proceeds from an extraordinary increase of population, which does not necessarily contribute one jot to the reduction of the relative value of money, but rather, on the contrary, to its augmentation, by increasing the number of hands capable of productive labour, is most strange indeed. Besides, how can we not suppose a depreciation, if the price of corn be so increased, when the price of labour and of all commodities must eventually, in a great measure, be regulated by that of corn? The same quantity of money could not possibly serve the purpose of circulating these as before such general rise of price. They must necessarily be diminished in price or quantity But it cannot be believed, that if the expence of producing them were augmented, whilst the utmost price at which they could be sold was diminished, they would not cease to be produced. That some of our goods have of late been much diminished in price, is true; yet from another cause,—the want of foreign markets. But the consequence has been, that of these the quantity produced is less, so that it is probable the price will soon advance. The price of British goods in general has, however, been enormously increased, and had been previously to their exclusion from the foreign markets.

* In the tables annexed to Mr. Vansittart's printed speeches on the bullion question, divers articles (the produce of our colonies) are specified, whose prices have of late been much diminished. But of British produce, all, excepting iron, seem to have been more or less increased. With regard to many of these, the supply, it is clear, must be uncertain, and depend in some degree on chance: and as to iron, the improvements in machinery have tended greatly to reduce the price of that metal, though, as I fear, the profits of the trade can hardly now sustain it. Upon the whole, it is surprising, that, with common information on the subject, and such documents before him, this gentleman should have arrived at such conclusions, as he has, respecting the state of our currency.

The question, why the price of corn (I speak not of times of real scarcity) is not by means of our vast foreign supplies reduced to its former average, is, however, easy of solution, when we consider the nature of an excessive or depreciated currency; which, at the same time that it affects the profit of the grower at home, may affect that of the importer from abroad; and, in a manner abridge both below what they would be supposing the same prices to exist, and be paid in an undepreciated currency. For as the natural consequence of such depreciation is at home the increase of the wages of labour, tithe composition, rent and poors' rate, so may be the depression of exchange. Though sold at a high nominal rate in our markets, the corn brought hither from abroad may yield not much higher profit to the foreign merchant, than might have been obtained for it in the country of its growth. Thus, estimating the price of wheat to be here 85s. the quarter, if the course of exchange be 20 per cent. against us, which it long has been, it is plain that this price is equivalent only to 68s. from which the expence of conveyance and insurance must be deducted; and the difference between the remainder and the price current of the country, whence the wheat is exported, is the sole profit attending the speculation of the merchant.

The price of wheat, however, has of late been much beyond the sum here supposed; and on exportations from countries bordering on the Baltic, as well as from America, the profit must evidently have been great. Accordingly, it seems that, under all the varieties of exchange, and price and difficulties of intercourse, vast supplies have been obtained from the former.*

* It is stated, that two million quarters of grain were imported in the course of last year; for which, eight millions sterling were paid in our currency. See Mr. Perceval's Speech, 13th April, 1812. And in arguing against the notion, that, our Orders in Council had prevented commercial intercourse between this country and the ports of the

All which but leads to this conclusion, that the depression of exchange yet bears a small proportion only to the depreciation of our currency.

Nor can there be a reasonable doubt that this traffic will continue so long as the depression of exchange continues to bear such small proportion to the depreciation of our currency; and it is the policy of foreign states controlled, notwithstanding, as those of Europe have been by the power of France, to permit the export to this country, and the policy of this not to prohibit it. Larger, and still larger supplies will be received by us, till in process of time the same cause operating in full force, will effectually drive the British farmer from his native market, leaving it open only to the speculations of foreign traders.

But to this point I have already turned the attention of the reader,*and endeavoured to shew the ill consequencewhich might

Baltic, Mr. Rose observed, that, "On the contrary, they gave facility to the supply in aid of the people: that grain principally came from the Baltic; and, that with the ports there, the orders had nothing to do." Mr. Rose's Speech, Courier, April 14, 1812.

With regard to our supplies from America, I have been informed, that the price of fine flour in Canada was, lately, seven dollars only per barrel. The expence of freightage being about 8s. per barrel, and insurance 3 per cent. The profit at which it might be sold in our markets is therefore enormous, even after allowing for the depression of exchange.

* P. 44, 45, of the Reflections.

It may be observed, that within these few months, the rate of exchange with the Northern States has been considerably improved, though still much below par. The cause of this improvment may be various. The currency of some of those countries may, lately, have become like our own, more or less excessive, or otherwise depreciated. Nay, our own may have been diminished in quantity, a supposition which the Bank of England notes in circulation, not long since, and

ensue; which, even at the present hour, it would, perhaps, have been in the contemplation of our enemy to bring to pass, did not his own difficulties, similar in their nature, press too hard upon him, and enforce reciprocal accommodation and concession. Had the depression of exchange kept exact pace with the depreciation of the currency, the danger to which we are exposed it is probable would never have existed.*

the probable consequence of extensive failures in our trade, and general want of confidence, resulting from it, may seem to justify. Again, the very reduced prices of some of our goods, brought reluctantly to market, and greatly overstocking it, may have produced the same effect on the exchange, as if the quantity of our currency were positively diminished; its value being increased by the quantity and value of the commodities it can purchase. Lastly, the real balance of payments having been (if they were) so long against us (for to this cause, many of the gentlemen who were examined before the Bullion Committee attributed the great depression of the exchange in 1810), may have become more favourable, as may the balance of trade itself, in consequence of a less restrained intercourse with the countries bordering on the Baltic. At least these causes all co-operating, might have considerable effect in improving the exchange.

* It may, perhaps, indeed be thought, that the depression of exchange (assuming the real balance of trade to be at par) is, together with the expence of conveying the precious metals, at all times, the utmost limit of depreciation. But understanding by depreciation, the diminution of the relative value of money, its inability to purchase the same quantity of labour as before, that notion does not appear to be correct. From the excellence of our machinery, and skill of our manufacturers, many goods may be produced here at a cheaper rate in reality, that is, by a less quantity of labour than elsewhere. Suppose, therefore, a superabundance of the precious metals to exist in this country, in consequence of our traffic in such goods, our almost exclusive intercourse with South America, our little intercourse with European States, and the use of paper money, only, for our internal commerce, but to an excessive amount, proportionate to the superabundance of the precious metals; the value of these, as well as our paper money, would doubtless be diminished in this country. They would be ex-

That effects, such as I have described, can arise from unlimited issues of paper money, many persons are, perhaps, prepared to doubt, and some positively to deny. Accustomed to consider the establishment of numerous banks, and facility of obtaining capital to an enormous nominal amount, (not more effective however, in reality, than under other circumstances, it would be though much smaller) they can hardly be prevailed upon to conceive how any excess of paper money can, by any mode of operation, either directly or indirectly, tend to the discouragement of the growth of grain at home, to the conversion of arable into pasture, or to the neglect of improving wastes; and, consequently, to the real injury of land-owners and the community at large. Yet, surely, it is plain enough, notwithstanding the high price which may be obtained for farm-

changed for a smaller quantity of other goods, than if the supply of, and demand for, gold and silver, had continued relatively unaltered. Yet if payment of any certain sum, or quantity of either were required to be made at Hamburgh, or elsewhere on the continent of Europe, and a bill of exchange were purchased for the purpose, 'tis plain, that on this simple transaction, the depression of exchange should not exceed the amount of the expence of conveying so much of either, to the place of payment.* And yet the actual depreciation of our currency might be double that amount. And even supposing a considerable intercourse to subsist between the countries, yet, by the imposition of heavy duties on all imports, excepting gold and silver, these may still be materially depreciated, without a correspondent, or even any fall of the exchange.† Nay, the prohibitory duties on corn, when below the stated prices, serve to shew that such depreciation might exist, and actually countenanced and confirmed it, at times, when the course of the exchange was not unfavourable, still more, when directly the reverse.

* See An examination of Sir J. Sinclair's observation on the report of the bullion committee, p. 20.

† In the examination of Sir John Sinclair's observations, the author did not advert to this difference, which may subsist between them. It was not requisite there to enter into the question.

ing produce, and the inducement, therefore, which there is to multiply it, that the expence of cultivation here is nominally much increased, whilst no such increase of expence is felt by the foreign grower; who, together with the merchant, receives all the benefit of advanced prices, without proportionate deduction on account of the exchange; nay, till of late, perhaps, has actually received the precious metals themselves in payment, as if there were no depreciation of the currency at all.

It is in that part of the produce of land which, in proportion to its bulk, is most valuable, and which, in other respects, is most fit for transportation, that the greatest advantage is generally to be derived to the merchant, from the depreciation arising from excess of currency, without a correspondent depression of exchange. Thus, if the price of wheat be raised by these means from 54s. to 108s. per quarter, and that of oats in the same ratio from 18s. to 36s. it is manifest, that the profit attending the importation of the former will be greater than that of the latter. For even allowing the freightage of wheat be to that of oats as 3 to 2, or as 12s. to 8s. per quarter: and that at this rate a reasonable and proportional profit was afforded to the importing merchant, prior to the depreciation, when the respective prices were 54s. and 18s.; but that, with the increase of price, the freightage had increased proportionably, (that is to say,) in both cases doubled, the additional profit upon the importation of wheat would be 42s. or more than two-fifths of the whole selling price; whilst that of oats would be 10s. only, or considerably less than one-third. It follows, therefore, that the importation of wheat, compared with that of oats, or any other inferior production, is likely to be much increased in consequence of an excessive currency, not accompanied by proportionate depression of exchange.

Hence it appears to be a circumstance well worthy of remark, that although the quantity of wheat which has been imported within the twelve years, ending with 1810, (including, it is true, two years of scarcity) has greatly exceeded that of the twelve immediately preceding them, (including likewise two years of scarcity) yet the quantity of oats, beans, and barley, imported in the course of these, was considerably greater than in the succeding twelve.* It serves to prove, in no small degree, the truth of those opinions, which I have ventured to offer, that the effect of our present policy is to encourage the growth of barley, oats, and beans, and other inferior productions, in preference to that of wheat; and in time, perhaps, (allow but the system to have its full sway) the almost total abandonment of tillage for pasturage. Though long before such an event can take place, the eyes of those, who are materially concerned, will partially at least be opened, if they are not so already. At present, the foreign merchant and grower will not so much dispute with the British farmer the sale of barley, oats, and beans, provided he yields to them the benefit of deriving much higher profit, than he himself enjoys, from an unfettered participation in the sale of wheat, from which, till the suspension of cash payments, they had been almost utterly precluded, except in times of real scarcity.

To account for this late alteration in the relative quantities of the several species of grain imported upon the supposition, that the condition of the great mass of people in Great Britain is so much improved as to enable them to consume wheat where before they were obliged to live on oats or barley, is to hazard, as I conçeive, a bold conjecture, without any proof of the fact. On the contrary, is it not notorious, that the wages of labour have not, of late, been increased in proportion to the increase of the price of corn? (I speak not of the present year particularly, but a series of years.) How then is the labourer become more capable than formerly of purchasing

* See the Account printed by order of the House of Commons.

the more expensive species for himself and his family? It seems impossible that he should be so. Then is not this an argument almost decisive against such an hypothesis?

Partly on the same principle that heavy duties have been imposed on almost all foreign-manufactured goods, the sale of which might come into competition with our own, have the prohibitory duties, (for such they must be considered, so long as they attach fully and effectually,) been levied on foreign wheat, and other grain. As in the one case, it was intended to encourage the manufacture, so in the other, was it the agriculture of this country. But, as there probably is no doubt at all that, in various instances, the manufactured goods of foreign countries, notwithstanding the excellence of our machinery, and the skill of our manufacturers, would, in case the duties imposed on them were repealed, be disposed of to a large amount, in the British market—so doubtless, however different it might formerly have been, is it now with foreign agricultural produce, the heavy duties upon which are virtually repealed, in consequence of the great depreciation of our currency. For the policy which, in effect, prescribed the perpetual exclusion of such foreign-manufactured goods under almost all circumstances, did not prescribe, in like manner, the perpetual exclusion of foreign grain—Goods, similar to the former, or which might serve in lieu of them, and of which we may stand in need, can generally be made at home, and augmented almost infinitely in quantity, so as to accommodate the supply to the demand; and no serious evil is likely to result, even though it sometimes should not. No relaxation, therefore, of the duties attaching to their importation, is allowed, except upon particular occasions. It is not so, however, in respect to grain, the due supply of which is absolutely necessary to the prosperity, nay, existence, of the people; and therefore, if, from unfavourable seasons, the home supply should prove deficient, recourse must instantly be had to foreign countries, and all impediments to importation set aside. The very scheme of laws themselves, by which, at first, bounties were granted on export, and heavy duties imposed on import, was grounded on the principle of encouraging the growth of grain at home, and thus rendering us independent of foreign supplies: of enabling us to provide, with greater certainty, more ample means for our subsistence; such as, in common years of plenty, should exceed our actual consumption—not of debarring us, in times of scarcity, from other sources of supply.

It has, indeed, been often questioned, whether greater benefit would not arise from the destruction of these bounties, and duties altogether, and making free the trade in corn. But, however simple the train of reasoning, which may have led to the adoption of the affirmative, it seems not yet to have met with the general concurrence of our land-owners; too many of whom, like the rest of mankind, are, perhaps, at all times more ready to promote what they consider their own peculiar interests, than those of the community at large; yet some of whom, it may be justice to add, do, in reality, conceive, that here at least they are in unison. It is not, however, to be wondered that, as soon as they perceive the price of grain to fall so low as to require a reduction of the rent of land, that their tenants cannot otherwise afford to bring their corn to market at the same rate as the merchant is willing to dispose of that which he has imported; instead of admitting the propriety of reducing, or foregoing any increase of the rent they have been accustomed to receive, and of thus enabling their tenants to enter into fair competition with the latter; they plead the policy, nay, the necessity of effectually prohibiting his entering our market to sell below the price at which British corn can be produced at the present rate of rent and labour—for the most part unmindful of the general interest of the community; whose general interest it is to obtain the necessaries of life at the cheapest rate possible—not much considering that, although their rents mighr be lowered, the quantity of commodities, which the amount of them might purchase, may yet remain the same; and, on the other hand, that though their rents may be advanced, no real advantage may accrue to them, but the price of commodities may be advanced precisely in the same proportion—that by cheapening or making plentiful the necessaries of life, the price of labour, and the poors' rates, would in reality be lowered, together with the nominal rent of land.—That hence the British farmer would be at length again enabled to enter into competition with the foreign trader, whose expence and risk of transportation, would always give the former a great, and probably sufficient, but, at the same time, natural, advantage over him.

Nor is this salutary order of things much disturbed by means of an excessive currency, which, (whatever may be its injurious effects,) is accompanied by a proportional fall of the exchange with those countries, whence exportations have usually been made. As the increase of price is proportionate to the depreciation of the money with which the produce of the land is purchased, the farmer is as well capable as before of cultivating it; and, in many instances, much better; but in these, no doubt, to the real prejudice of his landlord, who receives not his fair proportion of that produce.

Till the increase of paper-money had, in a manner, outstripped all bounds of moderation, it was matter of doubt, amongst many persons, (nay, it is so at present, notwithstanding all which has lately passed before their eyes,) what had been the cause of that change, which appears to have taken place in respect to the corn-trade—that instead of an exporting country, we should gradually have become importers to a large amount, particularly in respect to wheat. It was not, however, till of late, that any ventured to maintain, that this was owing to the increase of our population. So monstrous a proposition would have met with few supporters, till the last enumeration returns had appeared to give some colour to it, however faint and insignificant. The greater part of those who reasoned on the subject, seem to have attributed this change to the alteration of our corn-laws many years ago—to the restriction of the bounty on export, and of the duty on import, to cases where the prices of corn were below the sums for that purpose previously limited. Further encouragement, therefore, it was thought, should be given to the British farmer. And accordingly, the comparatively open trade, permitted by the act of 1773, was narrowed by that of 1791, and the prohibitory duty of 24s. 3d. per quarter, was also thereby imposed on wheat, in case the market price should be under 50s. This, for a while, seemed to answer the end proposed, of satisfying the farmer and the land-owner, and did not much distress the public. The prices yet remained almost low enough, till the defective harvests of 1794 and 1795 occasioned that great and rapid rise, which brought the average price of wheat, in the following year, to upwards of 77s. the price of labour making no proportional advance. Soon, however, in consequence of the suspension of cash-payments, followed at no great interval by two years of scarcity and an overwhelming tide of paper money, the nominal rent of land, the price of labour, and poors' rates, were so greatly augmented, (which they could not have been by the mere operation of preceding temporary scarcity, without such tide of paper money) that in 1804 it was deemed expedient by the legislature to pass a new law, attaching the heavy duty of 24s. 3d. per quarter on the importation of wheat, in case the market price should be under 63s. a price during the whole course of the last century, up to the suspension of cash-payments, unequalled, except in the two years of distressing scarcity immediately preceding it. However, it was thought, unless such heavy duty were imposed, our markets would be overstocked with foreign grain, and the British farmer undersold; in other words, that the nominal amount of new rents would be diminished. The excess of currency had not, indeed, at that time, become so generally apparent as in later years, else no doubt the public voice would have been raised against this legislative enactment, in respect to corn, as well as against the prolonged suspension of cash payments, by means of which alone it seemed to have become expedient. It would have been easy to have traced the evil to its source, and found a safe and speedy remedy, by the gradual reduction of the quantity of paper money, which being then less excessive than at present, the market price of gold might more quickly have been brought down to the mint price, and thus facilitated the return to cash-payments. At all events, it would have been for the true interest and honour of the nation, and therefore the true policy of the legislature to have recommended, and, if necessary, to have enforced, it.

We are not, however, to be astonished that, as matters stand at present, the same notions should still continue to prevail amongst the same class of men in respect to the expediency of prohibiting importation, unless the market price exceed the expence of cultivation, as prevailed before; and accordingly, that we should now hear the like arguments employed for extending the importation price from 63 to 80s. the quarter. Indeed we must, in common candour, now acknowledge that the foreign grower does, in fact, possess the advantage, as it were, of the repeal of the act of 1804; the excessive issue of paper money having, in effect, reduced the value of 63s. at least as low as, if not lower far than 50s. prior to the suspension; whilst, from the high prices which have, for some years, successively been obtained, the duty is rendered wholly ineffectual—So that our markets lie free and open for the sale of foreign grain. But what may be thought yet worse for the British farmer or his landlord, this depreciation seems not to be followed by a correspondent depression of exchange, which would, at least, have placed him on a level with the foreign grower.

It is the difference between depreciation and depression,

therefore, which demands so much of our attention, from the peculiar effect it has long had upon our corn trade, since it enables us to solve, in some degree, the difficulties in which the question was formerly enveloped. Had the relative value of the precious metals been reduced equally throughout the world, and our currency not exceeded its due amount, though our corn duties might have been rendered nugatory, yet the foreign merchant and grower would have possessed no other real positive advantage over the British farmer. The advantage arising to the former from this difference between depreciation and depression is, however, as I have attempted to shew, most important and decisive.

It was somewhat strange, that those who chiefly busy themselves in watching the interests of the land-owner and farmer—(since they could not but be conscious, notwithstanding the nominal wages of labour and poors' rates had been greatly augmented, much additional rent had been required on the expiration of every lease for life or years—therefore that, whatever the increase of the wages of labour and poors' rates might have been, the increased price of the produce of the land had more than compensated for the increased expence of cultivation)—it was somewhat strange, I say, that they were not conscious also that the relative value of money had been diminished, and that the advantage which the British farmer once possessed over the foreign grower, was lessened by reason only of that diminution. For it cannot be supposed, as was observed before, that if the increased price of the produce proceeded from the smallness of the supply compared with the demand, the Legislature would have passed an act at all impeding the supply from abroad. The depreciation of our currency is, however, now a fact so clearly demonstrated, and accounted for, that the question admits not of dispute, excepting as to the degree; and it may fairly be concluded, on the whole, that, in proportion to its excess beyond the depression of exchange, is its tendency to discourage the growth of grain at home.

But since the fact is ascertained, that the real cause of our large importations from abroad is the high price which may be obtained in our markets, it surely cannot be pretended that to remedy this evil the Legislature ought to raise the importation price. This would be a mischievous and cruel remedy indeed —to many much worse than the disease. We have seen how ineffectual, in the long run it has already proved. Under the present system of our currency, it would serve only for a time the purpose for which it was devised, though it would tend to confirm us in that system, and render its duration more permanent. It may be thought, perhaps, a trifling matter, after what has passed, that the consistency of the Legislature should be preserved. But having so lately, so solemnly, and so extraordinarily, pronounced the currency to be undepreciated, with what face can it sanction a measure founded on the suppositition of its gross depreciation? for it is on this supposition only that even the shadow of an argument for extending the importation price could rest. With such calamity as is spread around us, by means of the destruction of our commerce, and high price of the necessaries of life, and more particularly of those the supply of which would by such a measure be impeded, it would be bold indeed to try it.

So long as the heavy duties operated only towards the encouragement of the growth, and diminution of the price of grain, perhaps no reasonable objection could have been made to them; but in the present disordered state of our currency, new regulations to check the importation, if of any moment at all, would probably tend only to raise the price; since large supplies tend necessarily on the other hand to reduce it. And though without such regulations, 'tis true we may for a time remain dependant on foreign countries for supply, till the depression of exchange shall be duly proportioned to the depreciation of our currency; and we shall thus continue liable to the evils I have mentioned;* which, had the currency remained stationary in value, or the depression of exchange been proportioned to the depreciation, we should not have been; yet this ought rather to be imputed to an unreasonable reluctance which our land owners, from of old, have felt to reduce, if not from their eagerness to increase, their rents—the reduction whereof would better enable their tenants to enter into competition with the foreign grower, and, together with the increased importation from abroad, effect, within a short time, a reduction in the price of corn, and consequently of labour, and all commodities whatever. In other words, the relative value of the precious metals would be augmented.

In truth, the price which regulates our import is already much too high for an undepreciated currency, and perhaps would be attended with great public distress, if the law determining it were left unrepealed, so soon as the value of the currency were restored to its due level—its depreciation operating like a real scarcity to raise the price of grain, the law's repeal is now of no importance.

I have already had occasion to observe how small are the taxes imposed on the necessaries of life—compared with the heavy duties on foreign corn, whilst the market prices are below the limits prescribed for the enforcement of them, they are truly insignificant. Till the currency became depreciated by excess, the farmer paid not even in the accumulated shape of tax, tithe, and rent, so much as 24s. 3d. per quarter for the wheat he raised. Till the suspension of cash payments, he was well able to sell it, with reasonable profit, below the then importing price of 50s. except in case of very unfavourable harvests,

* P. 43.—supra.

which rarely occurred. Since that period but little addition has been made to the taxes, whereby the price of farming produce ought to have been materially affected. It is, therefore, mere idleness and absurdity to say the increased taxes had occasioned the necessity of laying the heavy duty of 24s. 3d. so long as the market price should be below 63s. the quarter, by way of due encouragement to the farmer. He before had full encouragement enough. Restore the currency to its former real value—reduce the rents to their former nominal amount—it will be still greater idleness and absurdity to say that he requires such duty to attach, though the market price exceed that sum to a considerable degree.

For had the price of labour continued at its former rate, (and there is no sufficient reason to believe it would have been materially increased, but on the contrary diminished, had there been no excess of currency) there is no doubt at all that the British farmer could have brought his corn to market nearly at the same rate as formerly. He would have had no additional rent to pay for his land, unless indeed it had been actually improved, and yielded a correspondent increase. The composition for his tithes would have remained the same; so also would his poors' rates, except perhaps that, in some instances, they might have been augmented in consequence of the dismission of so many persons from their manufacturing employments—which, by the way it may be remarked, would naturally have tended to lower the wages of labour in general, and thus encourage the better cultivation of his land. As it is, neither the landlord, the clergy, the labourer, nor the poor, have in reality been benefitted; but, on the contrary, like multitudes of other members of the community, have all been injured—not indeed in the same, but various degrees; oftentimes, however, seriously and cruelly.

It seems unnecessary, therefore, to say more on this head;

and, upon the whole, I trust it will appear that no sufficient argument of such extraordinary and alarming increase of our population, as has been pretended, is to be drawn from a comparison of the returns of 1801 and 1811, defective as the former were acknowledged, and still more so as they may reasonably be supposed to be; and even though such increase had actually taken place, still that this would not of necessity tend to raise the price of grain; but, under the circumstances of the times, exclusive of an excessive currency, ought rather to diminish it, by facilitating the employment of more hands in agriculture, and thus augmenting the supply;—that the great importations which now, for some years past, (I speak not of the present year* in particular) have been made from foreign countries, are no proof of the incapability of our own soil to produce sufficient for its inhabitants, but are merely the natural consequence of the high prices which have long been obtained in our markets, and which enable the foreign to undersell the British grower; that, nevertheless to prohibit the importation, or discourage it by extending the heavy import duties beyond the present limits, is mischievous and impolitic, whilst better means of encouraging the growth of grain at home lie plainly in the restoration of the value of our currency—a measure whence the greatest good would otherwise result.

But if, after all, the increase of our population be truly so enormous as to have rendered it necessary for us, as is pretended, to obtain supplies from abroad, our own soil being incapable of yielding a sufficient produce, how absurd to lay the least restraint on importation! Further encouragement

* The harvest of 1811, contrary to the expectations previously indulged, appears to have been defective, whilst the impediments to our obtaining supplies from the Baltic and America, have no doubt been considerable. The present high prices are, therefore, in part attributable to both these causes, but principally to our excessive currency.

to our farmers must be wholly useless—nay, almost impossible, upon the face of the hypothesis.

But let us not be deluded by this phantom of an excessive population, set up against the reality of an excessive currency. It is this which has augmented the price of the common necessaries of life, as of almost all other commodities whatsoever, though divers causes may have operated to reduce the price of some—which has increased the cost of agricultural, as well as almost every other species of labour, the poors' rates, tithe-composition, and rents, but these only in few instances in a like proportion. Reduce the quantity of paper money, you will reduce the price of the necessaries of life, and all other commodities whatsoever, the wages of labour, poors' rates, tithe-composition, and rents: you will enable the British farmer, without danger of being undersold by the foreign trader, to employ more hands in the cultivation of wheat, and other grain: lands, of late converted from arable to pasture, may be reconverted, and wastes be broken up, inclosed, and put into tillage, not only without loss, but with amazing profit, measured by the real, not merely nominal amount. The times are peculiarly fitted for the trial. Humanity and true policy demand it—smarting, as we are, under the severe affliction of real or pretended scarcity — looking to other countries to aid us with supplies, but dreading the effects of a stern policy, which would mock our sufferings even in the agonies of famished nature—with a large portion of our population already a victim to the same policy, but which, bereft of its wonted means of livelihood, and driven from necessity to any other which may offer, would receive, with eager hands, the plough or mattock—and henceforth happily become the means of effectually insuring a sufficient supply, so far at least as human prudence can provide.

'n Account of the Quantity of Corn, Grain, Meal, and Flour of all Sorts, imported into Great Britain, in Twelve Years from 1775 to 1786, both inclusive;—in Twelve Years from 1787 to 1798, both inclusive;—and in Twelve years from 1799 to 1810, both inclusive:——Distinguishing each Species and each Year; and stating the Annual Average Quantity of all sorts Imported during each Period.

EARS.	WHEAT and Wheat Flour.	RYE and Rye Meal.	BARLEY and Barley Meal.	OATS and Oat Meal.	INDIAN Corn and Meal.	BEANS.	PEASE.	MALT	TOTAL of All Sorts.	ANNUAL AVERAGES.
	Quarters.	*Quarters.*	*Quarters.*	*Quarters.*	*Quarters.*	*Quarters.*	*Quarters.*	*Qrs.*	*Quarters.*	
775	575,250	34,150	133,838	386,397	9,609	32,704	14,896	— —	1,186,844	
776	21,568	3,415	8,433	369,495	— —	19,055	19,133	— —	441,099	
777	233,905	18,454	7,981	366,465	— —	35,127	28,696	— —	690 628	
778	106,616	9,327	42,714	201,196	— —	30,165	27,769	— —	417,787	
779	5,254	1,693	7,088	354,710	— —	14,591	29,154	— —	412,490	
780	4,242	- - -	352	196,344	— —	7,407	17,716	— —	226,061	
781	162,278	10,743	56	109,103	— —	3,245	14,508	— —	299,933	
782	81,259	- -	13,180	37,920	— —	3,730	4,951	— —	141,040	
783	584,014	81,326	145,562	229,548	109	29,964	2,418	— —	1,072,941	
784	215,817	24,779	78,536	270,835	46	28,674	18,466	— —	637,153	
785	107,968	28,761	67,392	383,571	15	9,355	7,458	— —	604,520	
786	50,999	3,643	65,454	486,652	— —	34,013	1,697	— —	642,458	*Quarters.*
	2,149,170	216,291	570,586	3,392,236	9,779	248,030	186,862	— —	6,772,954	564,413
787	60,245	7,048	41.637	519,196	28	40,752	2,330	— —	671,236	
788	149,667	- - -	11,479	120,613	17	9,820	1,188	— —	592,784	
789	109,762	14,845	11,128	428,880	54	162	229	— —	565,060	
790	219,351	21,683	29,719	741,058	10,546	39,541	3,552	— —	1,065,450	
791	463,591	56,378	61,134	790,732	1,248	12,743	1,982	— —	1,387,808	
792	22,417	13,027	118,526	968,061	5,677	38,452	4,802	— —	1,170.962	
793	490,398	55,594	147,169	709,816	2	29,720	18,553	— —	1,451,252	
794	327,902	25,531	128,568	853,636	1,600	90,243	40,368	— —	1,467,848	
795	313,793	22,248	18,070	449,749	20,586	15,807	20.263	— —	860,516	
796	879,200	163,900	40,033	767,747	28,311	35,206	32,711	— —	1,947,108	
797	461,767	8,258	64,198	584,116	111	17,394	17,818	— —	1,153.662	
798	396,721	6,925	116,485	745,364	21	12,327	21,683	— —	[illegible]	
	3,894,814	395,437	788,146	7,978,968	68,201	342,167	165,479	— —	13,633,212	1,136,101
799	463,185	22,808	19,538	510,557	2	4,800	8,750	— —	1,029,640	
800	1,264,520	145,005	130,976	544,040	11,142	15,796	26,796	— —	2,138,275	
801	1,424,766	150,559	113,966	583,016	76,798	16,246	44,218	— —	2,409,569	
802	647,664	15,503	15,252	546,947	5,169	5,793	10,671	2,303	1,249,302	
803	373,725	4,099	14,027	501,633	710	1,738	23,992	25	919,949	
804	461,140	2,644	11,596	717.654	244	11,928	19,648	— —	1,224,854	
805	920,834	24,267	43,301	468,954	24	10,736	10,217	— —	1,478,333	
806	310,342	1,014	5,385	528,830	113	3,406	1,559	— —	845,649	
807	400,759	7,394	22,131	743,047	1,063	13,765	6,070	— —	1,194.229	
808	81,466	5,172	32,502	490,815	4,308	10,739	12,882	1,228	639,112	
809	448,487	13,602	27,887	1,098,322	1,262	29 966	33.109	533	1,653,168	
810	1,530,691	91,042	26,314	545,480	37	15,226	12,263	893	2,221,951	
	8,327,579	483,109	462,875	7,274,295	100,872	140,139	210,180	4,982	17,004,031	1,417,003

Custom-House, London, 15th January, 1812. } *William Irving.*

AN

EXAMINATION

OF

SIR JOHN SINCLAIR'S OBSERVATIONS

ON THE

REPORT

OF THE

BULLION COMMITTEE,

AND ON THE

GENERAL NATURE OF COIN OR MONEY, AND THE

ADVANTAGES OF PAPER CIRCULATION.

By P. R. HOARE, Esq.

London:

PRINTED FOR T. CADELL AND W. DAVIES, IN THE STRAND; HATCHARD, PICCADILLY; AND RICHARDSON, ROYAL EXCHANGE;

By George Sidney, Northumberland Street.

1811.

ERRATA.

Page 19, line 11, *for* the, *read* our. P. 27, l. 30, *for the full point insert a semicolon*; l. 31, *for* is, *read* may be. P. 51, l. 14, *for* of, *read* for. P. 56, l. 3, *for* fact, *read* facts; l. 6, *for* But, *read* and; l. 10, *for* its, *read* bank. P. 58, l. 6, *dele* be milled; l. 7, *for* basis, *read* bars; l. 21, *for* in our shops or our markets as seldom to be seen, *read* as seldom to be seen in our shops or our markets. P. 60, l. 25, *dele* as. P. 66, l. 4, *for* owner and cultivator, *read* owners. P. 90, l. 28, *dele the last comma.*

ADVERTISEMENT.

A CONSIDERABLE time has now elapsed since the publication of Sir John Sinclair's Observations on the Report of the Bullion Committee. Yet no reply of which the writer of the following pages is aware, has heretofore been made to them. Is it because the doctrines there promulgated are so manifestly ill-founded and preposterous that they refute them selves, or that they are so rational and conclusive as to be wholly unanswerable? If the former, on what ground have three editions been called for by the public, and passages of the work been quoted and referred to in print, as an authority which ought to be respected? If the latter, the reader will profit but little from this vain attempt to oppose those doctrines which, however rational and conclusive in his mind, and that of the multitude, appear to the author before him, not only answerable, but likely, if permitted to remain unanswered, generally credited, and practically observed, to be productive of consequences most pernicious to the community.

AN

EXAMINATION, &c.

The science of political economy, improved as it has been, and undersood without difficulty as it may be, in a limited degree, by all men of education and reflection, has yet in it something naturally, though more, perhaps, artificially, mysterious. It is not, therefore, with much astonishment that I have heard doctrines advanced upon some of the more complicated branches of this science, which my mind cannot immediately or deliberately assent to; though it can hardly, by mathematical demonstration, prove them to be erroneous. But, on the other hand, it is with much astonishment, indeed, that I find what I had conceived to be amongst the first principles of the science, openly doubted or denied by men practically most conversant with various parts of the subject; yet when I hear their scepticism and disbelief, encouraged and defended by men of studious enquiry and reflection, that astonishment subsides; and, not without sufficient confidence in the result, I feel myself urged to tread over again the steps, by which I had arrived at conclusions so opposite to theirs, being yet, as I imagine, so clear, satisfactory, and indisputable.

I will not accuse the author of the Observations before

me of any overweening self-confidence in venturing to attempt the overthrow of the acknowledged common principles of Locke, of Hume, of Steuart, and of Smith, by upholding a system practically and theoretically at variance with them. For it is good that all reasonable men should form and pronounce their opinions freely and without prejudice; and that the authority of great names alone should not shut the door against the candid enquirer after truth. If we have really been in error, following lights which have gone before us, to lead us only into deep perplexities and difficulties, it is time, indeed, that we recover the right road; and thankful we should be to those who will conduct us thither. Perhaps the leisure hours of Sir John Sinclair could not be more usefully employed than in so charitable, so patriotic an office as the endeavouring to find out some new and better path to riches, honour, and prosperity.---Should he, however, fail in his endeavours, and should no clearer lights, from whatever quarter, arise to direct us through the intricacies of our journey, we must, it is our misery, perhaps, proceed under the guidance of those which we have hitherto pursued, and the practical deviation from which has, I fear, already brought no small difficulty upon us.

Let us then examine this recent publication of Sir John Sinclair, and consider how far it is likely to assist us.---Whether the light which shines forth from it be true, genuine, and perspicuous, or rather dazzling, deceptive, and bewildering. But ere we enter upon the examination of the main question, it may be well to notice some of the preliminary observations, which the

Author has thought proper to introduce, touching the appointment of the Committee for inquiring into the high price of bullion, the character and conduct of its members, and the general tendency of their report.

" Inquiries," it is observed by Sir John Sinclair, " regarding points of so delicate a nature as the circu- " lation of a country, (on which the prosperity, and " indeed, the comfort and happiness of every individual in " it so much depend) cannot be too cautiously entered into, " nor the subject too maturely considered, before any " step is taken, or even remedies are suggested." [P. 4.] A sentiment which, perhaps, few persons would feel any hesitation to adopt, if it be understood that the maturity of consideration shall not interfere with the fit season for action. But to delay enquiries into matters of great and general importance, till sore and irremediable evil has arisen from the neglect of them, is neither wise nor commendable. Yet, whatever may be the construction which the Author intended should be put upon the above-quoted observation, it will hardly fail to recall to our minds the sudden and alarming step which was resolved upon,---the very violent remedy which was applied in regard to our circulation, now near fourteen years ago,---a step which, at that time, it was understood, would be speedily retraced,---a temporary remedy, as it was then declared to be, which the reviving confidence of the country would not long require to be continued. Where was the caution which reduced the Bank of England well nigh to a state of bankruptcy? Where was the mature consideration which did not provide the means of restoring it to its former elevated state of punctuality to its engagements, even after the lapse of so many years? Is it now to be treated as a new enquiry incautiously entered into,---as a subject which cannot yet be so maturely considered as it ought to be,---this, which regards the present circulating medium of the country? Is the system which now prevails, an anciently established system, handed down to us by our forefathers, from generation to generation, unimpaired and perfect,---a system, under which the nation has long prospered, and on which "the comfort and happiness of "every individual so much depend?" Are doctrines recommendatory of a circulation, consisting in part of the precious metals, and in part of paper money immediately convertible into them, new-fangled doctrines introduced by revolutionary theorists and speculative politicians, whose opinions are dangerous to the state, and ought, therefore, most watchfully to be guarded against? Little, indeed, was it to have been expected, that the inquiries which have been instituted, and the conclusions which have been drawn from them by the Committee, appointed by the House of Commons, should have given rise to insinuations, that the subject has not been "impartially investigated, and that the chimeras of "political speculation" have been "set up against "results of practical experience;" or should have excited any lamentation or regret that the Minister of the Crown "had consented to the motion for the appointment of a Committee, and taken hardly any concern in the nomination of its members, and no part in "its deliberations, until it was too late;---that the Members of the Committee had made up their minds regarding the points under discussion; and that, when the principles, on which the report was to be drawn up, came

" to be settled, the first Lord Commissioner of his Majes-" ty's Treasury found himself in a minority." [P. 5.]

Persuaded, however, as the Author of the Observations seems to be, that the Members of the Committee, though " certainly persons of distinguished abilities, " and competent to the task of conducting the proposed " investigation, could they have totally divested them-" selves of various prejudices, and had they given them-" selves time to carry on so extensive an enquiry;" [Ib.] not having so divested themselves, and given themselves such time, have materially failed in the due discharge of their office; we are, in a manner, invited by him to go over the report and evidence again,---or at least to attend to the comments which he has thought proper thus publicly to make upon them.

I will not say there is any want of due decorum in a Member of the House of Commons, thus apparently to deplore the absence of that influence in a Minister of the Crown, which might command a decision in a Committee of the House of Commons, as to the principles upon which the Report of that Committee should be drawn up. I will not insist upon the indelicacy of thus accusing the Members of that Committee of prejudices of which they could not totally divest themselves, or of heedlessly hurrying through an examination of so much importance. Neither will I detain the reader by any observations upon the two first of the "*most serious* "*objections*" which the Author has brought forward against the form and substance of the Report, viz. that the Committee have *stated their opinions, and* *suggested remedies*, " although authorized merely to " *report the result of their enquiries, and their obser-* " *vations thereupon*;"* and that they have reported the evidence of one witness whose name is not made public.† It is fit, however, that the third of these objections, a most serious one indeed, should be more particularly attended to, for it is no less a charge against the Committee than that of having reported " contrary " to the weight and mass of evidence before them." [p. 7] This is, indeed, a serious charge,---a heavy accusation.--- But let us see how far it is, in point of fact, substantiated.

In the first place then, we are referred, by a note, to a passage of the Report, (p. 4, l. 10 from the bottom) wherein it is stated, that " it will be found by the evidence, " that the high price of gold is ascribed, by most of the " witnesses, entirely to an alleged scarcity of that " article, arising out of an unusual demand for it " upon the Continent of Europe." And this, it seems, is to be construed into an admission, on the part of the Committee, that they have reported contrary to the *testimony* of witnesses. As if *testimony* and *opinion* were terms purely synonymous. But the testimony of witnesses, as to facts, may be perfectly true, though their opinions as to the causes of those facts may be perfectly erroneous. It was not for the Committee to be guided by the latter, but to form their own opinion upon the former; or, if not to form their own *opinion*, at least to pass their own *observation* upon them.

* P. 6. † Ibid.

Next, as to the instances of misstated or neglected evidence,---it is observed by Sir John Sinclair, that Mr. Merle (one of the witnesses) " states that a dollar is " worth four shillings and four-pence, at its standard " price; but that, at the time he was examined, it would " fetch four shillings and nine-pence; consequently," says Sir John Sinclair, " the difference was rather more " than five-pence per ounce, or *about* $9\frac{1}{2}$ *per cent. above* " *coinage price.*" And he adds, " No notice is taken of " so important a fact in the course of the Report." [p. 7, 8.] But was it in truth of any real importance that such a fact should have been noticed in the Report, when Mr. Merle himself, on that very day, Saturday, says, " I have " a very great demand for dollars, and, perhaps, must " give five and seven-pence on Monday, because they " are wanted to go out, and I, therefore, must get them " at the best price I can. Perhaps that may be for a " month, or perhaps only for a week."† Sir John Sinclair, however, goes on to observe, that " it was more " consonant to the prejudices of those, by whom that " Report was framed, to rely on Wettenhall's tables, " where the Committee found new dollars quoted at five " shillings and eight-pence per ounce; and that the " difference is then immediately mounted up to 15 instead of 13*l.* 6*s.* 4*d.* per cent." [p. 8.] And, in a note, he adds " 5*s.* 8*d.* per ounce would only be 13*l.* 6*s.* 4*d.* " which is nearly two per cent. less than the Committee " have stated." [Ib.] Now, although it be true, that the Committee have referred to Wettenhall's tables for the price of new dollars throughout the year 1809, noticing

* Minutes of Evidence, p. 40.

that it is there stated, that they fluctuated from 5*s*. 5*d*. to 5*s*. 7*d*. per ounce; and have also observed, that in the month preceding the date of the Report, dollars had been quoted as high as 5*s*. 8*d*. per ounce;* yet it does not follow from thence, that they intended to proclaim the latter as the average price; the natural conclusion to be drawn from their expression is, surely, very different. With regard, however, to accuracy of calculation, I am at a loss to know how 5*s*. 8*d*. per ounce would only make the difference between the mint and the current price amount to 13*l*. 6*s*. 8*d*. per cent. according to the text and the note of Sir John Sinclair. For if the standard price of dollars be 4*s*. 11½*d*. per ounce, as stated in the Report, I should conceive rather, that the difference would amount to nearly 14*l*. 5*s*. 8*d*. per cent. which is not so far from the 15*l*. per cent. of the Committee, as it is from the 13*l*. 6*s*. 8*d*. of the Author of the Observations. Yet I am not over confident of my own accuracy in this morsel of arithmetic. But should the reader take the trouble to find me in an error, I shall then console myself with the soothing reflection, that at least one of two greater men has failed in the same task.

In respect to the other instance which Sir John Sinclair has adduced of the carelessness of the committee, viz. in stating Spanish gold to be *better* instead of *worse*, than the standard;---the accusation seems just enough, and they themselves may answer it in the best manner they can. For such statement is directly opposite to the evidence of Mr. Goldsmid, [p. 2, of the evidence] and to the statement in page 36, of the Accounts, where Spanish gold is put at 21½ carats of fine gold, and 2½ of

* Page 3 of Report.

alloy, the standard ounce of gold being (if as stated in page 71 of the Accounts) composed of 22 carats of fine gold and 2 only of alloy.

It is not, however, such errors as these which should induce us to think unfavourably of the labours of the Committee; we have all probably, in our own experience, similar instances of mistake, in our own individual concerns. The first attentive reader of the Evidence, the Accounts, and the Report, was enabled, without difficulty, to correct those which Sir John Sinclair has discovered, and naturally would ascribe them to the dispatch which the Committee thought it expedient to employ, in order that their report might be before the House, previous to the termination of the then sessions, that the several members and the public might thereby have full leisure to consider it, previous to the opening of the next. The subject was of the first importance, and, therefore, not unnecessarily to be delayed.

But Sir John Sinclair seems not to have been moved by this consideration; on the contrary, "it is much to be lamented," says he, "that the drawing up of the Report should have been so hastily executed, before all the members of the Committee could possibly have had leisure thoroughly to consider such momentous questions in all their bearings, or minutely to examine all the evidence that had been adduced upon the occasion." [P. 9.] And there may certainly be much difficulty in ascertaining, with any sort of precision, the different degrees of information, which the several members of the Committee might happen to have possessed upon the subject, referred to them by the House of Commons, previous to their entering upon the examination of the several witnesses, who were about to give their evidence; and what space of time it therefore might, in all probability, require, to enable them satisfactorily to make up their minds as to the true result of this evidence. Yet it surely is not too much to suppose that, "persons of distinguished abilities, and competent to the task of conducting the proposed investigation," were not altogether ignorant of the subject of that investigation; that it was not wholly new to them,---but, that by paying due attention to the evidence as it arose, they could make themselves so thoroughly masters of it, that any long subsequent discussion upon it would become totally unnecessary; a supposition which the great length of time that elapsed between the commencement of the investigation and its close seems to justify as natural and reasonable. Indeed, the facts established by the evidence, appear at once so strong and conclusive, that, till the publication of Sir John Sinclair was made known to me, I had conceived no doubt could remain in the mind of any man, who had fairly, rationally, and thoroughly attended to the subject,---and even yet I am inclined to think, that the understandings and feelings of the people in general will zealously applaud this work of the Committee, as giving them a clearer insight into a subject so interesting to them, and as leading the Legislature, without delay, to adopt a measure highly necessary to the maintenance of justice, and the honour and prosperity of the state.

It is true, far different sentiments are entertained by the author of the Observations in respect to this measure suggested by the Committee, deeply impressed, as it seems he is, with a conviction that their suggestions, if "ever carried into effect, would do more mischief to the British empire, than the fleets and armies of Napoleon will ever be able to accomplish." [P. 10.] We shall have occasion hereafter to consider the grounds of this conviction. In the mean time we will proceed to consider the author's observations touching "the situation of the country in regard to its commerce and finance, as admitted by the Committee itself."---An admission which induces him to ask, "is it right that the state of a country thus situated should be at all tampered with?" And boldly to insinuate that the case before the Committee was not such as required any remedies. [P. 11.]

But not content with this admission of the Committee, Sir John Sinclair proceeds to give "some proofs" of the prosperity of the country, by bringing forward a "*comparison of the years* 1809 *and* 1796, *in regard to commerce, public credit, and revenue.*" He seems not, however, to be aware that the several amounts which he has there produced for the year 1809, if reckoned in a depreciated currency, afford not the same proof of increased prosperity, as if the value of that currency had remained unaltered;---and that, to ascertain with any tolerable accuracy the real improvement, which has taken place in regard to our commerce and revenue, the relative value of the currency should first be ascertained,---And here we might refer to the opinion (if opinion we need refer to) of one of the witnesses, whose evidence appears amongst the others annexed to the report,---and who stated, that "he conceived the paper currency of this country to be depreciated to the full extent of the 15 to 20 per cent." (before mentioned as the fall of the exchange,) " or rather, the difference in this country between the price of bullion and the rate by which the coin is issued by the mint;---and again, that " he conceived the balance of trade with the continent of Europe to be considerably in favour of this country, though not to the extent as generally stated in figures, those figures representing in his mind only about 80 per cent. of their nominal value." [Minutes of Evidence, p. 84.] But our own experience sufficiently informs us that the depreciation of the currency, within the above-mentioned periods, has been great indeed. Let it, however, be admitted, for sure it ought to be, that, notwithstanding the depreciation of the currency, the commerce, public credit, and revenue, of the country have, upon a fair and general estimate, and upon fundamental principles, increased, and greatly too, since the period of 1796. Does it prove that this increase has been effected by means of our present system of circulation, and that in any greater degree than it would have been, had the former system never been abandoned, or had we returned to it long ago? Our commerce, public credit, and revenue, have increased, notwithstanding, and in spite of the new system. The skill and industry, the well-directed energy of the people ---the ingenuity of our mechanics---the unrivalled spirit of our manufacturers and merchants---not to say the unfortunate condition of continental Europe in general---the numerous and extensive colonies, of which from time to time we have deprived our enemies, and possessed ourselves, have begotten our prosperity, and maintained and multiplied it. It is an assumption, therefore, most inadmissible to ascribe that prosperity to the new system of paper currency, unexchangeable for the precious metals, and a perversion of terms most extraordinary to denominate "that a new theory, unsanctioned by recent experience,"* which would limit the quantity of the former within its natural bounds, and at the same time introduce a reasonable proportion of the latter into the circulation.

It can hardly be imagined that Sir John Sinclair is so wholly ignorant of the nature of money, as really to be of opinion, that the one and twenty shillings, which, some years ago, were sufficient to purchase a given quantity of commodities of whatsoever description, were not worth more than the guinea note of the present day, with which we cannot purchase two-third parts of the same quantity of such commodities; or that, if the quantity of the circulating medium, consisting almost entirely as it is of notes of the Bank of England and country banks, were reduced to what it was previous to the restriction of payments in cash, by the former, the price of labour and things in general would not be réduced accordingly. Yet when he asks "how the immense trade and more extended agriculture of this country could be carried on, if the circulation of Bank notes were reduced to eleven millions and a half?"†---we may well be at a loss what to think of the principles upon which his doubts in that respect are founded. But our attention will more than once be directed to this branch of his observations.

* P. 18. † Note, page 18.

We will now follow Sir John Sinclair through his more minute consideration of the report.

" *Section* I. *The rate of Exchange.*" [p. 14.]---In the opening of this section we are taught what we are to expect from it, which is nothing less than a bold attempt to shew that, " the rate of exchange having been for some time past unfavourable to this country, it is that circumstance which has occasioned the high price of bullion, and the alleged depreciation of our paper currency." In the discussion of this subject, therefore, Sir John Sinclair very properly adverts to---" 1st. The causes of the rate of exchange being against this country: 2ndly. Whether the present state of our currency has any connexion whatever with that circumstance: and 3rdly. What are the most likely means of restoring the exchange to its former favourable rate;" and, accordingly, he proceeds to consider, first,

The " *causes of the unfavourable rate of the ex-* " *change;*" [p.15,] and here, after expressing a wish that the Committee " had favoured us with a distinct statement of the various circumstances which, in the opinion of the intelligent individuals who appeared before them, had occasioned that unfavourable rate;" the author himself enters into some detail of those circumstances, independent of the present state of our currency;---which latter circumstance, however, he afterwards endeavours to shew, has no material effect upon the exchange.---

" The causes of the unfavourable rate of exchange," then, says Sir John Sinclair, " are in a great measure *purely commercial;* though some of them are of a *mixed,* and some of a *political* nature, and some may be arranged under the head of *miscellaneous;*" and accordingly he immediately proceeds to enumerate *eight* purely commercial; two mixed, or those *partly commercial, and partly political;* he afterwards mentions the causes *purely political;* and lastly, those of a *miscellaneous nature.* But concludes, after all, that the rate of exchange must depend *not on the balance of trade, but on the balance of payments.*

And what comfort is it intended that this nation should derive from the distinction? "We grant that the balance "of trade is in your favor, that it has been so for many "years; that your exports have annually exceeded your "imports, by many millions sterling; but you are to "remember, that your expenses for the maintenance of "your fleets and your armies abroad, have been great, and "that money has been remitted, or bills of exchange have "been employed for that purpose. We do not say, the full "amount of those expenses has been nearly so great, as that "of the excess of your exports, beyond your imports; "No, but then you are not to forget that, although your "exports have so considerably exceeded your imports, "they have not been paid for;---that, notwithstanding "the former are in point of fact much more than suffi- "cient to balance the latter, yet the payment for these "must be prompt, whilst the payment for those must "be postponed, till it suits the convenience of the "debtor.---Aye, perhaps, till it pleases the fancy of the "French emperor forsooth; --*Usque ad Calendas Græcas.* "But, in the mean time you have the satisfaction to know, "that an enormous debt has long been due to you, and

" to hope that it may possibly some time or another " be actually discharged. And the lower the rate of " the exchange, the better will be your chance."

But is not this grossly trifling with us? Besides, have the gentlemen who were called before the committee--- Has Sir John Sinclair himself ventured upon any sort of proof, that, notwithstanding all those various causes, which have been enumerated---the *purely commercial*, the *mixed*, those of a *political nature*, and those which are *miscellaneous*,---should co-operate* (which it can hardly be pretended that, in fact, they do, to such an extent as he seems to suppose, without menancing very alarming consequences to our trade and manufactures) they are capable of lowering the rate of Exchange to the great degree of 15 or 20 per cent. against this country? Whatever the balance of payments against us may be,---from whatever causes, other than the depreciation of our own currency, that unfavourable balance may spring, how can they reduce the exchange so much below the

* According to Sir John Sinclair's specification of these causes, " the *purely commercial* are, 1. A greater amount of import " than usual, principally from the Baltic, from France, and " from Holland. 2. The trade having been carried on in " foreign ships, and at a very heavy expense of freight, some- " times to the amount of fifty per cent. on the original cost of " the goods. 3. The manner in which the prices of the goods " imported from the Baltic were drawn for; the bills being " negotiated immediately on the shipments taking place, with- " out consulting much the interest of the proprietors in this " country, who would naturally have wished to defer the

expense of transmitting the precious metals to the places where these payments are to be made, inclusive of the expense of insurance? It seems quite clear, upon every principle of reason, that they cannot. Nay, whatever may be the testimony afforded in the course of the investigation by the committee, even that of persons who seemed most unwil-

---

" negotiation, till a demand for such bills had taken place. " 4. The greater difficulty and hazard in carrying on bill and " bullion operations between this country and the continent, " and also between some parts of the continent and others, " which, consequently, require greater profit to cover those " risks, and occasioned thereby an augmented depression in " the exchange. 5. The want of middle men, who formerly " were accustomed to employ great capitals in exchange ope- " rations, but who, from the increased difficulties and dangers " to which such operations are now subject, are, at present, " rarely to be met with. 6. The small amount of exports " compared to imports in our trade with France and the Baltic. " 7. The long credit given to foreign merchants for goods " exported, the price of which, particularly those sent to " South America, has not yet come back. And 8. The " lower prices at which foreigners obtained their supplies.

" The *mixed* causes, or those *partly commercial and partly* " *political,* are the system of commercial warfare carried on " against this country, by which the admission of British goods " into the continent was checked; communication, even by " letters, became difficult and uncertain; whilst no suit at law " could be instituted in the courts of justice there, against any " person who chose to resist the payment of a returned bill, or " to dispute the charges of exchange. 2. The decrease of " foreign export, and, consequently, an unfavourable rate of " exchange, was also owing, not only to the decrees in " France, but to the Orders of Council in England, and to the

ling to admit the depreciation of our currency, no part of it has tended, in the slightest degree, to shake the solidity of that position;---whilst, on the other hand, we find that the continental merchant, whose name the committee have thought proper not to make public, when asked if he could state how much per cent. might be the expense and risk of transmitting gold from London to Amsterdam, or

---

" American embargo; to the last, in particular, by which the " Americans were prevented from carrying their own produce, " and the produce of the enemy's colonies, to the continent of " Europe, which would have operated upon the Exchange in a " great measure as an export from this country.

" The causes *purely political* are the payment of foreign " subsidies, the maintenance of our troops abroad, and the " prices drawn on our government for naval and other expenses " in foreign countries.

" The rate of Exchange," Sir John Sinclair adds, " must " also be affected by various circumstances of a *miscellaneous* " *nature,* as the interest on capital in England possessed by " foreigners, as well as on capital abroad belonging to inhabitants " of Great Britain; the contraband trade between Great " Britain and other countries, and the amount of bullion " exported and imported." [P. 16---20.]

No one can doubt that these causes, if existing, are sufficiently powerful to affect the course of Exchange, to a certain degree. Whether they have all satisfactorily been proved to exist, and to what extent, those who have perused the appendix to the report may not, perhaps, be perfectly agreed in determining.

Hamburgh, or any other principal places of trade on the continent:---answered, that "independent of the pre-"mium of insurance, it would be from 1½ to 2 per cent. "from London to Hamburgh;" and when further asked, what he conceived to be the average risk, he replied, "about "4 per cent."* And in like manner Mr. Goldsmid, when questioned, what was the expense of sending gold to Holland, and how much it varied, answered, "From "4 to 7 per cent. for all charges covering the risk as "well as the cost of transportation."† Yet, after all, how are we to reconcile the existence of all these various causes of the depression of the Exchange, or the great preponderating influence of any of them, with that state of commercial prosperity, which Sir John Sinclair himself has so formally announced?‡ It is of little moment to set before us, upon paper, the flattering comparative statements of this year and that year, if the result of the whole be unprecedented difficulty and distress---if certain ruin be, as it must, the consequence of the full and continued operation of those causes; even though their operation upon the exchange be not so powerful as is pretended.

It is next discussed by Sir John Sinclair,

"*Whether the present state of our currency has any* "*connection whatever with the state of the exchange?*" [p. 20.] Under which head we find it laid down, that "no "doctrine can possibly be more adverse to the evidence "annexed to the report, whether as containing matter "of opinion, or matter of fact," than, "that the "unfavourable rate of the exchange is owing to the "state of our currency; and that if we were to revert "to our old system, and remove all restrictions on the

* Min. Ev. p. 84. † Min. Ev. p. 115. ‡ P. 12.

" payment of cash, at the bank, a favourable state of " exchange would be the necessary consequence."

Now, although it be but too plain, that some of the gentlemen, examined before the committee, did not give it as their opinion, that the low rate of exchange was occasioned by the depreciation of the currency; but, on the contrary, held, that they had no connection with each other; yet it is also as plain, that their opinion upon this subject ought to be but little regarded, if at variance with the direct conclusions to be drawn from their own statements and concessions.

In support of his position, however, Sir John Sinclair has cited divers passages from the evidence,---and, first, from that of Mr. Lyne, who says, " I do not agree " with those who conceive that the depression in our " exchanges, and the consequent export of our specie, " are occasioned by our circulating medium being con-" fined to Bank Notes; inasmuch as bills on foreign " countries are here attainable, precisely at the same " rates of exchange, whether they be paid for in Bank " Notes or guineas."* Now, strictly speaking, our circulating medium is not wholly confined to Bank Notes, but consists both of Bank Notes and species; why may not the one, therefore, be depreciated, notwithstanding it continues to bear the same nominal, and, in this country, the same reputed value, by means both of general credit and the law, as the other? Both may be depreciated. The relative quantity of the whole circulating medium may be increased a third or a fourth part, and, therefore, its value diminished in the same ratio, without our being able to procure more corn or meat for a guinea note than for a

* P. 21.

guinea; and, on the other hand, the relative quantity of the circulating medium may be diminished, and consequently its value increased, so that, with either the guinea or the guinea note, we might purchase a third or a fourth part more corn or meat than we can purchase with either of them at present. And hence, that such bills as Mr. Lyne alludes to, are attainable at the same rates, whether they be paid for in Bank Notes or in guineas, is a proof only that Bank Notes are not, *in this country*, depreciated more than the coin itself. It is no proof at all that the general currency is not depreciated. Besides, the law prohibits the exportation of guineas; he, therefore, that has the guineas wherewith he might purchase a bill upon foreign countries, might as well purchase it with them as with notes, unless he is willing to risk the penalties of the law in attempting to transport the former; which, doubtless, is oftentimes the case. But, let it be asked, if Bank of England Notes were to remain not convertible into species; and species might legally be sent abroad, as well as bullion, by persons who have payments to make there, at the expense of from 4 to 7 per cent. only, would they not send it, rather than purchase bills at the expense of 15 or 20 per cent.; and would not bills upon foreign countries then become attainable at different rates of exchange, according to the nature of the money which should be paid for them? Would the bank note and species, then, continue of the same relative value? Is it not absurd to suppose the latter would not be more sought after, and become much more valuable than the former?

Next follows a passage from the evidence of Mr. Greffulhe, who says, "I conceive the state of paper cur-

"rency of this kingdom, and the state of the exchanges "upon foreign parts, are subjects almost unconnected, "and that have but little influence on each other. In "proof," he continues, "I beg leave to adduce two facts, "from which it appears, that at two several periods, "the exchange, for a length of time, improved in favour "of this country, whilst the amount of bank notes was "gradually increasing."*

It is from the want of due attention to a few leading principles that so much doubt and difference of opinion have arisen upon this subject.

Let us suppose that two countries, England and Holland for instance, have been for many years in the habit of trading with each other; that English produce is imported into Holland, and Dutch produce, in return, imported into England; that the money-price of commodities is the same in each country; that is to say, that a pound of gold or silver, in a coined state, will purchase the same quantity of wheat in one as the other; if a thousand quarters of wheat, or other commodities of equal value, be imported into England from Holland, and the like quantity of wheat or other commodities, be at the same time imported into Holland from England, it is plain, if this were the whole of the mercantile transactions, no payment of money, of gold or silver, would be necessary on either side,---the trade would balance itself. If, however, there should be an excess of import from Holland into this country, beyond the export from the latter to the former, gold or silver would be sent hence to settle the balance, or bills of exchange would b drawn upon this country by Holland, to the amount of that balance, and be sold for that amount, excepting, per-

* P. 21.

haps, a part of the amount of the expense of freightage and insurance; the amount of the expense of freightage and insurance, would be the utmost limit of the depression of the exchange on the one side, and of its rise on the other.

Let us now suppose the relative quantity of the circulating medium to remain the same in Holland, but in England to be increased one-fourth; so that, what before cost four hundred pounds, should now cost five hundred; but the trade with Holland continues exactly as first mentioned; the same quantity of wheat, or other commodities of equal value, being mutually exported and imported; still the balance will be equal; no money, gold or silver, need pass from one to the other; the exchange may still be at par. But if there should be an excess of import, beyond the export, as was afterwards supposed, though the exchange would be against us, yet the expense of freightage and insurance being, perhaps, the same as in that case, the course of the Exchange might be the same likewise; unless, indeed, the circulating medium of this country, be not only depreciated by means of its increased quantity, but consist of paper instead of the precious metals. If this be the case, then, in order to obtain the gold and silver requisite for the discharge of the sum due to Holland, as we have supposed, that gold and silver must be purchased like any other commodity; and the price of all commodities having increased one-fourth, one-fourth more must be paid for the gold and silver requisite for the above purpose;---or, which amounts to the same thing, bills of exchange upon Holland would be purchased by this country, at the rate of 25 per cent, and upwards, in addition to the sum owing to the former by the latter;---or, in other words, to entitle a person to receive any sum in Holland, in the currency of that country, we must here pay after the same rate of 25 per cent. and upwards, in addition to that sum; and, on the other hand, to entitle a person to receive a sum of money here in our currency, 25 per cent. and upwards, less than that sum would be paid in Holland, in the currency of that country, reckoning the *par* according to the relative standards of each. And the same thing might happen, though there were no trade at all, between the two countries, in case it were expedient, on any other account, that payments should be made in them. These effects of the depreciation of our currency could only be counteracted by a favourable balance of payments, and probably but in part even by that.

It is true, that in complicated transactions, means may oftentimes be resorted to, whereby the unfavourable rate of exchange may be diminished. As for instanee, if the balance of trade between this country and Hamburgh were favourable to the former, the course of exchange would also naturally be favourable to it; and the debt due from Hamburgh, might therefore be beneficially applied in discharge of that due to Holland; whereby any actual transmittance of the precious metals from hence to Holland might be unnecessary. For the bills of exchange upon Hamburgh would, if transmitted to Holland, tend to liquidate our debt there, and possibly to advantage, if the course of exchange between these countries happened to be in favour of the former.

It is plain, however, from what has been said, that the state of the paper currency of this kingdom, and the state of exchanges upon foreign parts, are subjects not so unconnected with each other, as Mr. Greffulhe seems to imagine. The proof, therefore, which he would adduce in support of his opinion, viz. that the exchange has occasionally improved in favour of this country, whilst the amount of bank notes was gradually increasing, though it may be a proof, perhaps, that the balance of trade, or of payments, was improving, yet seems to be a proof of nothing more.

And, surely, when we consider how greatly the general balance of trade appears to have been in our favour, it is not too much to suppose that, occasionally at least, the balance of trade, and of payments with the Continent, might also be favourable to us, and that the rate of Exchange might in consequence improve: it is, indeed, rather matter of astonishment that the Exchange should, notwithstanding the depreciation of our currency, have been so long against us; but it would be still more astonishing if, as Mr. Greffulhe believes, the currency were not depreciated. But does this gentleman, or any of the gentlemen whose evidence is reported, state that, since the vast increase of Bank notes, the Exchange has ever risen so high in our favour, as it has fallen low against us. No such thing---neither is one instance brought forward, that I am aware of, by which it can be made to appear, that the rate of Exchange ever did before that time fall so low, except in cases where the currency was acknowledged to be depreciated.

In the next place, we are favoured with an extract from Mr. Harman's evidence, who declares, that he "cannot conceive that the diminution of the paper of the "Bank, would, either immediately or remotely, tend, in "any shape whatever, to an improvement of the Ex-"change."* But the observations which have already been made upon what fell from Mr. Greffulhe, may be applied to the correspondent opinion of Mr. Harman.

With respect, indeed, to the opinion of Mr. Goldsmid, who is next quoted by Sir John Sinclair, as saying, "The "man, who takes a bill at Hamburgh on London, pur-"chases it for purposes of his own---either to purchase "a commodity, or to pay a debt;"†---it would surely require something more than this to shew, that even Mr. Goldsmid himself did not consider the low rate of Exchange to be occasioned by the vast issue of paper money. ---Nay, on the very day, in which he made the above observation, when asked whether it was his opinion that the circulating medium, as entirely confined to paper in this country, produces any effect upon the foreign Exchange, he answered, "I do not profess myself competent to give my opinion upon that."‡

Lastly then, with regard to the accounts alluded to by Sir John Sinclair, the one delivered by Mr. Whitmore, being an account of "the amount of Bank Notes in cir-"culation, on each Saturday night, in each week, in the "year 1797, and of the course of Exchange on the fol-"lowing Tuesday;" (a period, by the bye, when the Exchange appears, from that account, to have been decidedly in our favour;) and the other delivered by Mr. Pearse, being "a comparison of the amount of Bank Notes, "and rates of the Hamburgh Exchange at certain pe-"riods," that is, from the 27th of February, 1797, to Christmas, 1809; "both proving" according to Sir John Sinclair, "in the *most satisfactory manner, as a matter "of fact*, that there is no connection whatever between "the amount of paper currency issued by the Bank of

* P. 22. † Ib. ‡ Min. of Evid. p. 121. § P. 22,

" England, and the rate of Exchange;"§ do they not rather prove, that as the rate of Exchange was oftentimes considerably, and always something in our favour, from January 3, 1797, up to March, 1799, when the utmost amount of the Bank Notes did not exceed thirteen millions and a half; but had since that time, whilst the amount of Bank Notes had been gradually increasing to eighteen millions, been kept almost constantly, and considerably unfavourable, sinking so low as 28s. 6g. and never rising higher than 35s. 10g. and that only sometime between January 1803, and the end of 1807--- do they not, I say, under these circumstances, rather prove some most intimate connection to subsist between the amount of Bank Notes, and the rate of Exchange; and that the small, and rare occasional rise which is to be observed within the last-mentioned period, must have proceeded, as I have before observed, from the favourable balance of trade, or of payments, notwithstanding the depreciation of the currency, and the vast advantage which that depreciation afforded to the Continent, in its transactions with this country? But " nothing can be " more decisive," says Sir John Sinclair, " in support of " the doctrine, that the amount of Bank Notes has no " effect upon the Exchange, than the paper given in by " Mr. Pearse." " From January, 1803, to the end of the " year 1807, the Exchange on Hamburgh varied from " 32s. 10d. to 35s. 6d. becoming more favourable as the " amount of Bank Notes increased."* Yes, the Exchange did become more favourable, though the amount of Bank Notes increased. But mark what followed---the Bank Notes continued to increase,---and the Exchange fell, it fell to 28s. 6g. And this should teach us not to

* P. 23—Note.

judge of general causes from particular, but from general effects. We occasionally experience a warm day in the depth of winter. The quicksilver will sometimes in January rise above the *temperate* of Farenheit. But shall we therefore say, that the sun's absence from the northern hemisphere, is not the cause of our winter, and hence negatively of the fall of quicksilver in the thermometer?

Having now gone through that part of the evidence of Mr. Lyne, Mr. Greffulhe, Mr. Harman, Mr. Goldsmid, Mr. Whitmore, and Mr. Pearse, which Sir John Sinclair has thought proper to notice under this head, let us, hear some part of what these gentlemen have said; the notice of which Sir John Sinclair has thought proper to omit.

In the first place then, it is observed by Mr. Lyne, immediately after the first of the sentences before quoted from him, that " *he knows of instances* (and in which he " has had much practical experience) *where such effects*" (meaning the depressions of Exchanges, and the consequent export of species,) " have been produced by a " paper money circulation in different parts of the Conti- " nent of Europe; but that that has been produced, only as " such paper currency became of less value, than what by " law it was purported to represent. (P.53, Min. of Evidence.) What, however, are we to understand from this, but that the depression in the cases alluded to, was produced by means of the paper currency having become less valuable than the species? But with regard to transactions with foreign countries, the paper currency must necessarily be less valuable than the species, unless the former can be converted into the latter without loss. Notes of the Bank of England on the Continent of Europe are of no further value than the amount of gold or silver, which they can purchase. As by the law of this country, they purport to represent some certain specific quantities of the coin; so if they be of any value at all on the Continent, by the law of commerce, they purport to represent the quantities of gold or silver, which those specific quantities of coin contain, or to which they are generally allowed to be equivalent. What need of further proof then have we, that our paper currency has become of less value, than what by this law it purports to represent,---than that with Bank Notes of a hundred and five pounds, or a hundred guineas, which by law, they purport to represent we cannot purchase a hundred guineas weight of gold, but must give for it 120*l.* and upwards, whether in Bank Notes, or in specie, notwithstanding the value of gold abroad continues nearly the same as it formerly was? For although it must be acknowledged that there is great difference between the paper currency of this country, and that of other countries alluded to by Mr. Lyne; since in the former the credit of those who issue the paper is good, whilst in the latter it is bad; and, in the one, the paper holds equal value with the coin itself; but, in the other, falls below it,---so that in other countries, therefore, the value of the coin is preserved, perhaps increased; whilst in this country it is diminished, together with the paper which bears its denomination. Yet, with respect to the exchange, this distinction is of no importance.

But, to have done with Mr. Lyne, what does Mr. Greffulhe say? Why, he admits, that if a Bill of Exchange for 100*l.* is remitted from Hamburgh, the person to whom it is remitted receives a Bank Note; and if his correspondent desires to have gold for that 100*l.* the former must buy it; and that, reckoning the difference to be about 16 per Cent. if in the first instance the foreigner could receive gold, *he would give nearly* 16 *per cent. more in exchange.* [P. 73, Minutes of Evidence.]

Let us next hear Mr. Harman; he admits, that " an " augmentation of the paper currency generally, per- " haps, may tend to increase the price of commodities, " though he declares, that " he sees very few symptoms " of it." [Min. of Evid. p. 220.] In other words, he admits, that such augmentation may tend to depreciate the currency; and we have already shewn in what manner the depreciation of the currency may affect the Exchange. And though Mr. Harman declares, that he sees very few symptoms of the increase of the price of commodities; yet, those who are in the habits of attending to the price of the victuals which they consume, and the clothes which they put upon their backs, and of casting a retrospect upon the price which they paid for similar articles some few years ago; or, if their opportunities should lead them to the like consideration of articles of greater importance, in respect to the pecuniary amount, and they should compare the present with the former price of houses and of land, they will, I doubt not, perceive symptoms enough of its late extraordinary increase. What, indeed, is the article of luxury, of comfort, of necessity, which is not of higher, of much higher price than it was previous to the restriction of cash payments by the Bank? Few may be the symptoms which Mr. Harman may see; but turn which way they will, those who have fixed incomes and large families to maintain, can see nothing but symptoms, and most alarming and distressing they truly are.

With regard to Mr. Goldsmid, we have already heard his reply to the interrogatory of the Committee, respecting the effect produced on the Exchange by the paper medium of circulation. Mr. Goldsmid, however, when asked, whether it was not one of the effects of a forced paper currency, to raise in the country itself the nominal prices of all commodities, "begged to be excused from "answering that question," adding, that "he was not a "competent judge---that it was a political question." [Minutes of Evidence, p. 119.]

Let us now try Mr. Whitmore, the governor, and Mr. Pearse, the deputy-governor of the Bank. Do they say any thing more upon the subject? Yes, truly, and a great deal. For the former upon being asked, whether "a rise in the value of any species of money or "currency, mean a fall in the prices of commo-"dities;" in reply, among other things observed, that "he would rather wish to leave that to the judg-"ment of the Committee." And, when pressed immediately after as to his opinion whether, "supposing the "currency of any country to consist altogether of specie, "that specie would be affected in its value by its abun-"dance, or its diminution, the same as copper," &c. he answered, "I have already said I declined answering "questions as to opinion; I am very ready to answer any "questions as to matters of fact; I have not opinions

" formed upon the points stated in this, and the preced- " ing question sufficiently matured to offer them to the " Committee." [Minutes of Evidence, p. 124.] So, when Mr. Pearse was asked, whether " he conceived that " a very considerable reduction of the amount of the " circulating medium would not tend, in any degree, to " increase its relative value compared with commodities; " and that a considerable increase of it would have no " tendency whatever to augment the price of commo- " dities, in exchange for such circulating medium?" he observed, it seems, " that it was a subject on which " such a variety of opinions are entertained, he did not feel " himself competent to give a decided answer." [Minutes of Evidence, p. 187.] If the opinions of these gentlemen, therefore, upon such general principles, connected so intimately as they are with the subject of Exchange, were not sufficiently formed or matured; what are we reasonably to think of their opinions, that the state of the Exchange is in no wise materially connected with the circumstance of the restriction on payments in cash, and the consequent increase of Bank Notes.

On a preceding day, however, the same gentlemen, Mr. Whitmore and Mr. Pearse, being asked by the Committee, whether, in their opinion, the state of the Exchanges had at any time very materially operated *before the restriction* to increase the demand on the Bank for gold; ---" In my opinion," said Mr. Whitmore, " it has not; " the demand for gold for exportation depended upon the " price of the article in foreign countries;"---and " within the course of my experience, in the Bank," added Mr. Pearse, " the Hamburgh Exchange has never " been so much below par *previous to the Restriction Bill,*

" as to render it sufficiently an object of advantage to " individuals to make any material demand for gold " upon the Bank." [Minutes of Evidence, p. 155.] But, what is indeed very material to the point, on the subsequent day, Mr. Whitmore made the following declaration:---" Provided it was imperative " upon us to open, I should think a restriction of the " Bank issues would be necessary, &c." And immediately after Mr. Pearse too declared, that " in the con- " templation of the removal of the Restriction Bill, at " any definite period; it would become necessary for the " Bank to regulate the amount of its issues, with a refe- " rence to the course of Exchange with foreign coun- " tries, &c." [Minutes of Evidence, p. 186.] Thus in effect, acknowledging the very strong, if not conclusive, circumstance, that the quantity of paper money in circulation was never so great previous to the restriction, as to occasion so great a depression of the Exchange, as materially to increase the demands on the Bank for gold. Yet since the vast increase of paper money consequent upon that restriction, the depression of the Exchange has become so great, that were the Bank to be opened for payment in cash, there is much reason to apprehend, that the demand upon it for gold would be so considerable, as to render it necessary for the Bank to lessen the issue of its Notes; nay, to regulate the amount of them, with a reference to the course of the Exchange. And we find, Mr. Harman's, evidence not very different in this respect.

For, upon being asked whether, "supposing the Bank to " be paying in Cash, and the Exchange, as well as the " price of Bullion, to be as they then were, and conse-

" quently a drain upon the Bank to have taken place, it " would be his opinion, that the Bank ought to diminish " its paper or not?" Mr. Harman answered, that " he was " decidedly of opinion, that it would, and ought to make " the Bank very cautious." And again, being asked whe- " ther, " supposing the Parliament to enact that the Bank " of England should again pay in gold at a distant period; " say one, two, or three years, it would be his opinion, that " the Bank ought to resort to the measure of restraining " its issues, as a means of preparing itself to meet that " event, supposing the Exchanges, and the price of Bul- " lion to continue, as they then were;" he replied, that " he " conceived they must necessarily, if the exchanges were " to continue as they then were, which, however, he " deemed barely within possibility." [Minutes of Evidence, p. 219 and 220.]

Having paid due attention to what Sir John Sinclair has observed, and what it seems he has not observed, of the evidence given by those gentlemen, whom he considers as ranged upon his side of the question; let us now examine what he has observed of the evidence which is given by some of those who appear to be ranged rather upon the opposite side of it. And, first, as to Sir Francis Baring whose evidence Sir John Sinclair thus briefly notices, though he acknowledges that " much " weight is certainly due to so respectable a cha- " racter." " Sir Francis Baring," says he, " indeed, " states, " that the two great circumstances which affect " the Exchange in its present unfavourable state, are " the restrictions upon trade with the Continent, and the " increased circulation of this country in paper, as pro- " ductive of the scarcity of bullion; but he does not

" seem to have considered the various other causes enu-" merated in the preceding section." Yet are we not, therefore, naturally to conclude, that either Sir Francis Baring did not believe those other causes to have existence, or deemed them to be of little or no comparative moment or importance? Sir John Sinclair, however, makes no further comment upon the evidence of Sir Francis Baring, but straightway proceeds to observe, that " by another evidence," (referring to the gentleman whose name is not made public,) " the *whole deprecia-*" *tion* of the Exchange is ascribed *originally* to the mea-" sures of the enemy; and its not having recovered itself " is attributed to the circumstance of the paper of " England not being exchangeable for cash. But this doctrine," Sir John Sinclair continues, " is ably refuted by Mr. " Lyne, who contends that though gold, being of a more " portable nature, would sooner find its way to the Con-" tinent, and consequently would produce the *speediest* " *effect*, yet, that merchandize of lawful export would " produce a *greater effect* in reducing the difference of " Exchange." [P. 24.] But are not those very measures of the enemy which were alluded to, the cause of our not sending sufficient merchandize to the Continent? " I " will take your gold and silver," says he, " but none " of your merchandize: the balance of trade shall no " longer be in your favour." But though this balance were not in our favour, and never should be; yet, if our paper were convertible into cash, and any payment should be required to be made by this country to the Continent, gold and silver might be sent thither for that purpose, which would at once restore the Exchange to its proper level. Whether the gentleman referred to reasoned after this manner, I know not. But if he did, he will hardly acknowledge that his doctrine has been ably, or indeed in any manner at all, refuted by Mr. Lyne.

There can, indeed, be no doubt, that the rate of Exchange may be raised in favour of a country, by exporting from it the produce of its land and labour, as well as the gold and silver which it may happen to contain. But the more the currency of a country is depreciated, at the higher money price must its exported merchandize be sold, in order to bring a profit to the manufacturer and merchant; but the higher the price of the merchandize, the less will be the demand for it abroad. Whilst, on the other hand, the more the currency of a country is depreciated, the greater, it is likely, will be the quantity of goods imported into it, from abroad, for the sake of the higher price which may be obtained for them.

Much more of the evidence which has been printed, by order of the House of Commons, might have been brought forward to shew, that the low rate of Exchange proceeds principally, if not altogether, from the causes ascribed by the committee; but it is sufficient, perhaps, to have followed Sir John Sinclair in the path which he himself has chosen. And here I cannot but observe, with astonishment, to what different conclusions the minds of different men will sometimes lead them. So long as the Bank of England, and the Country Banks, shall be enabled to sustain their credit---so long as pound notes shall be exchanged for 20 shillings; be the amount of all the notes in circulation increased to twice, or ten times their present amount, it may be maintained, according to the notions of some of the gentlemen who were called before the committee, that there is no depreciation in our paper currency, though all commodities, whatsoever, be increased double or ten times in their price,---though the exchange fall twice, or ten times below its present rate; yet all this, it may be said, is no proof at all, that the currency is depreciated,---the pound note is exchangeable for twenty shillings, (such as they are) and the hundred pound note for a hundred notes for a pound. But what is meant by a depreciation of the currency, but a diminution in the value of the several pieces, or denominations, of which it is composed, compared with that of other articles, which it is employed to circulate? If the price of wheat, eighteen or twenty years ago, was, upon an average, but 6s. per bushel, and that of almost all other commodities in proportion, and although the demand for, and supply of wheat and other commodities, continue relatively the same, yet the price of the former has in the mean time risen upon an average to 10s. per bushel, and the price of the latter also proportionally;---if, within the same period, the rate of exchange with foreign countries, instead of being 3 or 4 per cent. in our favor, has fallen so low as to be 15 or 20 per cent. against us, though the expense of the actual transmission of the precious metals, including that of the insurance, amounts to no more than from 4 to 7 per cent. and although the balance of trade, appears upon a general view of the official statements made out as they are, without reference to the Bullion that is exported, or imported, to be very greatly in our favour; there surely is some ground to apprehend from these circumstances, that our currency is become depreciated, and that, whether it consists of the precious metals alone, or partly of the precious metals, and partly of bank paper, or wholly of bank paper. But if we know that since the period above specified, the quantity of bank paper and dollars, issued by the Bank of England, is increased two-fold, and we may have reason to believe,. that the quantity of paper issued by other banks, is increased in as great, or a much greater proportion, that there is little or no gold in circulation, and that its market price has risen 15 or 18 per cent. above its mint price, can we hesitate to believe, can we for one moment doubt, that the currency has been depreciated, and that the effects above stated, must have proceeded in great measure, if not altogether, from that cause? That the governor and deputy governor, and directors of the Bank of England, that English merchants of consideration, should not see this most clearly,---that an established writer upon political economy, should have his eyes shut against it, is, indeed, most extraordinary and unaccountable.

We come now to the third head of this section:

" *What are the most likely means of restoring the* " *Exchange to its former favourable state.*" [P. 25.] Wherein Sir John Sinclair, after noticing that " the " great corrective of every mischief, arising from an " unfavourable state of exchange, in the judgment of " the committee, is the repeal of the law, which sus-

"pends the cash payments of the Bank of England," and wishing, "most sincerely, that the committee had "examined the subject more minutely, before they had "hazarded such an opinion," adverts to the declaration which was made by one of the evidence, "that a free "circulation and liberty to export the coin, was, in his "opinion, the only effectual remedy;" "but he adds," says Sir John Sinclair, "if that is not deemed practi-"cable, I conceive that many palliatives may be applied." "Yet the nature of these palliatives," Sir John Sinclair observes, "the Committee never gave themselves any "trouble to ascertain." It is, however, very plain from the passage here cited, and from other parts of this gentleman's evidence, what he really thought upon the subject; and if the committee were convinced, that no very essential and important benefit would arise from the application of mere palliatives, whilst the currency is permitted to continue in its present state,---that the repeal of the law referred to, would of itself render them wholly unnecessary---that such repeal alone, as it would necessarily effect the reformation of the currency, would necessarily lead to the most speedy, effectual, and beneficial accomplishment of the end they had in view; why spend their time in searching for mere palliatives,---poor, meagre, half-measure palliatives?

The committee, perhaps, might have found out somewhat more that could be exported to France, and its dependant states, and somewhat less that might be imported from thence, than is at present; but without a strong system of interdiction and combustion, of which the French emperor himself has set us so worthy an example, is it likely we could insure a greater equality of trade, or the restoration of the Exchange to a par? For whilst the currency of this country is so considerably depreciated, and the balance of the trade, or of payments, (which in the long run, if the currency were not depreciated, might amount to the same thing,) is against us; that depreciation must, most seriously, affect the rate of the exchange; but it was to the root of the evil, not to a few of its branches only, that the committee directed their attention, and recommended that the axe should speedily be laid.

"Section II.---*On the high price of Bullion.*" [P. 27.]

The author, after some preliminary observations, declaratory of his opinion of the great absurdity of making any rise in the price of Bullion the ground of serious alarm, now ventures to submit to the reader's consideration, "some political axioms," or, as he afterwards denominates them, "general principles regarding Coin or Bullion." [P. 28.] These we shall hereafter have an opportunity of examining more particularly, if necessary, when we arrive at the appendix. In the section now under review, however, "the precious metals," it is said, "may be described as a species of merchandize, which, "by common consent, answers three important purposes: 1. That of enabling individuals to receive the "value of their labour, for an article *universally* "*exchangeable.* 2. That of transferring property in "goods, from one individual to another, or from one "nation to another, without the trouble of actual barter; "and, 3. That of enabling the government of a country "to obtain a revenue, and to defray the public expenses."

But we are soon after informed,* that " it is in early " ages of society alone, before the credit of a govern- " ment is established, and property is secured, that " the precious metals exclusively answer these important " purposes, and that in ages of civilization and refine- " ment, *a well-regulated paper currency*, with a small " proportion of these metals, in a state of coinage, is " equally useful, indeed, on many accounts, more " advantageous; and that the precious metals ought, in " commercial periods of society, to be accounted merely " as a species of merchandize; the increase or dimi- " nution of which has no decisive influence on the " wealth and prosperity of a country, and which, if left " to itself, soon finds its own level." And this, it seems, is presented to the reader, as one of the author's political axioms, regarding Coin and Bullion---as simple and as true, in politics, as that two straight lines cannot inclose a space, or that things which are equal to the same, are equal to one another, is simple and true in mathematics. But surely this political axiom requires some little explanation before we venture to apply it broadly to the solution of political problems. It ought, surely, first to be explained, what is meant by a *well-regulated paper currency*, and what degree of influence on the wealth and prosperity of a country, is that which may be considered as, and termed " decisive."

If by a well-regulated paper currency is intended that which is always convertible, without loss, into the precious metals, and which, together with the precious metals in circulation, never exceeds in quantity the amount of the precious metals which would be in circulation, if

* P. 29.

there were no such paper currency, we might be disposed to admit the first part of the above position as true; but with regard to the latter part of it, the author himself, in the very next following pages, seems to bring matter of argument directly in opposition to it. He there shows upon his own statement, taken from the appendix to the report of the Committee, that the precious metals are, even in the present age, something more than a species of mere merchandize, when he observes, "that the French, when they were in Portugal, "so drained that country of gold, that none could since "be procured from that quarter;"---"that in order to pro-"cure cotton" from the Brazils, "gold and silver were "exported to that country, both because in the Brazils "there were no takers of bills on England, and as the "importer could make his purchases more rapidly, "by sending cash;"---"that there has been an unusual "demand for gold, for the use of the French armies;"---and that, "above all the state of the times, the "failure of confidence, and the apprehension of future "revolutions, have led to the practice of hoarding, and "consequently the withdrawing of gold altogether, and "that to a considerable extent."* Or does all this look as if gold and silver were mere merchandize, like "sugar "or cochineal?" Do they not seem rather to be by one common consent, an article exchangeable for all other articles, at all times, and in all places in the civilized world---an instrument of barter peculiarly fitted for the circulation of all commodities whatsoever, and sought after, and applied almost exclusively for that purpose, and most valuable on that account? Yet, notwithstanding all this, the increase or diminution of the

* P. 30, 31.

precious metals may, perhaps, have no decisive influence on the wealth or prosperity of a country; that is to say, though the precious metals be imported into, if unproductive stock to the same amount in value be exported from a country; or, though on the other hand, a portion of the precious metals be exported from, if unproductive stock to the same amount in value be imported into it, the total capital, the strength, the industry, the enjoyments and happiness of that country, may yet remain the same, and therefore need not of necessity be decidedly influenced by the change. But that the precious metals, should find their just level when left to themselves, in a country where paper is substituted almost entirely in the stead of them, as a circulating medium,---where paper money is made well nigh equivalent to a legal tender, and is, in consequence of its excessive amount, together with the little coin that remains there, greatly depreciated in value,---is a notion somewhat novel and extravagant;---but that it should be received as a political axiom, the meaning of which it is only necessary to understand, in order to assent to, and which, therefore, can require no further demonstration, is somewhat contrary to the rules and practice of sound logic. What! shall we admit that the precious metals have attained their just level in a coined state when they are rendered less valuable than when uncoined? Should the king's image deteriorate the metal? Is it of the nature of an alloy which reduces its intrinsic value? But it is upon such principles as these, if I understand them rightly, that Sir John Sinclair would build his approbation of the present system of circulation in this country, and that he indulges in the notion, that whoever takes the trouble of considering his observations upon the subject, " will be of opinion, that we might as well " institute an enquiry into the price of diamonds, or " cochineal, or of sugar, as of gold; and that com- " pelling the Bank of England to pay in cash, were it " a practicable measure, could be of no service what- " ever in the present state of Europe." [P. 32.]

We will proceed, however, to " Section III.---*On the con-* " *duct of the Bank of England in regard to its circulation.*" [P. 32.]

In this section Sir John Sinclair, after having animadverted upon the language of the Committee, in respect to the Directors of the Bank of England, presents his readers with a short statement of the rules by which the Bank of England is regulated, in regard to the issue of its notes. These are to make advances to government on the security of Exchequer Bills, issued on the credit of taxes, or otherwise, under the authority of Parliament; on the loans of the year; and on what is called *legitimate mercantile paper*, payable within two months; never to advance at less interest than 5 per cent.; and lastly, " to consider not only the solidity of the paper, but also the amount of accommodation the individual applying for it already has."---He then immediately adds that, " it is owing to the Committee having kept this last rule entirely out of their view, that they triumphantly exclaim, " though the Directors state the broad principle that there can be no excess of their circulation, *if issued according to the rules of discount*, yet they disclaim the idea of acting up to it in its whole extent." But why should they not as triumphantly so exclaim, though this last rule of the Directors had stared them directly in the face? Does it at all contradict the assertion of the Committee? If it do, Sir John Sinclair should have stated how, and in what manner it does so. But instead of that, he tells us that the Directors "cannot act up to this broad principle in its whole extent, because they must restrict their advances to individual applicants, and must not risk too much property on the same security."*---Why not? Because it is contrary to the rules of discount. But do not the Committee expressly say, "if issued according to the rules of discount?" This, however, is not all; for, says Sir John Sinclair, "the instant any superfluous issue is made it reverts upon the Bank.---For no individual will ever think of keeping in his possession any paper for which he has no occasion, and for which he must pay an interest of 5 per cent." So, provided the Bank notes be employed, the issue of them cannot be superfluous! But if, by reason of the increase of Bank notes, the price of all things has been increased, at least one-fourth, is it not plain, that any individual will require Bank notes (supposing the circulating medium to consist of them alone) at least one-fourth more in amount, than he would in case no such increase had taken place; and, therefore, although all the notes may, notwithstanding their increase, be as much employed as the smaller quantity formerly was, yet that the one-fourth part increase of that quantity may be as superfluous and unnecessary as the one-fifth part of a pint and a quarter of water, in which a hen's egg may be boiled, but no better than if a pint only were used for that purpose?

* P. 34.

"But the best answer to any over-issue on the part of the Bank," we are told, "is this, that if the large notes of the Bank were to be diminished in the proportion of one-half, it would be impossible to conduct the affairs of the metropolis."* It would, indeed, be impossible to conduct them, supposing the present high price of things to continue, and the same payments to become due as at present. But it is not a sudden annihilation of Bank notes that the Committee recommend, but a gradual diminution of advances, which would occasion a gradual diminution of prices; and perhaps it would have been well for the trading part of the Community if those advances had been diminished long ago. What evil can arise to the prudent trader, though he should be able to get but six or seven hundred pounds where he may now get a thousand; if he can purchase the same quantity of goods with the former, under a really well-regulated system of paper currency, as he can with the latter under the system now tolerated?---a system which enables so many rash adventurers to enter upon speculations, which oftentimes prove not only highly injurious, nay, ruinous, to themselves, but also to others, whose prudence and caution ought to render them secure? With regard, indeed, to the scarcity of money, which, by one of the evidence referred to by Sir John Sinclair, is remarked to prevail at a period prior to the payment of the dividends; that is no doubt an evil necessarily attendant upon our system of finance, and which it is idle, or worse, to attempt to remedy, by increasing the circulating medium. The public debt has become so enormous, that a large sum is requisite to discharge the interest upon it. Taxes are raised, they are accumulated in the hands of the collectors before they are applied to that purpose---

* P. 3.

the fair and natural effect of our financial system. As well may complaints be made of the scarcity of money, arising from its accumulation in the hands of the tenants of lands and houses previous to the quarter-day, with a view to the payment of their rents. But what would landlords say to the issuing of vast quantities of paper money, as the means of facilitating the payment of those rents? Would they not in future increase their rents in proportion to the additional quantity of paper money that would thus be brought into circulation? Is it not the fact that they do so increase them, in consequence of that which has already been actually brought into circulation? If the public debt is so enormous, if the amount of the dividends, payable in respect of it, occasions so great a temporary scarcity of money in the metropolis, as to prove inconvenient to the mercantile interests of the nation,---if that be an evil of high magnitude, let it be remedied,---but let it not be remedied by working an injustice to the public and private creditor. Let not this description of person feel all the inconvenience and distress, but let them be equally apportioned amongst us all,---neither the mercantile nor any other interest should have any solid and exclusive ground of complaint against a system which the circumstances of the times have induced us to adopt.

" Section IV.---*On the amount of our Paper Circulation, and whether it ought to be diminished.*" [P. 35.]

In the opening of this section, Sir John Sinclair formally announces the paper which has been printed by way of appendix to his observations, and to which he had before referred in a note. He now apprises us of the general doctrines which he there lays down, but which we need not at present stop to examine, and states that the deduction from the whole is this, viz. "That an increase of labour " or industry, a more extended commerce, and an increas- " ed revenue, require perpetual additions to the circulating " medium of a country." And, " being deeply im- " pressed with the incontrovertible solidity of these " doctrines, he declares, that he cannot possibly concur " in any measures for reducing our circulating medium, " and thereby cramping all our exertions, and materially " endangering our security." From which we are, no doubt, to conclude, that all our exertions must be cramped, and our security materially endangered by the reduction of our circulating medium. But adds Sir John Sinclair, " Whether any regulations are necessary regarding coun- " try bankers for the protection of the public *against fraud*, " is an important subject different from the question " regarding the quantum of circulation." [P. 37.]

Yes, regulations may perhaps be necessary to secure the public from such frauds as insolvent country bankers now commit in issuing notes which, if returned, they cannot exchange even for notes of the Bank of England. But you who are not guilty of this, fear not. Scatter your paper like chaff before the wind; like seed it will take root and multiply, and replenish the earth. What though you lend nothing but your name! Are not the house which you inhabit, the fields which you proudly walk over, the stock you are possessed of, the navy and exchequer bills, the India bonds, and other bonds, the mortgages, policies, long bills, but more numerous short bills, and the many other parchment and paper securities, which are ranged in sacred order within your closet---all ready to answer the demands which may be made upon you, even to the very limit of your undertakings? Who, then, shall say that you defraud the public? What matters it, though you profit of your house and lands by living in and letting them, and of your stock, bills, bonds, mortgages, and other securities, by the interest which is payable on them,---though perchance the full amount of your whole capital be represented by your promissory notes;---though the currency be depreciated by the excess which the issue of those notes has occasioned, though a multitude of people are sorely aggrieved and suffer many privations in consequence of your practices.---Nay, though your notes represent the very property which is pledged to you, and though you receive interest from the persons who have pledged it for the loan of those notes,---yet who will say that the public, that any individual is defrauded? If the Bank of England be free from the imputation, if they are guilty of no fraud, they who promise but do not perform, well may the country banker be excused. And in regard to the Bank of England; " as it is proved no pains " are taken to force bank notes into circulation or " to retain them in it, no material excess, in the opinions " of the most respectable practical authorities, can take " place;" [p.[illegible].] and that the gentlemen to whom Sir John Sinclair alludes, are most respectable gentlemen there is probably no doubt at all; but that there are as respectable, whose opinions are different upon this subject, there is, probably as little doubt. I will not refer particularly to that of the late Sir Francis Baring, *to whose sentiments so much weight is certainly due*,* or to that of any other gentleman who was examined before the committee, but rather to the understandings of people in general, whether it be in the nature of things, that either a corporation or any set of individuals associated for the purpose of lending money at interest, but who are permitted to advance their promissory notes as money, and to receive

See p. 32, Sup.

the like interest upon them, but who are not compelled to pay them in cash, should not in such a country as this, where so many are willing to borrow, increase their advances to an excess so as to lessen the value of its circulating medium in general, and that most materially? It is in vain to attempt to argue with those who will persist in a contrary opinion. The question being plainly stated, it may at once be decided without further discussion. But the depreciation of money we shall, perhaps, be told, is no proof of excess; nay we are told, that "no "circulation, unless forced, can go beyond what the immediate wants of the public, require," and are pressed with this further observation by way of argument; "for if there is any redundancy, it immediately reverts to the bank that issues it." Yet what is really the meaning of all this, but that, provided loans are required and advanced (it matters not to what amount) the circulation not being forced, cannot be redundant, though thrice the quantity of money may be employed to circulate half the quantity of commodities that were circulated before, still there can be no redundancy. Does this argument require serious consideration? Does not any increase of circulating medium which reduces the relative value of that medium render it redundant? Does it not become more than sufficient?

"At length we arrive at Section V. *On the measures recom-* "*mended by the Committee.*" [P. 38.]

But ere he considers "the plan recommended by the committee, that of repealing the law which suspends the cash payments of the Bank of England, and removing any restriction on such payments, at the period of two years from the present time," Sir John Sinclair deems it prudent to make "some observations on the grounds on which that system is founded,"---and with such sentiments as we have already seen are entertained by him, we need not be surprized that after noticing the remark of the committee, "that any such general excess of currency as lowers its relative value is attended with disadvantages to the country;" he should turn round and reply, "If it was granted that to a certain extent such was the case, the question is, whether the advantages do not preponderate?"* Neither that he should exclaim, in the following strain of becoming pride, "If the new system which we have adopted, contributes "to the public safety, enables us to carry on the most "momentous war in which we are now engaged, increases "our agriculture, our commerce, and revenue, places us, "as admitted by the committee, [Report, p. 68.] in a high "state of mercantile and public credit, and makes us, "as I trust will continue to be the case, the admiration "of the universe; what matters it, then, whether the "circulation of gold or paper is the instrument of our "prosperity?"†

It is not, indeed, to be supposed, with such a glowing picture before him, and looking to the present system of our circulation, as to the sun, which scatters his benignant rays on all around him, that Sir John Sinclair should be much affected by the apprehensions entertained by the committee, that the excess of currency tends to deteriorate the situation of the country labourer,---apprehensions, which, it seems, according to Sir J. Sinclair, have no foundation whatsoever. On the contrary, he considers that their comfort depends "on their "having a regular and constant demand for their labour," and that "that can only be the case where a circulating

* P. 39. † Ib.

" medium abounds."* Yet he does not even attempt to shew that the price of labour has risen in proportion to the abundance of the circulating medium, or that the condition of the labourer is in any way benefitted by it. No, he refers rather to the laws, which, in England, secure to the labourer and his family their *subsistence*, by throwing them upon the parish; and to the practice in Scotland where the servants in husbandry are *chiefly* paid in kind. No very satisfactory argument, however, will this be deemed, as set against the conclusions of the committee. But what will Sir John Sinclair say of the situation of those town, as well as country, labourers, who, from the scanty savings of their scanty wages, may have accumulated something for their support in declining life.---Who may by their industry and frugality, with a meritorious love of independence, have hoped to abstain from calling on the tender-hearted overseers of their parish for subsistence?---Is their situation in no respect deteriorated? but of this hereafter.

Yet Sir John Sinclair seems still unwilling to admit, that our paper currency is depreciated. " As to the idea " entertained by the committee," says he, " that our " paper currency is depreciated, a number of the most " intelligent witnesses brought before it *have proved* the " direct reverse." I will not trouble the reader with again going over the evidence, which appertains to this part of the subject; enough of it, I think, has already been brought within his view. For, whatever value Sir John Sinclair may think proper to attach to the *opinions* of the individuals, whom he has noticed as witnesses,

* P. 39, 40.

who *have proved* that our paper currency is not depreciated; their evidence, excepting indeed that of Mr. Harman, goes only to shew that in respect to the coin, it still retains its former value in the country, a circumstance of which we, in a manner, have daily experience. We certainly do still exchange a guinea (if we feel inclined or are compelled to part with it) for one and twenty shillings, and a pound note for twenty. But, on the other hand, can it be denied, that coin has both been melted down for the sake of the profit attending its sale in the form of bullion; and, in some instances, been actually bought in its coined state, at a price exceeding its value as mere coin, for the purpose of being melted down for home use or of transportation?

"But we are told," says Sir John Sinclair, as if it could be made a question, "that a reduction of paper circulation would diminish the price of provisions." "Would it not, however," he immediately asks, "in a still greater proportion, disable the great body of the people from having the means of purchasing them? Would not lower prices also have a tendency to discourage the growth of grain, and to damp the exertions of the farmer?"* Thus neglecting, it seems, the contemplation of the very necessary consequence of the case put before him; that, if the price of provisions be diminished, the same means, the same quantity of money, would not be requisite for purchasing them; that the price of provisions would be reduced in proportion to the reduction of the quantity of circulating medium; that, as the same demand for grain would exist as does at present the farmer, though under the necessity of selling it at a less nominal price, would sell it at an equal real price. He

* P. 41.

could not fail to perceive the increased value of the money which would be paid to him, and that the greater the produce of his land the greater must be his gains. How then would the growth of grain be discouraged, or the exertions of the farmer be in any manner damped?

Sir John Sinclair, however, proceeds :--- "the won-"der," says he, "is not that the provisions are "high, but that with such a war against such an enemy, "with armies in every quarter of the globe, and fleets "commanding every ocean in it, we should be able to "carry on our agriculture, manufactures, and commerce, "in the manner and to the extent we are doing."* And, as we have before seen, our ability to do all this he ascribes to the abundance of our circulating medium. "Nothing "else," he tells us, "gives us ability to go on but the abundance of our circulating medium, which operates like blood in the human frame, nourishing every part of the system, and enabling it to perform its functions."†

Little, little indeed, was it to have been expected that out of the bed of sickness, in which the good lady of Threadneedle Street long since lay prostrate,---at that alarming period when the legislature, it was feared, could scarce provide a remedy to keep her just live, should come forth a progeny, whose multiplied myriads would prove the very safeguard of our country,---to which we should owe our life, our glory, and our prosperity. If the expulsion of the precious metals, and the substitution of paper money in their stead, have really, in Sir John Sinclair's opinion, such effects as he here proclaims, it would have been well if he had explained in what manner, by what process, those effects are wrought ---it is not the common faculty of mankind which can discern it. But if we are not convinced, let us not be lulled

* P. 42. † Ibid.

into a belief that it is to our abundant paper currency we are indebted for the victualling and procuring ammunition for our fleets and armies, and for their glorious success against our enemies, for the cultivation of our fields, the working up of our manufactures, and carrying on our commerce, rather than to the fertility of our soil, the excellence of our machinery, and the skill and industry, the determined enterprize and courage, of the people. A notion how monstrous, and, at the same time, if generally adopted, how mischievous! Whatsoever other goodly effects may be ascribed to our present paper system, let these, at least, be ascribed to better and to nobler causes. The crane which lifts the goods from the warehouse, the shuttle which is cast by the weaver, nay, the very dung cart, which is driven across the field by the husbandman, are of far more intrinsic value than the whole pile of promissory notes, of which our paper currency consists; these are not the instrument, passive or active, that produces what is valuable. If they were annihilated to the very millionth part of their present amount, the same quantity of grain, and of meat, of clothing, and of every article of necessity, utility, and luxury, excepting perhaps that which is formed of the precious metals, might be produced, as is at present. How unaccountable is it that beings who are endowed with reason should not understand this.

We come now to the more immediate discussion of the measures recommended by the Committee,---but as if it were intended to stop us in the very threshold, and prevent all further question on the subject, the following branch of it is first to be decided: viz.

"*Is it practicable to open the Bank in two years?*" [P. 42.] And by way of establishing the negative, it is demanded, "since it was found necessary to prevent the payment of cash at the Bank of England, when the exchange was in our favour, and when the notes in circulation, including Bank post bills, amounted to the sum of only 8,640,250*l.* (which was the case on the 27th February, 1797,) how is it possible to remove the restriction when the amount of the Bank circulation is now stated by the Committee at 24,249,980*l.* making a difference of 12,609,730*l.*, besides an addition of at least 10,000,000*l.* by the paper of country Banks, and when the exchange is against us?" But if we can with any patience bear with such an argument as this, let us ask, why, in the name of common honesty, if the Bank of England could not pay in cash, when its issues amounted not to nine millions,---it has dared to increase its issues till they have amounted to more than one and twenty? It is, indeed, a sad and woful consideration that the Bank should have reduced itself to such a state. But let us not, therefore, neglect or be dismayed by it. Though the outstanding demand against the Bank of England be so much increased, though the price of gold and silver, the medium of payment, be so greatly enhanced, yet let us not, I say, despair of its ability to accomplish this so arduous an undertaking; not, indeed, by the means proposed by Sir John Sinclair, by exporting goods to the amount of twenty millions, and getting bullion to the same amount in return, for I fear means such as those would, most unquestionably, fail.---But by discontinuing the excessive issues which have heretofore of late been made. --By reducing the amount of discounts, nay, of advances to the government, if that, indeed, should be necessary, which it perhaps would not.---So, that at the end of two years, a competent portion of the notes, which are now in circulation, and of those which may be issued previously to tha period, being paid into the Bank by the persons to whom it has made, or may, in the mean time, make advances; such a proportion only of notes may remain in circulation as would, together with the species then also in circulation in the country, equal the quantity of species which would naturally be in circulation, in case there were no paper currency at all. As the circulating medium would be diminished, in quantity so would the price of silver and gold be diminished, in like manner as that of every other commodity. And thus would the Bank, when called upon, be enabled to procure them at a rate but little if at all exceeding the mint price. In fact, it should seem, no danger could arise to the bank, unless the amount of its issues should exceed the amount of its credits, which Sir John Sinclair would hardly contend to be the case. It is true, the profits of the Bank would, by these means, be considerably reduced. But its profits have already been sufficiently great. It is time they should no longer be enjoyed to the prejudice and detriment of others. Nay, indeed, if it should most unaccountably so happen (which, till it does, ought not, perhaps, to be supposed) that the market price of bullion should not fall exactly to a level with the mint price, notwithstanding the great diminution of the quantity of our present circulating medium;---I know not upon what ground of justice the Bank of England could complain, though it should ultimately be compelled to refund to the holder of its notes a part of those enormous gains, of which it has made no secret, and of which the following fact may enable us to judge. On the 27th February, 1797, the price of Bank stock was about 133 per cent. the 3*l*. per cent. Consol. Ann. being about 51 per cent. But, on the 2d November, 1809, the price of Bank stock was about 288 per cent. the 3*l*. per cent. Consol. Ann. being about 69¼. So much, of late, had the profits of the former been increased, by means of the circulation of its notes.

But the period, which by the Committee is recommended for opening the Bank, Sir John Sinclair seems to think ought not to be so limited; "the Committee itself," says he, "admit, that in the present state of our circulation it would be hazardous to compel the Bank to pay cash in six months, and acknowledge that it would be found wholly impracticable. They, therefore, recommend that, the space of two years should elapse before the restriction is removed."* But it is asked by Sir John Sinclair, "what reason have we to expect that the measure would be more practicable two years hence, than at present?" And by the mode which Sir John Sinclair would adopt, perhaps it never would be practicable; but by that which has been stated above, and which might, not unnaturally, have occurred to Sir John Sinclair on the perusal of the report, and the evidence upon which it is founded, the space of two years can hardly be considered as too confined. It is ample for the calling in of securities and for the forming of all the necessary arrangements, which would attend a recurrence to the old system. To allow of any needless long delay, would be productive of nothing else but mischief.

* P. 44.

With respect then to the next branch of this section,--- "*Would it be of any use to open the Bank for payment* "*in cash?*" [p. 45.]

"But were the measure practicable," Sir John Sinclair begins,--- "I do not see any possible advantage that "could be derived from it. The value of gold instead "of falling, must rise in consequence of the greater "demand for it; the exchange would only be affected "by it, in so far as the Bullion that was exported could "go, and not a step farther." This, however, it is to be observed, is all upon the supposition, that the Bank of England, instead of calling in its securities, and narrowing its issues, would continue to keep afloat the same quantity of paper as at present, which, indeed, might render it necessary for the Bank to purchase bullion at the present high price, in order to satisfy the demands which would perpetually be made upon it. But that, as was attempted to be shewn, would not be, if its securities were called in, and its issues sufficiently narrowed. On the contrary, the quantity of the whole circulating medium being by these means reduced to its natural level, the price of gold, together with that of all other articles, would be reduced accordingly. And the exchange, therefore, would naturally rise till it arrived at *par*, or at least would not continue below what the expense of transmitting the precious metals would warrant, how much soever the balance of trade and of payments with certain countries might happen then to be against us. The gold imported directly or indirectly from South America, or from the countries with which we carry on a favourable trade, would probably be ample for the settlement of our balances on the continent of Europe, so that it might at any time be purchased at the mint price, and transmitted to the continent, if requisite, at the expense only of the freightage and insurance against risk. And it may therefore, further be remarked, that in such be milled case it would be unnecessary to have recourse to the expedient of exporting our coin or the basis into which it may be melted; with a view to which Sir John Sinclair supposes an argument has been drawn, in favour of the measure proposed by the committee, and thence takes occasion to observe, "that there is a great fallacy in the "argument, that opening the bank, would improve the ex-"change, by the exportation of Bullion," because, forsooth, "by the existing laws, no gold can be exported, but in the "shape of foreign coinage or of bullion, not melted into "bars from the coin of this country."* To which, indeed, it might have been sufficient to have replied, that whatever the law may be, it is plain that guineas are exported, and that to a very considerable amount; else, whence is it that they have become so great a scarcity in our shops or our markets, as seldom to be seen? They cannot all be hoarded. From what has been said, however, it does not appear necessary, that much, if any gold coin should be sent from this country, for the purpose of improving the exchange. It would be improved, and necessarily, by that considerable reduction of our circulating medium, which would be the necessary consequence of the repeal of the law restricting cash payments at the Bank at the period recommended by the Committee. The Bank taking such precautions as common discretion may suggest.

* P. 45

"But compelling the bank to give gold and silver in ex-"change for notes," says Sir John Sinclair, "would "induce the nation in general to believe, that there "must be some considerable advantage in possessing "coin instead of paper." Yet is it not, surely, much more reasonable to think, that as soon as the nation shall perceive that the paper is at all times without difficulty exchangeable for coin, it will, on the contrary, more generally believe the one to be of equal value with the other? nay, is it not a thing almost unaccountable, even when every circumstance is considered, that the Bank of England should have been able, so well to support the credit of its notes, that they should still be, in general acceptance, of equal value with the coin itself? How long they may continue so, if the measures suggested by the committee, should be spurned at or resisted, we will not here stop to enquire.

At length, we arrive at the third branch of this section,---"*Whether it would not be, instead of an advantage, "a material detriment to the public, to open the Bank?*" [P. 47.]

"And here again," Sir John Sinclair refers to that passage in the evidence of Mr. Whitmore, which I have before had occasion partly to notice, viz. that "provided "it were imperative on the bank to open, he should "think a restriction of the bank issues, would be neces-"sary, notwithstanding the fatal consequences that "might arise from it, to the commerce and revenue of "the country," upon which Sir John Sinclair immediately observes, that "with this declaration from the "greatest practical authority, staring them in the face, "the committee do not scruple to recommend a mea-

" sure, that *would* be attended with fatal consequences " to the commerce and revenue of the country." Thus converting the uncertain, cautious, *might*, into the positive, the decisive *would*. And by a bold reiteration of the language, formerly employed, he asserts, " there " is nothing that speculative politicians, who entertain " a peculiar prejudice in favour of a particular doctrine, " will not approve of, if it has the effect of establishing " the system they wish to recommend. All the imme- " diate mischief is overlooked from the expectation of " future advantages which may never be realized." Thus apparently exemplifying the truth of the assertion. For what is there less worthy of approbation, than some of those doctrines which we are examining? the vast mischief which has already arisen from the depreciation of our currency, is overlooked from the expectation it seems, of I know not what advantages, but such as I suspect, ought, in justice, never to be realized.

Without stopping, however, to consider this mischief, Sir John Sinclair chooses rather to express astonishment at the coolness, as he is pleased to term it, with which one of the witnesses examined by the committee, " talks of individuals being put to an inconvenience, " by the want of the circulating medium; in other " words, as (according to Sir John Sinclair's construction) " of money to carry on their business," and hence an opportunity is seized of pathetically describing the situation of the merchant, who is unable to pay the demands, which are made upon him.

I do not, indeed, profess myself to be much conversant with the modes in which the business of our merchants is usually conducted. It may be true, and I believe it is so, that there are many who have occasionally some need of temporary advances, with the view of making purchases of merchandize, previous to the sale of such of their goods, as may be in their warehouses, or upon the seas. It may be their interest either to postpone the sale of those goods, with the hope of obtaining a better price for them hereafter, or to hasten the purchase of others, from the apprehension that the price of these may be enhanced. It is therefore easy to understand in what manner the merchant and the country at large, may be benefitted or injured by the facility of obtaining money for those purposes, and what is the nature of the convenience, referred to by the above-mentioned witness. Yet it may at the same time be questioned, whether by the gradual and judicious reduction of the notes of the Bank of England, by the iminution of their discounts, which would naturally tend to the reduction of the price of all merchandize whatever, any serious inconvenience at all would be felt by those individuals, to whom advances are now made, upon what are called "fair, mercantile transactions," supposing them to be such as I have just adverted to. But it seems on the other hand, somewhat difficult to understand,how such diminution of discounts by the Bank of England, should have the effect of rendering merchants, those thousands of respectable individuals, to whom Sir John Sinclair has alluded, unable, as he supposes, to pay the demands upon them, and of thus reducing their wives and their families, and a number of their dearest connexions, to beggary and ruin.* There must be some other cause besides the diminution of discounts to work such an effect as this. The Trader may be unfortunate,---he may bring his goods to a bad market,---he may be undersold and lose a part of his accustomed profit,---nay, he may lose his whole cargo, by wreck or by capture at sea. But what ought the bank to have to do with all this, and what in fact has it? It cannot be our wish, that foreign goods should be sold here at a price the highest possible. It is no great essential service to the public, to support our merchants in their enormous gains, when drawn from the public purse. And if a trader lose his cargo, it is not the Bank of England that will discount his bills upon such a security, as the wreck or the chance of a timely recapture may afford. Why then imagine such sad effects would be the consequence of the diminution of bank discounts;---such dire distress to thousands of respectable individuals?---Is it with promissory notes that they are all actually fed and clothed? Or is every one, who seeks occasion to borrow, at a time when, if prudent and intent upon moderate gains only, he possesses ample means of conducting his business with safety and regularity, though he borrow not a shilling, to become bankrupt, because he should find but few who have money to lend him? That such distresses as are likely to be occasioned by the diminution of bank discounts, should be regarded as nothing more than inconveniences, and that such inconveniences should be talked of with coolness, is natural enough; but that the ruin of thousands of respectable individuals should be the consequence of that diminution, seems hardly to be credited. What

* P. 49.

prudent merchant will suffer from it? What injury will it do the public at large? Perchance, indeed, it may put a check to monopolies and other adventurous speculations, and prevent the ruin of many families.

But the inconveniences to arise from the restriction of the bank issues, would not, in Sir John Sinclair's opinion, be confined to commercial men. "The landed "and farming interests," he says, "would suffer, per-"haps, in a still greater degree. They are at present," he adds, "enabled to go on, notwithstanding the "increased expense of cultivation, and the pressure "of heavy taxes, in consequence of the additional prices, "which their commodities fetch, and the facility with "which they obtain payments, *owing to the abundance* "*of the circulating medium.*" So it seems that even Sir John Sinclair himself, is pretty well aware, that the currency has suffered some depreciation, by reason of its abundance. Yet observe, what further he says upon the subject. "But if the taxes remain as "they are, and if, in consequence of the diminution "of the circulating medium, their commodities should "become unsaleable, except at low prices, and with "payments either distant or uncertain, *the agricultural* "*interest would be undone*;" adding that "to this "important subject, I earnestly request their par-"ticular attention, before it is too late." "Let "them recollect that they are fully as much inte-"rested as any other class of the community, in keep-"ing up an abundant, rather than a diminished medium "of circulation." [P. 49, 50.] Now, although it be true, that if the circulating medium were considerably reduced in quantity, the landed and farming interests would be unable to maintain the present high price of grain and other produce of their land; yet let it be remembered, that the whole produce of their land would not thereby be lessened; that the poor's-rates, the price of labour, of horses, and implements of husbandry, and of all manufactured goods, and all articles of consumption, would be proportionally diminished. With regard, indeed, to the taxes, supposing them to continue as they are, as the nominal income of those classes would be reduced, those duties which do not fall within the description of *ad valorem* duties, might, in effect, press somewhat more heavily upon the owners and cultivators of land than they do at present; yet, in respect to the former, not comprising in themselves the latter character, it is probable that the advantage they would derive from an increase in the value of money, and, consequently, of their stipulated rents, would far exceed what they now enjoy in consequence of any partial evasion of taxes, by reason of the depreciation of money. What heavy loss has been sustained by landlords of every description since the period of the restriction on cash payments at the Bank, in consequence of that depreciation, may easily be conceived from the prodigious rise which has taken place in the rent of land and of houses throughout all parts of the kingdom. The total amount of the several differences between the amount of rent actually paid, and the value of the land or houses computed, from time to time, according to the amount of rent which, for the time being, could have been obtained for them, is the amount of the loss which each landlord has sustained in the single article of rent.

But is it become a mere question of interest between different classes of the people, who shall contribute least to the service of the state? Would the landed and farming interests put conscience aside, and strive to throw the chief burthen of maintaining our government and our laws, the independence and glory of the nation, upon those who have fixed annuities, or capital, on mortgage, or in the funds? Would they wish favour to themselves and iniquity to others? Or have they eyes of compassion for the rich self-distressing merchant; but will not weep for the poor worn-down, helpless, mechanic, or common labourer, who, by the skill of his hand, or the sweat of his brow, had earned some small provision for his declining years? Will they turn obdurate from the widow and the orphan, well nigh bereft of their scanty pittance? Will they exult in the niggardly allowance which is doled out to those whose blood has been shed, and whose limbs have been sacrificed in the stubborn defence of their country? Will they indulge in no liberal feeling for those men of learning and mental skill whose days, and much of whose nights, have been devoted to most anxious pursuits, and whose long-delayed success in their avocations, has at length procured them but slender means of maintaining their families in decent independence? Will they see, without compunction, useful members of society, from time to time, despoiled of the property they rightfully possessed, and console themselves with the thought, that it is they themselves who wrongfully participate in the spoil? Why, in common justice, is the property of the stock-holder,* the mortgagee, or the annuitant, perpetually to be deteriorated by this continued excess of paper currency? On what principle of right, or of policy, are the owner and cultivator of land to stand exempt from the charge of contributing equally, not nominally, but really and effectually, for the service of the state? In vain will they endeavour to maintain the credit of an excessive paper currency. In vain will the legislature, looking partially to the interest of the landowner and the farmer, by its severe compulsory edicts, declare the Bank-note a legal tender to all intents and purposes. Like the paper of Revolutionary France, it will fall till it become merely nothing-worth. The total destruction of public credit will ensue, and men generally will regard less what has hitherto been deemed right, than what they will feel absolutely necessary. The landed and the farming interests will not then, perhaps, stand secure from all assault. But let us, for a while, turn from a spectacle so disgusting,---let us not yet imagine evils, for the prevention of which, I trust, the legislature will speedily provide most effectual remedies,---such as the common honesty, the common prudence, if not the disinterested patriotism of the country at large, will, upon mature deliberation, unanimously approve. For I will not think so meanly of the proprietors of land as to suppose them capable of intentionally shrinking from the burthen which we all, according to our respective abilities, should be forward to sustain.

From the splendid view, indeed, which the author before us has permitted his imagination to take of the

* It is unnecessary, perhaps, to say, that I exclude from this description the proprietor of Bank Stock.

subject of our abundant paper currency, he has brought his mind to contemplate, and, it seems, would alarm us with the apprehension of the many mischievous effects, which a diminished medium of circulation might have on the public revenue and credit of the country. "If," says he, "our circu-"lating medium were reduced one-half, (which must be "the case if the bank were opened) the revenue would "fall in proportion." And, he adds, "It would then "be necessary either to diminish the interests of "the public funds to one-half, or to dismiss one-half "of our fleets and armies." Now, granting for the sake of argument, that if the banks were opened for cash payments, the circulating medium should, as Sir John Sinclair asserts, be reduced one-half, a circumstance, by the bye, which would sufficiently prove the propriety of opening the Bank, how is it that the revenue must also be reduced one-half? Part of the revenue which arises from *ad valorem* duties, no doubt might be thus reduced; but not so the revenue which arises otherwise; nay, that which arises from the duty on property, which is an *ad valorem* duty, would not be reduced in this proportion; since a considerable part of that property consists of stock in the public funds, the proprietors of which would, upon the whole, contribute as much as, nay more than, they do at present to the revenue of the state.

From the method, which of late years has wisely been adopted, of raising a large portion of the necessary supplies within the year, or of providing for the speedy repayment of the sums which are borrowed, by means of the heavy duty upon property, the additional permanent charge which has been created, by way of interest upon the public debt, since the depreciation of our currency, in consequence of the suspension of cash payments by the Bank, is much less than it would have been, had the former method been exclusively resorted to. The revenue, therefore, originally made applicable to the discharge of the interest upon the public debt, might still be nearly sufficient for that purpose, though the circulating medium were reduced to its just level, and that the rather, by reason of the great improvement which appears to have taken place in the trade and commerce of the country. But if any should yet entertain apprehensions that the revenue would prove insufficient, it is to be remembered, that the funds now appropriated for the purpose of reducing the public debt, might be made subservient, in the first instance, to the purpose of making good the deficiency; an expedient, however, which ought not to be adopted without mature deliberation.

But it is further to be observed, that if the circulating medium were to be reduced one-half, or, in other words, if the price of commodities, exclusive of the duties that might be payable on them, were to be reduced in that ratio, the necessary expense of maintaining our fleets and armies, nay, the necessary salaries to the several officers of government, might be proportionally diminished; and, consequently, a much smaller revenue than is at present requisite for those purposes would then be sufficient, without any way diminishing in effect, the energy, or splendour of the state.

The notion, however, that the circulating medium

would be reduced one-half if the Bank were opened at the end of two years, as recommended by the Committee, may be thought somewhat extravagant, when it is considered what was its probable amount long previous to the restriction of payments in cash, and composed, as in a great measure it then was, of species, as well as notes. Be that, however, as it may, in no case does it appear that the dilemma, which Sir John Sinclair has been pleased to put before us, would in reality exist. And, after all, should it be proved that the resources of the country would be inadequate to the maintenance of the power and authority of the state, unless the heavy load of debt, which at present incumbers it, should, in part, be cancelled.---The sacrifice, I repeat it, ought to be ordained upon just principles, not iniquitously confined to the creditors of the public, and others of fixed incomes, or capitals, in money.

But it is not with the feigned dilemma alone which Sir John Sinclair has brandished, that he would alarm us; he would terrify us also with the notion, that if the restrictions were removed the Bank could never be enabled to advance any money on the loan of the year. But if, as Sir John Sinclair supposes, the circulating medium should, in consequence of the removal of the restriction, be reduced one-half, and the price of the commodities should fall proportionally, the loans which might be required would not exceed in amount the half of what are required under the circumstance of an excessive currency like the present, and yet be full as efficacious, whilst, at the same time, an equal facility of providing them would exist. And wherefore should not the Bank of England advance them, as it has advanced them heretofore? Or should it so ill consult its own interest, to refuse such assistance to the government, wherefore might not other modes be speedily devised, equally advantageous to the government, though much less so to the present Bank?

Upon the whole, therefore, notwithstanding the probable decrease in the revenue, which a diminution of the circulating medium would occasion, (for the risk of injuring or affecting the system of our public loans, and the means of providing for our public expenditure, which is apprehended by Sir John Sinclair, seems nothing but ideal) it seems to be a great deal too much to assert, without much more proof than is to be found amongst the Observations which have been examined, ---" That the suggestions of the Bullion Committee, if " carried into effect, would do more mischief to the " British Empire than the fleets and armies of Napoleon " will ever be able to accomplish,"* how small soever that, I trust, will be. Whilst, on the other hand, it seems there is strong ground for reasonable apprehension, that if those suggestions, or others of a tendency equally efficacious, are not carried into effect without much further delay, our manufactories will be abandoned, our commerce prove unproductive, and public credit be altogether ruined.

But to come in due form to the

" *Conclusion.*" [P. 52.]

In which Sir John Sinclair states his full conviction, " That if Parliament will consider the measures proposed " by the Bullion Committee as perfectly unnecessary, " and will resolve to maintain the present system of cir- " culation unimpaired, there will be no difficulty in " finding pecuniary resources for carrying on the war in

* P. 10. 51. 52.

" which we are at present engaged, for as many years " as may be essential for our safety." And, " On the " other hand, that if we attempt to overturn our present " system of circulation, and to try any new experiments " with our paper currency, it would occasion mutual dis- " trust, and would create a want of confidence in the " stability of our resources, and thence would be pro- " ductive of such scenes, both of internal misery and " external weakness, as would terminate in general anar- " chy and total ruin."

If the grounds of these several convictions, which I have already with some care endeavoured to scrutinize, as yet, to the reader, appear hardly tenable, when we come to examine the Appendix, they will, perhaps, appear still less so. In short, the theory upon which Sir John Sinclair would build his system for procuring resources for carrying on an eternal warfare seems, in effect, nothing better than, by the partial and arbitrary cancellation of interest upon our old debts to provide for the temporary payment of interest upon our new debts,--- these, in their turn, to be cancelled in like manner as the former. Nay, the very apprehension which he entertains for the consequences of overturning our present system of circulation seems to betray a consciousness of its want of stability and inherent durability. No such scenes as he imagines could arise were our currency, as it ought to be, composed of the precious metals, or of paper immediately convertible into them. By adopting the measures proposed by the Committee, such would our currency speedily become. We have distantly been witnesses of the dire effects of a paper currency, upheld by successive governments, though most ruinous to the people. We have seen how it originated, and with horror have observed its progress. We have seen but too nearly, that in consequence of temporary and partial calamities, indiscreet arrangements, or extraordinary emergencies, it was expedient for our own government, near fourteen years ago, to declare the Bank of England exempt from the liability of paying their promissory notes in cash, at a time when the exchange was favourable to us, when the market price of gold was lower than the mint price, when the number of country banks, it is believed, was only *two hundred and thirty*, when the amount of paper of the Bank of England then in circulation, scarce exceeded *eight millions and a half.** Since that period the rate of exchange has fallen so low as *fifteen*, nay *twenty* per cent. against us; the market-price of gold has risen *fifteen or twenty* per cent. above the mint price; the number of country banks, it is believed, has been increased to *seven hundred and twenty-one*; and the paper of the Bank of England alone has been augmented to nearly *one and twenty millions and a half.*† In the mean time the advance in the price of provisions has been most rapid, alarming, and distressing to multitudes of the people. The people are not blind to all this.---Surely the Parliament cannot remain blind to it.---Let the Parliament then take heed.---" *Ne aliquid detrimenti* " *respublica capiat.*"

---

* P. 46 Accounts.—But the average amount for a few years preceding was between ten and eleven millions.

† P. 48. ib.

We have previously had occasion to touch upon some of the principles with which Sir John Sinclair has been pleased to present us in the form of an Appendix.

" ON THE GENERAL NATURE OF COIN, OR MONEY, " AND THE ADVANTAGES OF PAPER CIRCULATION." [P. 53.]

In the examination of this Appendix, therefore, it is not to be expected that the reader should be indulged with matter that is perfectly new. The same principles will lead to the same conclusions. The same line of argument will be applied to the same topics. But as it is in this Appendix that we are to look for the sources of those doctrines, upon the authority of which the measure proposed by the Committee is so vehemently condemned, and the present system of paper currency modified, indeed, in some respect is so highly to be applauded, it demands our more particular attention.

We have already noticed what are the author's conceptions with regard to the precious metals in the early ages of society, and what are the three important purposes which they answer. We have also been apprized of his sentiments regarding a well-regulated paper currency; how, in ages of civilization and refinement, it is, with a small proportion of the precious metals in a state of coinage, equally useful, indeed, on many accounts, more advantageous. But it is fit we should here take a nearer view of his doctrines upon this subject.

" Money," says Sir John Sinclair, " (by which is " meant a well-regulated paper currency, with a small

" proportion of coin) becomes in a civilized state of " society the medium of barter, both for labour and " goods, and, in a manner, the source or basis of public " revenue. It is necessary, therefore," he adds, " to " preserve *a due proportion* between its amount, and " 1. the quantity of labour that must be paid for; 2. " the quantity of goods or merchandize, the property of " which must be transferred; and, 3. the total amount " of the demands and expenses of the Exchequer, whe- " ther arising from taxes, public loans, or any extraor- " dinary species of contribution."

Now it may be difficult to collect from this statement, formal as it is, but not so simple as it ought to be, presented in the form of principles, what is the author's true idea of money, so described, in a civilized state of society. It is a medium of barter, both for labour and goods; in other words, it is a token, whereby the holder of it may obtain from any one labour, or a commodity equal in value to the labour or the commodity, which the holder has performed for, or rendered to another. But how is this the source or basis of public revenue? It seems, according to the common acceptation of the terms, to be neither one nor the other, any more than it is the source or basis of private income. 'Tis true the owner of land lets it to the farmer for money; the farmer sells the various produce of the land, the manufacturer the several pieces of his workmanship, each of them for money; but land and labour, therefore, not money, are the source or basis of their wealth and their revenue; and so too the land and labour are, in like manner, the source or basis of the public revenue of a country. But money is the medium by which the produce of the land and labour is circulated; it is the instrument by which the resources are conducted and applied to their appointed purposes. Money, therefore, is the article in which the taxes are paid, as being the means by which all other commodities, and labour itself, of every kind, are to be obtained. We shall soon see to what erroneous conclusions the principles of Sir John Sinclair will lead him.

But to proceed orderly to the first and second positions, that "*it is necessary* to preserve *a due proportion* between, "1st. the amount of money and the quantity of labour "that must be paid for; and, 2dly, the quantity of "goods or merchandize, the property of which must be "transferred." Now, if by a due proportion he meant a certain fixed ratio between several quantities, as a general principle, this does not appear to be correct; and will, in fact, be found to be at variance with Sir John Sinclair's own doctrines. The quantity of labour, in consequence of the increased industry of the inhabitants, or of increased population itself, may be increased, which would of course produce an increase in the quantity of goods or merchandize, yet need there, of necessity, be no increase in the absolute quantity of money. The mines may fail, and only a limited quantity of paper money might be allowed; perchance there might be none at all. On the other hand, the quantity of labour and of goods or merchandize may be diminished, whilst the quantity of money may remain the same, or be increased. It is true, the relative value of money would, under these circumstances, be altered; any given portion of it would purchase a greater or a less quantity of labour and goods than the same portion of it would have purchased prior to the increase or diminution of the quantity of labour and goods, as the case might be; but that hardly proves the necessity whatever might be the general utility of preserving the same relative quantity of money in every case.

With regard, then, to the 3d position, that it is necessary to preserve a due proportion between the amount of money "and the total amount of the demands and expenses of the Exchequer," it seems that the order of things is here a little inverted, and that we should rather read, that it is necessary to preserve a due proportion between the total amount of the demands and expenses of the Exchequer, and the amount of money in circulation, or, in other words, the price of goods in general. For, let us suppose that the circulating medium of a country amounts to forty millions of pounds sterling, and the government requires ten millions annually for the public service; that sum is raised, we will say, by a tax upon the inhabitants, equal to one-tenth of their income;---of what real utility, if this tax be intended to operate fairly, is any addition to the circulating medium likely to prove? When it is stated that ten millions are requisite for the public service, the efficacy of this sum of ten millions is estimated upon the supposition that the price of labour and merchandize continues the same, and therefore will not be sufficient, if the price of labour and merchandize be augmented. If the circulating medium be increased in proportion to the increase of the taxes, whilst the quantity of goods remains the same---the taxes, previously imposed, will be rendered less availing, and, consequently, a necessity will arise of imposing still further taxes upon the people; and hence it would soon be found, that such increase of the circulating medium afforded neither the people nor the government any real aid whatsoever, excepting in the case o which it is proper that I should advert.

In states, indeed, where money is raised by way of loan, payable at a distant period, with interest in the mean time, or by way of perpetual annuity, it is clear that, supposing the quantity of goods to be increased, but the quantity of money to remain the same, the public would pay more than in strict justice they ought, were they to repay the very sum originally advanced for their service. And so, on the other hand, would they pay less than they ought, if the relative quantity of money were to be increased.

It is somewhat remarkable, that Sir John Sinclair, after having stated as a principle, that it is necessary to preserve such due proportion, as above noticed, should presently add this qualification: "The quantity of the "medium of circulation, however, instead of being "stationary, ought to be increasing. 1st. To promote "a greater quantity of labour, which," he observes, "is "always increasing where a circulating medium abounds. "2d. To facilitate the transfer of a greater quantity of "goods." "3d. To enable the people to furnish, without "inconvenience, greater supplies to the Exchequer." But that we might not be left to guess in what manner, physical or moral, the increase of the circulating medium promotes any greater quantum of labour,---a notion which the examples of Spain and Portugal notoriously contradict,---and by way of informing us how a pound-note, which can purchase only the fourth-part of a quarter of wheat, facilitates its transfer more than ten shillings formerly facilitated it, when it might have been purchased for that price,---and that we might not remain totally ignorant with regard to the true equitable proportions in which the various classes of people ought to contribute to the service of the state---the author proceeds to apply "these" his own "general principles, 1, to the case of an *increased* quantum of labour; 2, to an *increased* commerce in a transfer of goods; and 3, to an *increased* revenue, &c. concluding with some observations on circulation and paper currency."

With respect to the first, "*The increased quantum of labour.*" [P. 55.] Sir John Sinclair observes, that "an "increased medium of circulation, is of more consequence, "with a view of facilitating the convenient payment of "labour, and furnishing the credit or capital necessary for that purpose, than, perhaps, in any other respect." He admits it is true, "that labour properly applied is the "basis of national prosperity." Yet when he adds, "but "who will labour unless by his exertions he can be fur-"nished with the necessaries he may require, *which can* "*only be effected through the medium of an abundant cir-"culation?*" He spoils a fair passage by its conclusion. *Desinit in piscem mulier formosa supernè.* For if, without any further increase of circulating medium, that which exists is already sufficient for the payment of such labour as is demanded, what advantage can arise from the merely ideal additional facility which any further increase of that medium may afford? If labourers are to be obtained at the rate of ten shillings a week, what benefit to them, or to the country, though their employers should be rendered capable of paying, and should actually pay them fourteen, if, with those fourteen, they can purchase no more bread and meat, no better lodging and clothes, than they before could with ten? What additional quantity of commodities the increased labour of the people can furnish would, if the mines continued to yield their accustomed produce, and the commerce were open, naturally attract an additional quantity of circulating medium. But if this be, in the first instance, introduced, the natural consequence is an increase in the price without a necessary increase in the produce of labour. And though the industry of a nation should be on the advance, and, consequently, the quantity of its merchandize be increasing accordingly; yet it, nevertheless, should fail to draw towards it an additional quantity of the circulating medium; or if the former should increase in a greater proportion than the latter, the relative value of this would be increased proportionally. So that, in either case, there would be sufficient means for discharging the wages of labour, however considerable in effect they might be.

It seems to have been an error into which many other persons besides Sir John Sinclair have fallen, but which I thought, ere this, had nearly been exploded, to suppose that, if the medium of circulation be diminished, the interest paid for the use of it must be higher than if it continued as abundant as it is at present. That the medium itself must acquire an increase of value from being scarce is true; but so also must the interest which is payable for the use of it, and exactly in the same proportion. It, therefore, appears quite unreasonable and inconsistent to suppose that the same proportion should not be observed in the regulation of the rate of interest, whether twenty or fifty millions of money were to be employed in the circulation of a given quantity of goods. For it is not the great or the small nominal amount of the money, which may be in circulation, that renders it in this respect plentiful or scarce,--- its plenty or scarcity depends rather on the great or small unemployed capital, measured by the quantity of productive labour which it can purchase.

The question, therefore, whether money is to be obtained at a high or a low rate of interest, depends rather upon another circumstance than that of its great nominal amount, viz. upon what may be the profit of money employed as active capital. If labour is to be procured cheap, the profit of the capital, by means of which the labour is rendered productive, is great, and a high rate of interest, therefore, can be afforded for the loan of that capital. On the contrary, where hands are scarce, the profit upon capital is small, and, consequently, a low rate of interest only can be afforded for the loan of it in such case. And, hence it matters not much, in this point of view, what may be the nominal amount of the circulating medium, but what the quantity of productive labour which can be procured. Whether, therefore, it be a "temporary command of money that is required," "for "common commercial purposes," or "with a view of "effecting lasting improvements," that money be required for a long period of time;---the rate of interest (notwithstanding Sir John Sinclair conceives it ought, in the latter case, to be moderate) cannot depend much upon the amount of the circulating medium. New roads, harbours, mines, buildings, together with all the various branches of agricultural improvements, which he has specified and alluded to, may be as speedily and profitably undertaken, though there be no increase whatsoever in its quantity, provided labourers are to be had, and there is capital to employ them.

Sir John Sinclair, however, insists that there cannot be a more mistaken opinion than " that the prosperity of a country depends but little on the quantum of its medium of circulation;" and he asserts, that " an industrious nation must prosper in proportion to the quantity it possesses or circulates." [P. 56.] But how does he set about to prove this? Why, he supposes the total circulation of Great Britain to be forty millions sterling, in coin and in paper, bearing an interest of 5 per cent. " Then," says he, " if it were reduced to thirty millions, bearing an interest of 6 per cent. how much would not the industry of the nation be cramped? Whereas, were it raised to fifty millions, bearing an interest of 4 per cent. and the whole of it actively employed in various industrious pursuits, it cannot be doubted that the prosperity of the country would increase with a celerity, and be carried to a height which would not otherwise have been attainable." Thus taking for granted what is positively denied, both upon principles of reason and experience. The question we have already considered upon the former ground, and we have only to contemplate what is passing before us to satisfy us upon the latter. Has not our circulating medium been, of late years, prodigiously increased? Yet, has not the rate of interest continued as high as the law permits? It is strange that, with such facts immediately before his eyes, Sir John Sinclair should have ventured on such an argument. The truth is, an industrious nation will prosper however small may be the quantity of its circulating medium, unless there be other causes to counteract the natural effect of its industry. The smaller the quantity of this medium, the lower is the money price of labour, and the less, therefore, is the capital necessary for employing it. The efficacy of capital is inversely as the quantity of money in circulation.

Next as to " *Increase of Commerce.*" [P. 57.]

When we are told by Sir John Sinclair, that " nothing can be more evident than that an increased commerce, or the transfer of an increased quantity of goods cannot be carried on to advantage without an increased medium of barter; if we had not before had occasion to doubt such very evident propositions, we might have been fearful of expressing any doubt on this. But how shall we believe that it is not advantageous to one industrious nation to export the surplus of its produce to another, after retaining sufficient for its own supply and consumption, how much soever that surplus may, from time to time, be increased, and to receive in return an equivalent of the surplus produce of the latter; even though there should be no increase of the circulating medium in either of the countries so trading with each other? Is it not most evident that such commerce is highly advantageous to both?

Sir John Sinclair, however, admits that, " to a certain extent commerce itself furnishes this increased medium of barter by means of bills of exchange, and the rapid circulation of money which they occasion." " But still," he adds, " that accommodation is not sufficient, and commerce has experienced, and must experience, frequent checks, unless there is at all times plenty of money in circulation in proportion to its increase or extent." In answer to which latter observation, it is enough to remind the reader of those circumstances which seem chiefly to occasion a demand for money on the part of the merchant, and a consequent advance to him.* The reader will hardly be of opinion that they are such as imperiously demand any increase of the circulating medium, beyond its true natural level. Cases, indeed, of rare emergency, may arise, when it may become expedient to uphold, in a special manner, the manufacturing and mercantile interests of a nation; but these ought not to be permitted to grow into use. In ordinary times the extreme facility of obtaining large sums of money, in consequence of its depreciation, which Sir John Sinclair so approves, seems, upon the whole, to be of no essential benefit whatever. He is aware of the ready reply that may be made to his doctrine, in favour of an increased medium of circulation, as being requisite for the merchant, to enable him to bear up against the checks which he may sustain,---"Let him sell his goods cheaper, "and he will always find a market;" and observes, therefore, that "unless the sale of merchants' goods is attended not only with indemnification, but with profit, there must be an end to commerce; and, unless a merchant can procure money on loan, until a sale can be made on fair aud adequate terms, he may be ruined." But may it not justly be presumed, that the loss upon one speculation would be made up by the success of another? Or is it really to be desired, I mean by the community at large, that the profits of the merchant should be more than what upon general average are fair and reasonable? Nay, Sir John Sinclair himself, in the

* See p. 61, Sup.

very next passage to that which we have been just examining, allows, that all the encouragement of speculation that is wished for is, " that merchants may have " the command of money at the legal interest of 5 per " cent. when they have occasion for it, and can produce " good security." But the question whether money may be obtained at that rate, or a higher or a lower, does not, if the foregoing observations on that subject be correct, depend only, as Sir John Sinclair supposes, upon the quantity of money in circulation, but on causes altogether different? How great soever may be the increase of the circulating medium, it follows not that the rate of interest would, in the smallest degree, be diminished in consequence of that increase. Whether it be not desirable that the quantity of the circulating medium in a country, conditioned as this is, should be increased in proportion to the increase of the quantity of merchandize or commodities which it is employed to circulate, is another question, which, perhaps, it may be requisite hereafter to consider.

With regard then to " *Increased Revenue.*" [P. 58.]

In this curious subdivision, curious on account of the matter it contains, it is first stated, in words somewhat different from those which we have already noticed,* that " the public revenue of a country, unless derived " from property in land, evidently arises from the goods " or merchandize, or the value thereof, which the individuals of a nation can furnish, after supplying them" selves with the necessaries and conveniences, and, " what some would call, even the luxuries of life;"--- but it is then immediately added, that " after a public " revenue has reached a certain standard, let us suppose

* See p. 46, Sup.

" that ten millions of additional income is necessary for " the public exigencies: how," we are asked, " is that " sum to be raised, without, 1, more goods or wealth; " or, 2, a higher price for them; or, 3, a greater faci- " lity of barter, by means of an increased medium of " circulation ?"

Now, though Sir John Sinclair admits, and strange should he not, that " an additional quantity of goods, to a cer- " tain extent, may be obtained by greater industry and " improvements in agriculture and other arts;" yet he contends that, " unless there is a more extended mar- " ket for them, the price diminishes, and the result " proves, on the whole, rather a loss than an advantage " to the community." But whilst commerce is free, or not fettered by a barbarous policy, are not markets always to be found, in which, whatever may be the additional quantity of goods which the industry and skill of a people may enable them to produce, they will never fail to be purchased? I speak not of times like the present, when the rulers of empires will sacrifice the common interests of nations, and, in order to accomplish an injury to their enemy, voluntarily court ruin to themselves; but of ordinary times, when the general interests of civilized society are mutually respected by states warring with each other.

Yet, though no more extended markets should be provided for such additional quantity of goods as is here supposed, observe how it is attempted to be proved, that a loss rather than an advantage results to the community;---it is thus:---" Let us sup-

"pose," says Sir John Sinclair, "that the goods annu-"ally produced in the United Kingdom are worth one "hundred millions sterling per annum; if the quantity "were increased one-fifth, and if the price were low-"ered in proportion, we should not, *in a pecuniary point "of view*, be one farthing richer; and, in regard to "finance, the people at large would, in fact, be less "able than before to furnish supplies to the Exchequer. "All the classes of the community, by whose industry "the goods were made and brought to market, would "not be able to pay near so much as they did before, "and would necessarily be impoverished." But is it not plain, (as the reader has already had occasion more than once to consider) that if, as is here supposed, the increase in the quantity of goods is the cause of the diminution of price, the less will be the amount of the additional revenue required---that the old revenue, continuing the same in amount, will be more effective than when the price of goods was higher? that if the circulating medium amounted to twenty millions, and the value of that medium, in consequence of the increase in the quantity of goods, were raised one-fifth, and the price of goods were proportionally lowered, instead of ten millions, the sum, according to the former value of money requisite for the public service, eight millions only would thenceforth be requisite for the same purpose;* and, consequently, that the various classes of the community might be exonerated from the nominal amount of the former taxes in the same proportion? And hence is it not plain that none would be impoverished in the manner which Sir John Sinclair would lead us to

* I here leave out of consideration the circumstance of interest being payable upon a public debt, and confine myself to the case, as simply stated by Sir John Sinclair.

imagine; though all would, doubtless, be essentially benefited by the increased industry and produce of the country?

It would, indeed, have been a curious phænomenon in political economy, that the increased industry and improvements in the agriculture and other arts of a nation, should be rather a loss than an advantage to it; and that, because they possibly may not, in a pecuniary point of view, make it one farthing the richer, they may not make it substantially richer in all the additional wealth which increased industry and improvements are ever capable of affording.

2. To proceed, however, to Sir John Sinclair's second supposition.---" Let us next suppose," says he, " that " the quantity of goods remains the same, but that " the price increases one-fifth; the amount of the an- " nual income of the nation would then rise from one " hundred to one hundred and twenty millions in value, " and there would be a much larger fund for paying the " demands of the public!" But here also is the like fallacy in reasoning,---for is it not clear, that if ten millions were requisite for the purposes of government, when one hundred millions only were the amount of the circulating medium, one-fifth more, or twelve millions, would be requisite for the same purposes, when the price of commodities were increased one-fifth,---and that each individual would pay one-fifth more in money, not only by way of taxes, but for every article of which he might stand in need?

3. Still, however, Sir John Sinclair persists with another, his third supposition, *viz.* " That the

" price not only increases, but there is also an ad-
" ditional quantity of the medium of transfer, by which
" a good market or rapid sale is secured. The country
" is then," Sir John Sinclair proclaims, " in the highest
" possible state of prosperity." Indeed!---Yes. For
" abundance of merchandize, at a high price and a rapid
" sale, constitutes the summit of national felicity, in so
" far as regards income or revenue; and a nation enjoy-
" ing such advantages can pay, without difficulty, taxes,
" to an amount that seems hardly credible to nations which
" have not been placed in the same situation." Now, though abundance of merchandize and a rapid sale may, indeed, in a great measure contribute to national prosperity, in so far as regards income or revenue, whether private or public;---yet, the prosperity of a country, in regard to its income or revenue, is not to be measured by the numerical amount of that income or revenue alone, but by the quantity of service and commodities which it will purchase; for of what importance is income or revenue, except with reference to the services or commodities it enables us to obtain? Its sole utility depends upon the quantity of these which it can command. It is, therefore, somewhat hard to discover, though the revenue be never so large, in respect to its nominal amount, how it is preferable to one that is smaller, if the same services and commodities can be procured by means of this as of that. Surely our statesmen are not more eminent for their wisdom or their virtue,---our judges for their learning and integrity,---our fleets and armies better disciplined and equipped, because eggs and butter bear a higher price?

In proportion to the increase of the relative quantity of the circulating medium must the taxes, for the common purposes of government, be increased. In states, therefore, where there is no public debt, the depreciation of money is, on the whole, no way conducive to the easy payment of taxes: it is so only where such depreciation operates in like manner as a cancellation of the debt. As to the facility, therefore, which any additional quantity of circulating medium,---one of the splendid advantages to which Sir John Sinclair alludes,---can afford for the payment of taxes; it can afford no facility whatsoever which is not detrimental to the interest of, and in some degree proportionate to the injury sustained by, the public creditor. But is this the advantage which enables a nation enjoying it to "pay, without difficulty, taxes to an amount hardly credible to nations which have not been placed in the same situation?" Shame upon the nation which would intentionally aim at such an advantage! which would deprive, defraud, the public creditor of a fair equivalent for the advances which he has made for the service of the state in times of difficulty and danger! an ignoble conduct! a violation of the principles of justice, of honor, and of policy! a practice most studiously and anxiously to be avoided.

To these effects of a depreciated currency no one, who for a moment considers, can be blind. Sir John Sinclair is himself aware of them, of how small importance soever he seems to hold them. "Those with fixed incomes," says he, "may, in some respects, suffer, but," to console them, he adds, "they are sufficiently in-"demnified by the certainty and the regularity with "which those incomes are paid; the high price "which their capitals, either in the funds or in "land, fetches; and the easiness with which they can

" obtain credit, or capital to increase their wealth by " industry." Sufficiently indemnified! sufficiently indemnified for the loss of the third, or the half part of their property! And if the system be continued, for the loss perhaps of two-thirds, three-fourths, nay, of the highest fractional part of every pound which they possess! Is the certainty and regularity with which the remainder may be paid, and the high nominal, but low real profitable price at which they may sell their capitals in the funds: even supposing that price in any degree to depend upon the quantity of the circulating medium, -- is the ease with which they may obtain credit or capital to an enormous nominal amount, but no more effectual, than that which they can obtain at present; nay, not so much---for the security which they could afford would not in reality be so great---to be held out as a sufficient indemnity for such severe and heavy loss as has just been intimated? What though our land, if we have any, should be sold fifty or an hundred, nay, a thousand per cent. above its cost to us;---if the difference proceed only from the depreciated state of the currency in which we receive payment for it; are we therefore foolishly to fancy ourselves the richer? Are any of us so infatuated, as to be misled by such reasoning as this? No, we shall doubtless believe, rather, that the fair and full enjoyment of our property, whether in land on mortgage, or in the funds, might as effectually be secured to us, though no such heavy mulcture, much more, than second income tax, were imposed upon us. If the quantity of the circulating medium of this country, instead of having become relatively, as well as absolutely, more abundant than formerly, had been relatively diminished, and, consequently, its value increased---probably no question at all would have been made, whether the public debt ought not to be diminished proportionally. Both justice and policy would have required it. This would, indeed, have been a case in which, as far as the creditors of the public were concerned, the circulating medium might to that end very properly be increased---in which promissory notes or assignats, to a certain extent, might honestly be employed, so as to reduce the value of the circulating medium to its former scale. Nay, I apprehend it must, upon principles of general expediency, be admitted, that when the expence of maintaining a government, and of providing for the punctual discharge of the debt which it has contracted, or the interest thereon, has increased to such a pitch as well nigh to exhaust the whole produce of the land and labour of a country, and nothing is left but a bare subsistence for the bulk of the people, the cultivators of the soil ;---for in such a state of things manufacture will decline and perish :---it then may become a question, if it has not before, whether a government so circumstanced ought not to be dissolved; or, at least, whether the interest of the public creditor ought not to be sacrificed, either partially or wholly, for the public good. It is not likely, indeed, that a government should either be willing, or able, to protect the interests of its creditors to the extent here supposed. It would become bankrupt long before it arrived at the utmost possible limit of taxation. The people would not bear a load so oppressive.

But, surely, Sir John Sinclair does not mean to maintain, that we have already exceeded what the nation can bear;---that it is necessary even now to withhold from the public creditor some, and indeed no small portion, of the stipulated return for his advances, besides what he must contribute out of the residue in common with the rest of the people.---For if such be verily the case, how can Sir John Sinclair contemplate, with such high degree of satisfaction, the mere flattering, dressed-up, outline which he has drawn of the present situation of the country; and disregard the pale, and death-like countenance, and all the sure indications of decay, in the original?

But, to proceed with our examination of what further Sir John Sinclair has to advance upon the several branches of this subject.---After concluding from the preceding train of argument which we have noticed, that "three things are essential for public prosperity;" viz. 1st. "An additional quantity of labour or goods." 2d. "An adequate price for goods;" and 3d. "An increased medium of barter."---"Let us consider," says he, "how "the last, which is by far the most material, can be "obtained; for the greater the quantity of circulating "medium, the better the price of goods will necessarily "become, and the better the price of goods, the more "they are likely to become abundant; for good prices "necessarily promote the raising a greater quantity of "goods, whilst, by improvements in machinery, they can "often be manufactured cheaper." But is not all this very strange reasoning? At least, it would have been thought so not long ago,---for till of late it was thought, that the lower the price of goods, the greater would be the demand for them; that the increased demand would tend to increase the price, which, on the other hand, would tend to increase the supply, and yet, at the same time, to lessen the demand. So that a due balance would ere long be naturally restored between the supply and the demand. It was, moreover, thought likewise, that improvements in machinery were truly beneficial to a country, as being productive of a greater quantity of goods, by means of the same, or even a less quantity of labour,---thus enabling the manufacturer and trader to tender them at lower prices in the market, and hence to render them more generally attainable. What additional profit does the manufacturer enjoy, though he sell his cloth a shilling per yard higher, if he must pay proportionally higher wages to those whom he is under the necessity of employing in manufacturing that article, and a proportionally higher price for every other article which he may be under the necessity of purchasing for the carrying on his business---and for the maintenance of himself and his family?

It should seem, indeed, from Sir John Sinclair's mode of treating the question, that money, no matter whether it be gold or paper, has virtues which, many as they are, it never was before supposed to possess,---that the greater its abundance, the greater must be the prosperity of the nation in which it circulates;---but though millions, and billions, and trillions of pounds sterling, not in paper, but in precious metal, lay like mud in the middle of the streets, so plentiful that all might take their fill, is it to be contended that this additional medium of transfer would insure a better market, a more rapid sale for the goods now lodged in the shops and warehouses of our tradesmen and our merchants,---for the grain in the barns, or the flocks and herds in the pastures, of our farmers? Would they part with them the sooner because money had become a drug---a mere oyster-shell for boys to skim across the water? What, then, shall we say of such a circulating medium as we have at present, composed as it is of mere scraps of paper---of no intrinsic value whatsoever? Abundance of merchandize, and a rapid sale, are, indeed, symptoms of prosperity; but wherefore should not these exist, even infinitely beyond their present extent, though no addition were ever made to the quantity of the circulating medium,---nay, though it were positively diminished? Would not its value increase in proportion to the diminution of its quantity?

Lastly,---" *On a Medium of Barter, or Circulation and Paper Currency.*" [P. 60.]

It would not have required any very miraculous spirit of prophecy to have foreseen how these principles, which we have examined, would be applied, though we had been ignorant of Sir John Sinclair's previous observations upon the Report of the Bullion Committee. But let us hear it from himself:---" In countries," says he, " where " mines do not exist, if the precious metals alone are " the medium of circulation, an increase of coin or " specie cannot be obtained, except by means of com- " merce; but in that case goods must be exported to " purchase bullion for the purposes of coinage,---and " the nation is to that extent impoverished, merely " to procure a medium of barter. For instance, if

" in consequence of additional taxes ten millions of " money would be wanted for additional circulation, " were gold and silver necessary for that purpose, ten " millions worth of goods must be exported merely to " procure the representative of circulating wealth."

" Hence," he adds, " the advantages of paper money. " Gold and silver, represent property actually sent abroad, " and in the possession of foreign nations; *whereas paper* " *money, when issued upon proper principles*, represents " property at home, and in our own possession." But before any pains were taken to shew how an additional quantity of either gold and silver, or paper money might be procured, it ought to have been shewn, that such an additional quantity of either would really be requisite; for it does not appear that the supposed case of additional taxes would necessarily make it so.

Now, although by the employment of paper money, instead of species, at home, a nation is enabled to trade with the latter abroad, wherein consists one great advantage derived from the use of the former.---Yet how is it that a nation is impoverished to the extent of the goods exported to purchase bullion for the purpose of coinage---and what in this respect is the real advantage of paper money? Surely it cannot be made a question, but that the gold and silver, which are imported into a country in exchange for the produce of its industry, are not merely the representative of, but, considered as merchandize, (according to Sir John Sinclair's own notions)* are substantially property itself, and the more valuable as being immediately exchangeable in all civilized countries for property of other

* P. 54. See p. 38, 39, Sup.

descriptions---and in this view, that it is as beneficial to a nation that it should have in its possession its due proportion of them, as heaps of baneful commodities which last not beyond a season, and add nothing to the sustenance, the health, and vigour, but are subservient only to the luxury and vice, and conducive to the ruin of its inhabitants---nay, as any other species of unproductive capital whatever.

But the paper money, it seems, should be issued upon *proper principles.* Yet what these proper principles are, we do not find precisely stated; we are rather left to collect them as we can from Sir John Sinclair's subsequent observations. No easy task. "Paper currency," he remarks, "which, strictly "speaking, may be defined any *security payable* to "bearer *on demand,* is of three sorts;----the first "issued by the government of a country: the second "by private individuals: and the third by corporations, "erected for that special purpose." Hence, therefore, we should naturally conclude, that the paper money which is not payable to bearer on demand, is not of that description which falls under the denomination of paper currency issued upon proper principles. And what, then, shall we say of the notes of the Bank of England---that they are issued upon improper principles? Be that, however, as it may---After considering various objections to the paper money which might be issued by the government,---the many favourable, as well as lamentable, consequences, which, in Sir John Sinclair's mind, seem to have attended the issue of paper money by private persons; but admitting "that it might be so "issued with much national advantage, if they were

" put under proper restrictions, in regard to their fur-" nishing security to the public for the paper they is-" sue;" he concludes that, " the issuing of paper by " corporations, erected for that special purpose, is by " far the most eligible plan :" observing, that " any " abuse of this privilege will be checked by government, " whereas no government will check any enormity in its " own issuing. Want of credit," he proceeds, " which " must frequently overturn private banks, is not likely " to affect a public establishment, investing a large " capital in a great undertaking. A corporation," he adds, " is more likely to detect forgeries than the ma-" nagers of any national concern, and less specie is " necessary to circulate a million of paper belonging to " one great body, than to a number of private bankers, " separated from each other, and each of whom must have " a separate hoard." Now all this, in itself, is very well. The plan here approved is that which another writer of totally different sentiments, with regard to almost all the doctrines which are professed in the work under examination, has proposed as most proper to be carried into effect.*---But, besides the advantages which Sir John Sinclair has enumerated, one other very important advantage might be derived from it, namely, the appropriation of a large portion of the income to arise from the exclusive issue of paper money, to the service of the public.

* See " A Letter, containing observations upon some of the effects of our paper currency," &c. P. 77. The chief object of this letter to shew, that the present high prices proceed from the excess of currency,—the injurious consequences to individuals and the nation at large, and the remedy proper to be applied.

We have, too, plenteous reason, however, for believing, that even the paper issued by a single corporation, would greatly exceed its due amount, unless it fall strictly within the description which Sir John Sinclair has, rather inadvertently, I think, admitted into his definition, *viz.* that it be *payable to bearer on demand*.---I say, rather inadvertently,---for, notwithstanding that important, I would say, that indispensable, condition, which he has theoretically annexed to paper currency, we have seen how strenuously he has supported the new system of a paper currency not payable on demand,---how highly he approves the consequences of that system, for the assurance it gives of easy credit, increasing prices, and an ability to sustain unlimited taxation. But hear his own words.---" On the whole," says he, conclusively, " there " is no means by which a nation can be rendered more " prosperous, or can be better enabled to bear up under " any pressure of taxation, than by such additions to the " circulating medium of the country as can be admitted " without inconvenience." What, indeed, may be here meant by " inconvenience" it is not, perhaps, very easy to determine,---but it can hardly be conceived, after what has already fallen from the pen of Sir John Sinclair, that he should allude merely to such inconvenience as might possibly be felt by those classes of the people, who have only fixed incomes to depend upon for their support. Neither can he allude to the still more trifling inconvenience which might eventually arise from the indefinite increase of figures in the books of our bankers, merchants, and public accountants. With regard, however, to the means of attaining the important ends above specified, ---though increased industry and improvement in the arts add largely to the stock of comforts and luxuries in which a people may innocently indulge,---though they afford more ample resources for raising and equipping our fleets and armies, and supplying them with every article on which they can stand in need,---though the abundance of produce, raw and manufactured, occasion large reductions in their money price, and the means of decent subsistence to the labourer, the mechanic, the tradesman, and the gentleman, are, in all respects, facilitated,---though the taxes are, therefore, felt less severely, nay, rendered capable of absolute reduction in their nominal amount;---yet, these benefits so arising to the community, from the causes I have mentioned, may be as well obtained by means of an abundant circulating medium,---by the mere increase in the price of all commodities whatsoever;---and lest we doubt it, "What," we are asked, "is the foundation "of the taxable income of the nation, but the annual sale "of goods? and if, by increasing the circulating me-"dium you facilitate the sale of goods, or increase their "price; do you not augment the income of the people, "and, consequently, enable them, with infinitely more "ease than otherwise would be the case, both to pay "their taxes and carry on their industry?" In other words, by reducing the value of the circulating medium, do you not enable them, with infinitely more ease, to pay the debts they owe, than if the value of that medium remained the same?---If this be the real end in view,---if it be for this that our present system of paper currency is to be supported,---that the public creditor, instead of receiving the compensation solemnly agreed upon,---the fair acknowledged debt due upon the bargain, may be under the necessity of receiving what is equivalent only to its half, its third, or any less proportional part, let it at once be boldly and openly asserted,---let the champions of this Jacobinical system of finance come forth, and declare the object they are intent upon, and prepared by these means to accomplish. The question would then be simplified indeed. But, perhaps, it is already plain enough. If such, however, be not the meaning of Sir John Sinclair, the real ground on which his reasoning, in the passage now before us, is built, must be abandoned,---for all the necessary expenses of a government, (exclusive of defraying the public debt, or the interest payable upon it) and consequently the taxes, must necessarily be increased in proportion to the relative increase of the circulating medium, as already has been shewn. It has likewise been shewn, what little additional facility is afforded for the sale of goods by means of that increase; and, therefore, how little, in the long run, it can, in that respect, contribute to the encouragement of industry.--- We shall, ere long, see, perhaps, how much it may contribute to a directly opposite effect.

Already has it been the opinion of some of our merchants,* that, with regard to our trade with certain parts of the continent, our exports have been exceeded by our imports, and that, to this cause is partly to be ascribed the low rate of the exchange; and, indeed, it is sufficiently evident, that if the quantity of circulating medium, though composed partly of paper and partly of the precious metals, become so abundant in any country as to occasion the price of goods to rise much above their

* Min. of Evid. p. 52, Mr. Lynch. Ib. p. 63, Mr. Greffulhe.

price in other countries, it is the interest of the merchant to import such goods into the former from the latter, and from the former to export the precious metals, rather than the produce of its soil and industry.---Whereas, if the quantity of the circulating medium be kept within its due level, and the price of goods remain moderate, it would be more profitable to the merchant to export these, than the precious metals. To export that surplus of the precious metals which exceeds our wants at home, and which, from time to time, we have acquired upon the balance of our trade, which superior skill and industry in the manufacture of various goods had rendered favourable to us,---to ease ourselves of that which affords us no sustenance or clothing, and little scope whereon to employ our industry and art,---and in return to pour into our laps the necessaries and comforts of life, and the materials for productive labour from other nations, is a real and important benefit. It moreover tends to restore the general equilibrium of the medium of circulation, and to check its depreciation at home. But all attempts to do this effectually, must necessarily prove fruitless, so long as our paper money continues to be issued to such an excess, as for ever to retain our own medium of circulation much above its natural level. Whilst, on the other hand, it is to be feared, our manufactures will be rejected, by reason of their high price,---the consequence of that excess. Thus, at least, it is, that high prices, of which Sir John Sinclair has formed so favourable an opinion, have a natural tendency to check the industry of a nation, much more than to promote it.

Perhaps indeed, it may not, on the whole, be very material to a nation, though its medium of circulation be depreciated to a certain fixed extent, by reason of the known reduced intrinsic value of its coin, due provision being made for the fair adjustment of the claims of creditors;---yet, where the currency is depreciated by reason of the great, but still growing, abundance of paper money, which yet retains the same value as the coin itself, (a rare case if they long abide together;) or where the medium of circulation consists of paper money alone, of merely nominal value, indefinite and perpetually increasing in amount,--as there is no fixed standard whereby to adjust the respective claims of creditors, or to regulate the price of goods,---the inconveniences and difficulties which must be experienced in a country so situated, though at first, perhaps, almost imperceptible, must, in time, and that not distant, grow up into great and direful calamities.

The peculiar operation of our present system of circulation upon certain classes of the community, we have more than once been led to consider in the course of this Examination; we have observed with what apparent anxiety the landed proprietor, the manufacturer, and the merchant, have been roused to the contemplation of their respective interests; and now again, towards the close of his Appendix, Sir John Sinclair particularly selects them as the fit instances to prove the benefits theoretically resulting from an increasing abundance of the circulating medium---how worthy their support is our present paper system. "Let us take," says he, "the case of a landed proprieter of 5000*l.*

" a year. His tenants, from a scarcity of money, may not " be able to sell their produce, or may be obliged to take " an inferior price, or to agree to a distant payment. In " that case, how can he receive his rents punctually, or " pay regularly the demands of the Exchequer. *Increase* " *the circulating medium,* and these difficulties will vanish. " By an increased price, and greater demand, he may be " enabled to raise his rents, and to pay any additional " demands from the Exchequer, without materially di- " minishing his own expenditure, and, consequently, " without much inconvenience." The trading part of the community, "whose success," it is declared, " entirely depends on a command of capital, or on credit," is then summoned to attest the benefits of this increasing flood of paper currency:---" *Open a bank* " where the manufacturer, or the merchant, can discount " their bills with certainty, when the security is good; " and they will find no difficulty in paying the taxes, to " which they are subjected, and extending their com- " mercial concerns." But to sum up all.---" The same " observations," Sir John Sinclair adds, " are applicable " to almost all the various other classes of society." But can we patiently bear with such language and doctrine as this? Increase the circulating medium!---Open a bank! Go, dig a well for some water. Sink a pit for some coals. You may raise money more easily.

How far the landed proprietor may feel disposed to fall in with the adoption of such principles as these in practice---how ready our legislators (whose wide-extended domains constitute their wealth) may be to incline their ears to such doctrines as are here promulgated, I will not venture to determine. Sure I am, that the country is not without men who would scorn every opportunity of depriving those to whom they are honestly indebted, of one shilling of their due;---that it is not without men, warmed with a jealous desire of contributing their share, their full and equal share, to the service of the state, to the maintenance of the honour, the independence, and the glory of the nation,---to the fair and just recompense, and indemnification, of those who, in great emergencies, have come forward with the accumulated savings of their industry, or their patrimonial fortunes, acquired by the like means, to provide for its honour, its independence, and glory, in the times which are past. But if any there be, deaf to the dictates of justice, if not of gratitude,---let him consider also such other consequences of the depreciation of money which I have before represented to the reader. Let him consider the rent which he receives upon leases granted long ago--- how much annual income he loses by means of that depreciation, and how much more he is likely to lose should any further depreciation take place. Lastly, let him present to his imagination, the awful crisis which an ever-increasing depreciation of paper money must inevitably produce. He will then, perhaps, when it is too late, hesitate and doubt whether he may not altogether suffer much more than profit from this increasing abundance of the circulating medium.

And, what are the important benefits arising to the manufacturer, or the merchant, from this increasing abundance of the circulating medium? In proportion to that increase, will not the supplies of which they may stand in need be increased? Is it not the price of the raw or manufactured articles, which regulates the amount of the sum requisite for the purchase of them by the manufacturer or merchant? But does not the price depend upon the quantity of the circulating medium? Should it happen, that there were any considerable diminution of its quantity, would not the price of those articles soon fall?---Would not the manufacturer and merchant, then require less money to make their respective purchases? Finally, is it not plain, that whatever may be the amount of the taxes, it is not the manufacturer and merchant, but rather the consumers of the articles which are furnished by the manufacturer and the merchant, that eventually pay them; unless, indeed, in such extraordinary cases as may in truth affect the capital of the one and the other; and which, if they be equally burthened with the rest of the members of the community, they ought not, and I trust would not repine at, or endeavour to avoid?---Generally, whatever the amount of taxes may be, the manufacturer and merchant must at all times be allowed their reasonable profit. They will cease to expend their labour, and the profits of their capital, in the country where these are not secured to them. They will quit the land where they cannot reap the harvest they have sown. "Their own feet will carry them afar off to sojourn."

In regard, indeed, to "the various other classes of the community," we are left to ourselves to discover in what manner they also are thus highly benefitted by this increasing abundance here spoken of. We have considered sufficiently in what manner the interests of the farmer, the labourer, and the mechanic, are affected by it; and may be well satisfied that no argument is thence to be drawn in its favour. It remains, however, to say something more of its effect upon the interests of those generally whose property consists of stock in the public funds, of mortgages and annuities, or money vested in any other securities which yield only a fixed income. The partial and oppressive operation of a perpetually-augmenting currency upon all those, is but too plainly discernible to our understandings and our senses; it is demonstrable by strict calculation upon paper; it is exemplified amongst our acquaintance, and in our families. In permitting the unlimited issue of notes not payable in specie on demand---you not only preclude the holder of those notes from the benefit of his contract, whilst you absolve those who issue them from the liability to discharge their part of it; but you confiscate the property of a numerous class of individuals for the benefit of their debtors. Does it become a nation jealous of its honour, proud of its credit, and boasting faith to its engagements, thus to deal out injustice one to another? What maxims of prudence can sanction proceedings so highly injurious to the community at large? You would overwhelm, and annihilate, the public and the private creditor. You would urge him, by rendering his property here less available, and in time almost valueless, to seek an asylum elsewhere; thither to carry all his capital, not in the form of perishable paper, but of solid gold and silver,---there to establish it in security, and there, in person, fully to enjoy it. But you will prevent this justifiable act of self-defence---you will pass laws directly violating your own solemn engagements---you will alter the denomination of the coin, or if you have not already done so, you will make that, which is intrinsically worth nothing, a legal satisfaction of the claims of the public and private creditor---you will legalize fraud. Who will then regard your fair promises---your solemn engagements? Who will advance loans for the maintenance of your fleets and armies? What will become of your 3 per cent. consolidated, and 3 per cent. reduced annuities; your navy, and your Exchequer bills; your paper and your parchment? Your credit will crumble into dust. Your adopted paper currency will not be received, but at a discount, except by those who may be compelled to receive it at its nominal amount. The discount upon it will become greater and greater, till it become valueless. Hordes of wretched creditors, with their dependant families, hungry and houseless, will be scattered about the country, and prowl about the towns with good for nothing scraps of paper in their pockets; deprived of justice, and seeking for revenge. All the accumulated horrors of bankruptcy, ruin, plunder, and bloodshed, will mark your progress. Then shall it be said, "Who hath taken this counsel against Tyre, the crown- "ing city; whose merchants are princes, whose traffick- "ers are the honourable of the earth?"

Let us not, then, be dazzled by the false glare and splendour of the vast nominal pecuniary amount of our exports and our imports, our public credit, and our public revenue; magnified, as it apparently is, by means of our paper currency. Let us not fondly imagine; let us not be foolishly beguiled into an opinion, that mere nominal value is necessarily real value---that sound is equivalent to substance. But let us rather contemplate, and I trust we may with confidence and satisfaction, what have been the material, the solid, and intrinsic improvements, which have taken place in our agriculture and manufactures; the great increase which they have yielded, and the generally successful commerce in which we have been engaged throughout all quarters of the globe. These are our true subjects of consolation---notwithstanding the aspect of our affairs may, for a time, be clouded by the barbarous policy of a wide-extended despotism. But, at all events, let not our prosperity, nor our misfortunes, be made a ground for public iniquity and fraud, which must necessarily tend to the serious injury, if not the absolute ruin, of the state.

What, after all, shall we say of the results which Sir John Sinclair would deduce from his observations "on the "general nature of coin or money, and the advantages "of paper circulation," viz. "that an increase of labour "or industry, a more extended commerce, and an in- "creased revenue, require perpetual additions to the cir- "culating medium of a country;*---that such additions

* "It is incredible," says Sir John Sinclair, in his final note referred to in this place, "how so plain a proposition can be "controverted." "Will not 10,000 labourers require more "wages," says he, "than 5000? or 1000 vessels more money "to fit them out than 500 of the same size? or a revenue of "50 millions, a greater mass of circulating medium than one "of only 20 millions?" But need the reader be reminded that our labourers are not usually fed and clothed with gold

" cannot possibly be obtained to the extent that may be " necessary, but by means of a well-regulated paper cir- " culation;---and that if such paper circulation is properly " regulated, the periodical returns of commercial dis- " tresses will, in a great measure, be prevented, and the " demands of the Exchequer, however great, will be paid " without any material difficulty." What, I repeat, shall we say of these results?--Shall we admit, that the further

---

and silver, or with paper; that our vessels are not usually fitted out with one or the other, but with those things for which gold and silver, or paper, may be exchanged; and that the greater the mass of the circulating medium, the greater is the revenue required? He will surely see that, since the smaller the relative quantity, the greater is the relative value of the circulating medium—that if the quantity of the circulating medium remain stationary, whilst the quantity of goods which it is employed to circulate, is increased, the value of that medium will be proportionally increased; and hence that the same absolute quantity of money may serve to pay the wages of 10,000 men, as well as the wages of 500; that the money requisite for fitting out 1000 vessels, need amount to no more than is requisite for fitting out 500; and that a circulating medium requisite for the production of a revenue, in effect equivalent to 50 millions of the present day, need not be absolutely more than for the production of one in effect, equivalent to 20 millions in times which have passed.

In a former part of this examination, we were led to consider the facility which the present system of circulation afforded to the government, of obtaining advances from the Bank of England, upon the credit of Exchequer Bills.—Perhaps it was unnecessary to contend that an equal facility might exist, though the Bank were compelled to pay in specie.—For in truth it may be a questionable point, whether upon the whole any solid advantage arise to the nation in consequence of such facility or practice.

increase of the human species, or even the better, the more profitable application of its energies depends upon the increase of the precious metals, or of paper, or of whatsoever other substance the circulating medium may in this, or in any other country, at this, or at any other time, happen to consist;---that the passions and powers of men, and the natural order of things, are limited in the direct ratio of the amount of pounds sterling, of dollars, or of ducats, in paper, or in specie, for the time being, in circulation? Shall we admit the utter impossibility of procuring as much of the precious metals; but the possibility of procuring as much of paper money as may be necessary for the circulating medium; when "paper "currency, strictly speaking, may be defined any security "payable to bearer on demand,"*---thus implying its immediate convertibility into those precious metals which it is impossible to procure? Again, admitting the paper circulation to be properly regulated; therefore, at all times convertible into species, and together with the remaining species not materially exceeding the quantity which would be in circulation in case there were no paper money; shall we admit that the periodical returns of commercial distresses would be prevented, in any much greater measure, or the demands of the Exchequer paid with any much less material difficulty, than if species itself were in circulation? Or lastly, and (perhaps more according to the general tenor of the doctrines which we have examined) admitting that to be a well-regulated paper currency, which may be augmented at the pleasure of corporations and individuals,

* P. 61, and P. 96.—supra.

but is not convertible into species,---which may, in a moment of alarm, be rendered, both absolutely and relatively, altogether valueless, or may be, and is, perpetually diminishing in value by means of its growing excess;---yet is at the same time to be considered as the measure of the value of things which are always truly valuable, and to be held in all cases exchangeable for them;---shall we admit, that commercial distresses can, in any measure, be prevented,---that the payment of the demands of the Exchequer can, in any measure, be facilitated,---(I mean not merely for a day, or a year; but in the long run, and for a series of years,)---by such a paper currency as this; pregnant as it is with monstrous confusion and mischief,--- indicative, as it is, of real bankruptcy and ruin? Upon these points I will leave the reader himself, in some deep metaphysic mood, to determine.